TODAY, when all concerned citizens are attempting to understand the crucial issues dividing our nation, Robert F. Kennedy's TO SEEK A NEWER WORLD offers a clear-cut, readable analysis of America's most urgent problems.

With the unexpected announcement of Senator Kennedy's candidacy—and increased public demand for an up-to-the-minute definition of his stand on the major campaign issues—Bantam Books put publishing operations into high gear. Employing the overnight production and distribution techniques it pioneered with such urgent national documents as THE REPORT OF THE WARREN COMMISSION and THE REPORT OF THE NATIONAL ADVISORY COMMISSION ON CIVIL DISORDERS, Bantam has rushed the release of this low-priced paperback book in order that it reach the largest number of people in the shortest possible time.

This special Bantam Extra edition of TO SEEK A NEWER WORLD includes an expanded, up-to-date analysis by Senator Kennedy of the situation in Vietnam—with his specific recommendations for policy changes.

Books by Robert F. Kennedy

TO SEEK A NEWER WORLD

THE PURSUIT OF JUSTICE
(*edited by Theodore J. Lowi*)

JUST FRIENDS AND BRAVE ENEMIES

THE ENEMY WITHIN

TO SEEK
A NEWER
WORLD

ROBERT F. KENNEDY

BANTAM BOOKS
TORONTO · NEW YORK · LONDON

TO SEEK A NEWER WORLD

*A Bantam Book / published by arrangement with
Doubleday & Company, Inc.*

PRINTING HISTORY
Doubleday edition published November 1967

Portions of this book appeared in LOOK *November 1967*

Newspaper serialization by PHILADELPHIA BULLETIN,
CHICAGO'S AMERICAN, WINNIPEG FREE PRESS WEEKLY,
and OTTAWA JOURNAL

Bantam edition published April 1968

Lines of "Peace" from Collected Poems of Rupert Brooke. ©
*1915 Dodd, Mead & Co., Inc. Renewed 1943 by Edward Marsh.
Reprinted by permission of Dodd, Mead & Co., Inc. and Sidgwick
& Jackson, Ltd.*

Lines of "Politics and the English Language" from Shooting an
Elephant *by George Orwell. Reprinted by permission of Harcourt,
Brace & World, Inc. and Martin Secker & Warburg, Ltd.*

*Lines from Lecture #1 from a series of three lectures given by
Teodoro Moscoso at Mills College, Oakland, California, Fall of
1964. Reprinted by permission.*

Cover photograph courtesy of Lawrence Fried

*Bantam Books are published by Bantam Books, Inc., a subsidiary
of Grosset & Dunlap, Inc. Its trade-mark, consisting of the words
"Bantam Books" and the portrayal of a bantam, is registered in the
United States Patent Office and in other countries. Marca Registrada.
Bantam Books, Inc., 271 Madison Avenue, New York, N.Y. 10016.*

PRINTED IN THE UNITED STATES OF AMERICA

This book is dedicated

to my children

and

yours.

Perhaps we cannot prevent this world from being a world in which children are tortured. But we can reduce the number of tortured children. And if you don't help us, who else in the world can help us do this?

Albert Camus

The lights begin to twinkle from the rocks:
The long day wanes: the slow moon climbs: the deep
Moans round with many voices. Come, my friends,
'Tis not too late to seek a newer world.
Push off, and sitting well in order smite
Of all the western stars, until I die.
The sounding furrows; for my purpose holds
To sail beyond the sunset, and the baths

Alfred, Lord Tennyson

Acknowledgments

IN THE PREPARATION OF this book and the speeches and the thoughts contained in it, I am grateful to many people. It would be impossible to name them all. Literally hundreds contributed in various ways, large and small, to the chapter on the urban crisis. The chapter on Vietnam is as much the product of work and associations during my days in the Executive Branch of the Government as it is from my work and experience since 1965.

Certainly my views on what the military can and cannot accomplish date from my experience during those days, and what I learned from my association with representatives of the military establishment.

There were many, both in and out of the Government, who contributed ideas and thoughts on nuclear control, China, and the Alliance for Progress. Therefore it is not only impossible, but it would be unfair, to attempt to list all those who in some way were of help on the various subjects of this book. I hold none of them responsible for what is contained here; the views are my own. But to each of them who helped formulate my thoughts or who later gave critical suggestions and ideas, I am most grateful.

The only way I can adequately repay them is if this book, because of their help, stimulates new thoughts, different approaches, provokes discussion, and most importantly, action in the areas of their particular concern—and thus perhaps in some small way helps to xii TO SEEK A NEWER WORLD

make a better life for the next generation of Americans.

I extend my thanks to the personnel at Doubleday, and particularly to Ken McCormick whose ideas were so valuable. My appreciation also to Joyce Goodman for her help in typing; to Jean Main for her efforts and skill and, most importantly, her cheerful patience in typing and retyping this manuscript, and so many others that preceded it; and to Angie Novello, my secretary these long years, who does everything, and who everyone who knows her realizes is a saint.

I am most particularly grateful to my two legislative assistants, Peter Edelman and Adam Walinsky, for all the effort and work that they have contributed in gathering and assembling the material on which this book is based. To Adam Walinsky for his assistance, guidance, and advice as well as his perseverance, I express my special gratitude.

And to my wife, my appreciation can never adequately be expressed.

Author's Note To Bantam Edition

Since *To Seek A Newer World* was first published in November 1967, the world has seen many changes, particularly in Southeast Asia. For this edition, therefore, I have expanded and updated the chapter on Vietnam, and I have also added portions of my formal announcement of candidacy for the Presidency.

March 20, 1968

Contents

MY ANNOUNCEMENT OF CANDIDACY

I am announcing today my candidacy for the Presidency of the United States.

I do not run for the Presidency merely to oppose any man, but to propose new policies. I run because I am convinced that this country is on a perilous course and because I have such strong feelings about what must be done that I am obliged to do all I can. I run to seek new policies—policies to close the gaps between black and white, rich and poor, young and old, in this country and around the world. I run for the Presidency because I want the Democratic Party and the United States of America to stand for hope instead of despair, for the reconciliation of men instead of the growing risk of world war.

I run because it is now unmistakably clear that we can change these disastrous, divisive policies only by changing the men who make them. For the reality of recent events in Vietnam has been glossed over with illusions. The report of the Riot Commission has been largely ignored. The crisis in gold, the crisis in our cities, the crises on our farms and in our ghettoes, all have been met with too little and too late.

No one who knows what I know about the extraordinary demands of the Presidency can be certain that any mortal can adequately fill it. But my service on the National Security Council during the Cuban Missile crisis, the Berlin crisis and the negotiations on Laos and on the Nuclear Test Ban Treaty have taught me something about both the uses and the limitations of military power, about the value of negotiations with allies and with enemies, about the opportunities and dangers which await our nation in the many corners of the globe to which I have traveled. As a member of the Cabinet and a member of the Senate I have seen the inexcusable and ugly deprivation which causes children to starve in Mississippi, black citizens to riot in Watts, young Indians to commit suicide on their reservations, and proud, able-bodied families to wait out their lives in empty idleness in Eastern Kentucky. I have talked and listened to the young people of our nation and felt their anger about the war they are sent to fight and the world they are about to inherit. In private talks and in public, I have tried in vain to alter our course in Vietnam before it further saps our spirit and our manpower, further raises the risks of wider war, and further destroys the country and people it was meant to save.

* * *

. . . My decision reflects no personal animosity or disrespect toward President Johnson. He served President Kennedy with the utmost loyalty and was extremely kind to me and members of my family in the difficult months which followed the events of November 1963. I have often commended his efforts in health, education, and many other areas; and I have deep sympathy for the burdens he carries today. But the issue is not personal; it is our profound differences over where we are heading.

I do not lightly dismiss the dangers and difficulties of challenging an incumbent President; but these are not ordinary times and this is not an ordinary election. At stake is not simply the leadership of our party or even our country—it is our right to moral leadership on this planet.

Washington, D. C.
March 16, 1968

Introduction

THE ESSAYS IN THIS book primarily grow out of work, travel, and speeches in the Senate since I first took my seat there in January of 1965. The Senate is a place where problems are dealt with as they arise, and attention and effort are devoted to the crisis of each moment. Therefore these essays set out no grand embracing scheme, no comprehensive plan for America or for the world. They discuss our response to those challenges that have come before us most urgently and demandingly in the last two and one-half years.

Nevertheless, that these are the problems which have most insistently claimed our attention tells us much about the world we live in; a world, above all, of change. We have given our children unrivaled opportunities for learning, leisure, expression: yet they seem to grow further apart from us every day, striking off in directions of which we—and sometimes perhaps they —know only that they are different from our own. We have passed civil rights legislation of a reach and detail unknown since the Civil War; yet never has there been a greater sense of alienation or more open hostility between the races. We have found material wealth, and government programs, far beyond our dreams of a few years ago; yet perhaps we count the wrong things—for the new wealth and activity seem to destroy as many pleasures as they bring us, and the new programs seem irrelevant, even hostile, to many of the purposes they were designed to achieve. I have chosen in this book, then, to discuss these problems—youth, race, the city and our public response to its challenge—because they have been urgent problems; but also because they pose the question of change in its most stunning and difficult form.

In the world, we are the most powerful of nations, controlling a destructive capacity we almost shrink from counting; yet our young men struggle, and many die, in a war in a small far-off country where our power often seems impotent. We seek the friendship of the good neighbor with the nations near our borders, and enter into a great Alliance against the age-old enemies of man; yet we are constantly called further abroad, and our neighbors are strange to us when we return. The most populous nation in the world grows ever larger in our thoughts, with new power and wracking convulsions; yet we know little of it save a consciousness of rising danger. And above all loom the new weapons of war, threatening at every moment to destroy all they were designed to defend.

These subjects, too, have chosen themselves to be objects of our attention and concern; these too are symbols of a changing and churning world, recalling to us the words of Abraham Lincoln: "As our case is new, so must we think anew and act anew. We must disenthrall ourselves." As we move into the last third of this century—dangerous and bloody, but also liberating and exhilarating—that is our best guide to the future.

TO SEEK
A NEWER
WORLD

Youth

NOT SINCE THE FOUNDING of the Republic —when Thomas Jefferson wrote the Declaration of Independence at 32, Henry Knox built an artillery corps at 26, Alexander Hamilton joined the independence fight at 19, and Rutledge and Lynch signed the Declaration for South Carolina at 27—has there been a younger generation of Americans brighter, better educated, more highly motivated than this one. In the Peace Corps, in the Northern Student Movement, in Appalachia, on dusty roads in Mississippi and narrow trails in the Andes, this generation of young people has shown an idealism and a devotion to country matched in few nations and excelled in none.

We have shown our admiration for them in the sincere flattery of imitation, in ways large and small. Café society and country clubbers follow their fashions in slang and skirt lengths, listen to their music, and dance their dances. Detroit styles its cars and designs its engines on the model of those built by teen-age "hot-rodders" of a few years ago. The sit-in movement, which energized the Negro of the South and resulted in the Civil Rights Act of 1964, began with a few college students. And it was a small group of Northern students, in the Mississippi Summer Project, who taught thousands of adults how to make personal witness for civil rights in conditions of difficulty and danger.

Yet for all the inspiration, all the freshness and imagination our young people have given us in the last few years, we are now profoundly troubled by them; and so we should be. For the gap between generations, always present in the past, is suddenly widening; the old bridges that span it are falling. We see all around us a terrible alienation of the best and bravest of our young; the very shape of a generation seems turned on its head overnight. Bob Moses Parris is gone, Stokely Carmichael and Rap Brown stand in his place—and beyond them are others more militant, offering dark visions of an apocalyptic future. Peace Corps recruiting is not so easy as it was; and we read less of tutoring programs in the ghetto than of trips, festivals, and drugs with strange new names. There are riots on the Los Angeles "strip" and in dozens of colleges; hundreds of young men dodge the draft in Canada, and unknown numbers effectively do the same in years of graduate study; the suicide rate among young people is rising, and so is the rate of juvenile delinquency. Bob Dylan, the troubador of their generation, who once sang of the changes that were "Blowin' in the Wind," now dismisses our pronouncements as "propaganda, all is phony."

This rejection we see most clearly in the growth of a youthful "underground" culture. Its essence seems to be that participation in public affairs is a "hang-up"; that all power corrupts absolutely; and that salvation is to be found with a wholly new life style, sparked by drug-induced fantasies and preoccupation with self. This small minority not only preaches total estrangement, it lives it. In new communities that have sprung up from New York's East Village to Haight-Ashbury in San Francisco, this "underground" community preaches the message of total alienation: "turn on, tune in, drop out." Their life style is in every way a repudiation of modern American life.

These communities are small; but many more young people are sympathetic to the message of estrangement and disillusion even as they reject total alienation. The premises of the underground are, I am afraid, shared by far too many of those young people on whom we depend to commit themselves personally to public change. Time and again I have heard these young leaders—whether college editors or community-action organizers—express their dissatisfaction with the direction of American society.

They seek change, but with an increasing sense of futility; theirs is not the estrangement that leads to complete alienation, but a despair that leads to indifference. Even those young people who are anxious to make a personal effort to alter conditions they oppose, retreat in the face of inflexible institutions with overwhelming power, to become no different from the majority of their generation. These, too, drop out—but by becoming part of the "system" they deplore. They join the corporation, or the multiversity, or the law firm, not because they think they can contribute to those institutions, but out of resignation, out of the conviction that commitment to anything broader than their private welfare is fruitless.

Thus more and more of our children are estranged or indifferent, almost unreachable by the familiar premises and arguments of our adult world. The task of leadership, the first task of concerned people, is not to condemn or castigate or deplore; it is to search out the reason for disillusionment and alienation, the rationale of protest and dissent—perhaps, indeed, to learn from it. And we may find that we learn most of all from those political and social dissenters whose differences with us are most grave; for among the young, as among adults, the sharpest criticism often goes hand in hand with the deepest idealism and love of country.

SOURCES OF DISSENT

What estranges these young people? What are they dissenting from, and what do they tell us about ourselves? They begin, of course, with the war in Vietnam. Let me emphasize that I am not talking about all our young people; after all, Vietnam is a young man's war. The men who fight and die there, with bravery and endurance equal to any in our history, are young. There are others, as I have seen on many campuses, who are in favor of escalation through increased bombing of the North—though many who favor escalation also favor continuation of the student deferment, their seeming slogan "Escalation Without Participation," or at any rate "Without Me." But when a hundred student-body presidents and editors of college newspapers, hundreds of former Peace Corps volunteers, and dozens of present Rhodes Scholars question the basic premises of the war, they should not and cannot be ignored. Among these protestors, most will serve, if called upon, with courage and responsibility equal to any. Still, their basic loyalty and devotion do not and cannot obscure the fact of dissent.

These students oppose the war for the same reason that many Americans do: for the brutality and the horror of all wars, and for the particular terror of this one. But for our young people, I suspect, Vietnam is a shock as it cannot be to us. They did not know World War II, or even Korea. This is a war surrounded by rhetoric they do not understand or accept; these are the children not of the Cold War, but of the Thaw. Their memories of Communism are not of Stalin's purges and death camps, not even the terrible revelations of the Twentieth Party Congress, or the streets of Hungary. They see the world as one in which Communist states can be each other's deadliest enemies, or even close to the West, in which Communism is certainly no better, but perhaps no worse, than many other evil and repressive dictatorships with which we conclude alliances when that is felt to be in our interest.

Even as the declared foreign policy of our government is to "build bridges" to this new Communist world, they see us, in the name of anti-Communism, devastating the land of those we call our friends. However the war may seem to us, they see it as one in which the largest and most powerful nation on earth is killing children (they do not care if accidentally) in a remote and insignificant land. We speak of past commitments, of the burden of past mistakes; and they ask why they should now atone for mistakes made before many of them were born, before almost any could vote. They see us spend billions on armaments while poverty and ignorance continue at home; they see us willing to fight a war for freedom in Vietnam, but unwilling to fight with one-hundredth the money or force or effort to secure freedom in Mississippi or Alabama or the ghettos of the North. And they see, perhaps most disturbing of all, that they are remote from the decisions of policy; that they themselves do not, by the nature of our political system, share in the power of choice on great questions that shape their lives. These, at any rate, are some of the sources of their dissent from the war. It is not difficult to understand them.

It would be tempting, but it would be wrong, to trace all the problems of our disaffecting youth to the war. Nor can this problem be traced to any individual, or to any administration, or to a political party; the challenge is deeper and broader.

Consider for example our economy: the wondrous production machine that has made us richer, as we count, than any people in history, and within which we all find sustenance and support. It is a business economy, which is to say that most Americans are engaged in some form of business. Indeed Coolidge was accurate, if not notably edifying, when he said that "the business of America is business." Yet we know that in a recent survey only twelve percent of all college seniors hoped for a career in business, or thought such a career would be worthwhile and satisfying.

Part of the reason, surely, is that the great corporations that are so large a part of American life play so small a role in the solution of its vital problems. Civil rights, poverty, unemployment, health, education, these are but a few of the deep crises in which business participation, with a few important exceptions, has been far less than might be expected. We can recognize, and applaud, the work of the National Association of Man-

ufacturers in job training, or the work of foundations
like Ford and Rockefeller, or the efforts of individuals
like Dan Kimball or Thomas Watson, or corporations
like Smith Kline & French. But certainly business as a
whole has not sought out the challenge of the nation's
frontier. Of course, it may well be argued that the
business of business is to make a profit, that to attempt
more is to do less than its stockholders deserve. But
does such an argument have relevance, ask the young,
when a single company, like General Motors or AT&T,
has annual profits greater than the gross national product of any one of seventy nations in the world?

Even more distasteful to the young, as it has been to
moralists for thousands of years, is the ethic that
judges all things by their profit. They have seen high
officers of the nation's largest corporations engage in
conspiracies to fix prices, gathering in shabby secret
meetings to steal pennies a month from each of millions of Americans. They have seen us send people to
jail for the possession of marijuana, while refusing to
limit the sale or advertising of cigarettes, which kill
thousands of Americans each year.* They have seen us
hesitate to impose the weakest of safety standards on
automobiles, or require that a "respectable" store or
lending company tell the simple truth about the interest rate it is charging on loans. They have sensed that
organized crime, an empire of corruption, venal greed,
and extortion, continues to flourish: not only tolerated,
but often in alliance with significant elements in labor,
business, and government. It is perhaps for these reasons that many of them, in their contempt for the excesses of materialism, echo the teachings of another rebellious young man: "The rich He hath sent empty
away."

It is more than these abuses of the profit motive that
they reject; often it is the very nature of materialism in

---

* At hearings before the World Conference on Smoking and
Health, Emerson Foote—who had resigned a major position in an
advertising firm because he could not, in conscience, continue to
advertise cigarettes—remarked, "I guess I just don't think it's right
to make a profit out of killing people." A representative of the U. S.
Department of Agriculture shot back: "Do you mean that you
don't believe in the profit system?"

our society, and what it has brought us. The suburbs are "little boxes on a hillside . . . all made out of ticky-tacky, and they all look just the same." "Money can't buy me love," they sing. In their eyes, we too often measure the worth of a man by the size of his salary or the number of his possessions. In short they think their elders have surrendered community values and personal excellence, in exchange for the tailfins and trinkets that Westbrook Pegler once called "a variety of dingbats for the immature."

Nor, painful as it may be for liberals to acknowledge, are these young people enchanted with liberal institutions. Most Americans over the age of thirty, when they think of labor unions, have as a frame of reference the long struggle to establish labor's basic rights, to make the workingman something more than an industrial serf. Labor has been in the forefront of many a great battle; but youth looks with other eyes, and its view is very different. They think labor has grown sleek and bureaucratic with power, sometimes frankly discriminatory, occasionally even corrupt and exploitative, a force not for change, but for the status quo, unwilling or unable to organize new members, indifferent to the men who once worked the coal mines of Appalachia, a latecomer to the struggles of the grape pickers of California or the farm laborers of the Mississippi Delta. This is a one-sided picture, without the dimensions of fifty years of struggle, and the undramatic yet vital work of labor in many parts of the nation today. But there is enough truth in some of it for us to be concerned about our children's view, and not to ignore the need for change.

We have treasured our educational system also as a firm pillar of the liberal community. This faith, however, is not unanimously shared. One critic has said: "Education [is] by its very nature an individual matter . . . not geared to mass production. It does not produce people who instinctively go the same way . . . [yet] our millions learn the same lessons and spend hours before television sets looking at exactly the same thing at exactly the same time. For one reason and another we are more and more ignoring differences, if

not trying to obliterate them. We seem headed toward
a standardization of the mind, what Goethe called 'The
deadly commonplace that fetters us all.' " This speaker
was not part of a Berkeley rally; it was Edith Hamilton, one of our greatest classicists.

We hear much the same from our young critics—as
in this comment from a student representative, speaking to a meeting of the Board of Regents of the University of California: "We have asked to be heard.
You have refused. We have asked for justice. You
have called it anarchy. We have asked for freedom.
You have called it license. Rather than face the fear
and hopelessness you have created, you have called it
Communistic. You have accused us of failing to use legitimate channels. But you have closed those channels
to us. You, and not us, have built a university based
on distrust and dishonesty."

It is impossible to mistake the anguish of that voice.
There may be many things in that cry, but one of them
is surely a protest of individuality against the university
as corporate bureaucracy, against the dull sameness
Miss Hamilton saw also. For in bureaucracy and sameness is the denial of individuality, and the denial that
human beings matter; if all are the same, why listen to
what anyone says? If we are not prepared to listen,
then men cannot be recognized as more than numbers
in statistical collections, a part of the gross national
product like so many coffee cups or carpet sweepers.

The suppression of individuality—the sense that no
one is listening—is even more pronounced in our politics. Television, newspapers, magazines, are a cascade
of words, official statements, policies, explanations,
and declarations. All flow from the height of government down to the passive citizen: Who can shout up
against a waterfall? More important, the language of
politics is too often insincerity, which we have perhaps
too easily accepted but which to the young is particularly offensive. George Orwell wrote a generation ago:
"In our time, political speech and writing are largely
the defense of the indefensible. Things like the continuation of British rule in India, the Russian purges and
deportations, the dropping of the atom bombs on

Japan, can indeed be defended, but only by arguments which are too brutal for most people to face, and which do not square with the professed aims of political parties. Thus political language has to consist largely of euphemism, question-begging and sheer cloudy vagueness. Defenseless villages are bombarded from the air, the inhabitants driven out into the countryside, the cattle machine-gunned, the huts set on fire with incendiary bullets: this is called *pacification*. Millions of peasants are robbed of their farms and sent trudging along the roads with no more than they can carry: this is called *transfer of population* or *rectification of frontiers*. People are imprisoned for years without trial, or shot in the back of the neck or sent to die of scurvy in Arctic lumber camps: this is called *elimination of unreliable elements*. . . . The inflated style is itself a kind of euphemism. A mass of Latin words falls upon the facts like soft snow, blurring the outlines and covering up all the details." In this respect, politics has not changed since Orwell wrote. And if we add to the insincerity, and the absence of dialogue, the absurdity of a politics in which elected officials find sport in joking about children bitten by rats, we can understand why so many of our young people have turned from engagement to disengagement, from politics to passivity, from hope to nihilism, from SDS to LSD.

DOES IT MATTER?

Some, while admitting the disillusion of youth, discount its importance. There has always been generational conflict, they say; always it has been resolved, as the flaming youth of twenty matures into the father, breadwinner, and community member of thirty. Youth may be more noticeable now, because there is more of it and because of its new opportunities for self-expression, not to say irresponsibility. To exaggerate its importance, however, is only to distract attention from the real and serious work of the day—thus the critics.

This view, in my judgment, is as wrong as it is

seemingly comforting. At the most simple and direct level, the contributions of young people are sorely needed by the nation. Their work in the Peace Corps is our greatest asset in dozens of nations. Their willingness to work in VISTA, or other volunteer efforts, is critical to the solution of our domestic problems. And even if young men do not run the country, they are needed to fight its battles.

More significantly, the protest of the young both reflects and worsens their elders' own lack of self-confidence. Self-assured societies, confident of their wisdom and purpose, are not afflicted with rebellions of the young. But if the young question our involvement in Vietnam, surely this in part reflects their elders' own division and uncertainty of opinion. If the young reject a life of corporate bureaucracy and suburban sameness, surely this reflects their parents' dissatisfaction with their own lives, the realization at forty or fifty that money and status have not brought happiness or pride along with them. If the young scorn conventional politics and mock our ideals, surely this mirrors our own sense that these ideals have too often and too easily been abandoned for the sake of comfort and convenience. We have fought great wars, made great sacrifices at home and abroad, made prodigious efforts to achieve personal and national wealth: Yet we ourselves are uncertain of what we have achieved and whether we like it. Most of us can remember, after all, when the aim of youth was to grow into the society of its elders. Now it seems that the young no longer want to exchange their innocence for responsibility; instead many adults seek to recapture childish things. Thus to the extent that we confront the question of our disaffecting the young, we confront also our own dissatisfactions and problems, as individuals and as a society.

We cannot discount the disaffection of the young, finally, because there has occurred an important shift in the nature of modern society. Youth is now an identifiable and separate group; for while it is true that many change as they grow older, it is also a fact that their separate and special values are passed on to still larger generations of their younger brothers and sisters who follow them. The young will always be with us. And the estrangement of such a group is a serious strain on a society already stretched by the disaffection of many divergent interests.

Before the spread of mass education (secondary school and college), children passed more or less directly into adulthood, from strict parental control to the full responsibility of earning a living and raising their own children; thus it is on his thirteenth birthday that the Jewish boy proclaims in the Bar Mitzvah ceremony, "Today I am a man." One important feature of this pattern was that values were passed directly from one generation to the next, with change only slow and gradual. As Erik Erikson tells us, the archetype of human progress is in the story of Moses, who brought his people within sight of the promised land and then died, leaving to Joshua the leadership in achieving goals that both completely shared.

The twentieth century, however, has interrupted this ancient progression. A new time—adolescence—now separates childhood from the adult world. Adolescence by definition is a period without either the strict adult control of childhood or the full responsibilities of adulthood. It is a time, we are told, when the most important codes and standards are those of fellow adolescents; and thus it is a break in the chain that once directly transmitted values across the generations. It is a culture of its own, free of the restraints and demands that shape the vision of the rest of society—almost another country.

America is the nation where adolescence holds greatest sway. First with compulsory secondary education, now with more than half our children attending college and many going on to graduate study, we have lengthened the time and extended the scope of this unique period. In doing so, we have invited ever-greater separations between generations, ever-more rapid changes in values, attitudes, and beliefs. But continuity of values, shared beliefs, are vitally important to any society. Indeed it is these common attitudes that create and define a society, make it more than a collection of strangers occupying the same geographical territory. When I went to school, the unique success of the American experiment in democracy, and the stability of the two-party system, were explained as being based on our widespread sharing of values and beliefs, as opposed to a country like France or Italy, where men still differed widely on such basic questions as the role of the Church, the institutions of representative democracy, or private versus state enterprise.

It is just this sense of basic agreement that is now rejected by our youth, and at a time when many others are also denying the fundamental premises and processes of the nation. Great gulfs now yawn between black and white, right and left; the Minutemen share nothing with the Revolutionary Armed Movement—except a conviction of their own right to use guns and violence against fellow citizens with whom they disagree. These divisions spring from different causes, and may exist entirely apart from one another: The "hippie" rejecting affluence and action is far away from the Negro sharecropper or his unemployed brother in the city slums, who are in desperate need of action to achieve a minimum share of the affluence and acceptance the other scorns. But the effect of the two divisions is more than the sum of each. For at some point—who can say where, or under what strain—there is the danger that too many will not share the same goals, the same understanding of the present or vision of the future; that our politics and our life will lose much of their capacity to move forward, because we will not agree on where we want to go—or even where we are at the time.

Some profess not to fear, but to welcome, such basic divisions. In the "politics of confrontation" they see opportunities for basic change, which, like all revolutionaries, they assume will be favorable to their aims. I do not share this blithe confidence. It is undoubtedly healthy for us to confront ourselves and each other, *together,* and with a consciousness of shared aims and good will. But to confront each other across gulfs of hostility and mistrust only invites disaster, as does the intemperate and emotional rejection of general standards of decent speech and behavior.†

OTHER NATIONS, OTHER YOUTH

The estrangement of young people is not unique to America. Latin American students have been militant, angry critics of their societies for decades; students in Korea, Turkey, and Indonesia helped to overthrow their governments. South African students stand against the steadily increasing power of their government. Europeans are also perturbed by the growing phenomenon of adolescent apartness; English students rebel against the august London School of Economics, explicitly modeling their theory and tactics after the rebels of Berkeley. Even in the Communist world, the rumblings of a disaffected, youthful minority are heard, denouncing hypocrisy, demanding authenticity. The students of Prague chose not a Marxist-Leninist hero, but the American beat poet Allen Ginsberg as the king of their annual festival.‡ Soviet youth do not listen to Komsomol, but to poets like Andrei Voznesensky, whose rejection of a world of poverty and official lies sounds remarkably like voices in America:

---

† The past provides grim lessons in the consequences of total disaffection. Consider the following description of Europe in the years before World War II: "The cultural proletarians of twentieth-century Europe responded to men who offered millennial promises, secret knowledge, missions of stupendous historical importance overriding all the convictions and moralities of the past. And they reviled those who preserved the standards or prejudices of an old society. Communists, Nazis, Fascists—their most frenzied attacks were reserved for the bourgeoisie of their own societies and of the remaining European democracies who, blind and incompetent though they were, nevertheless clung to the battered framework of nineteenth-century liberalism, of Enlightenment humanism, of traditional Christianity" (Stillman & Pfaff, *The Politics of Hysteria*). The emotions described are more than a little reminiscent of some present radical attitudes within the United States.

‡ It is perhaps interesting that Ginsberg, who has sometimes been attacked as an extreme leftist, was expelled from both Czechoslovakia and the Soviet Union. Established Communists, like other bureaucratic totalitarians, have no fondness for revolutionaries.

When I go down and see
the way some people live,
and look around dismayed,
shame scorches my cheeks
like the back of a flatiron.

How shamefully we hold our tongues,
Or, at the most, we hem and haw . . .
Lies are written on fat faces
that should be hidden in trousers. . . .

Clearly these are different phenomena, different youth. The Latin or Asian student may face brutal repression and the stagnation of centuries. But he need not be estranged from all his leaders, nor from the conventional politics of his nation. The political and intellectual currents of his own country encourage his rage to flow outward, in a passionate reactive nationalism—fighting against the dominant, successful West, and especially against the United States, and against those forces and elements in his own country identified with it. These feelings are shared by parties and movements of all generations in his country. He can protest, he can be revolutionary, without total estrangement.

The role of the rebellious youth in Communist nations is shaped by its own dynamic and circumstance. It is to join the battle against bureaucrats, political censors, and the hard-core totalitarians, to achieve greater freedom of personal expression, whether in speech or poetry or dress. This is in many ways a less complex, if sometimes more difficult, struggle than that which faces American youth; still it is producing its own generational separation, as every Communist leader is discovering. Just as George Kennan predicted fifteen years ago, the staggering deceits and crimes of totalitarianism have ended up by disgusting and boring everybody, including those who practice them.

But the American youth has moved far beyond these battles. He cannot look elsewhere for the sources of his society's ills—for he is within America, not a poor and struggling nation. Nor can he battle for the right to express himself—he has that right; but he believes it irrelevant to changing his land for the better. One of their spokesmen once said that the absence of censorship is a sure sign that no one is saying anything worthwhile. Moreover, the youth of other nations can still see their task as the work of economic development: whether by revolutionary internal change, or by ending the economic domination—even if fancied—of the West. But the American youth, like the American nation, already knows an affluence far beyond the distant dreams of others. He only does not know what it is for.*

THE NEED FOR ACTION

Therefore, it is not enough to understand, or to see clearly. The gap between generations will never be completely closed. But it must be spanned. For the bridge across the generations is essential to the nation in the present; and more, it is the bridge to our own future—and thus in a central sense, to the very meaning of our own lives. Whatever their differences with us, whatever the depth of their dissent, it is vital for us as much as for them that our young feel that change is possible, that they will be heard, that the follies and cruelties of the world will yield, however grudgingly, to the sacrifices they are prepared to make. Above all, we seek a sense of possibility.

Possibility must begin with dialogue, which is more than the freedom to speak. It is the willingness to listen, and to act. To the extent that the young only mirror dissatisfactions common to their elders, they are raising matters that should concern us in any case. To the extent that they demand the observance of long-proclaimed ideals, they perform for us the ancient service of the prophets. And as they ask for opportuni-

---

* Obviously the problem of Negro youth in America is not a surfeit of affluence or freedom. Young Negroes, like youth in the former colonies of Africa or Asia, can turn their frustration outward, toward white society; they can join in a common rage with at least some of their elders, such as the late Malcolm X. Their special handicap, however, is that in the last analysis they are more American than Negro: they are entitled to the affluence and power of white America, but are unsure of whether they can share in it, or whether they should want to.

ties to contribute to mankind and shape their own fate, as so many have done in the Peace Corps, or in the Civil Rights movement, they lend greater urgency to a concern that all of us share: that our lives should make a difference to ourselves and our fellow men.

Thus to achieve the vital sense of possibility, to take up the challenge our young pose to us, we must remember that idealism and morality—in politics, and in the conduct of our lives—are not just a hope for the future, and must not be a thing of the past. Even in their style of total estrangement, many of our youth do propose to improve, and not abandon, society. In their "free universities" in the United States they are trying to offer exciting and substantial alternatives to conventional education. The bizarre "Provos" of Amsterdam have elected one of their leaders to the city council, and have offered serious, if unorthodox proposals, to solve some of the city's dilemmas, such as air pollution and traffic congestion. We can help link the practical idealism of such youths with our tradition of moral dissent; and we should remember how difficult it must be for the young dissenters of today to have before them only the example of the beat and silent generation of the 1950s.

We may find some of their ideas impractical, some of their views overdrawn. Still, there is no question of their energy, of their ability, above all of their honest commitment to a better and more decent world for all of us. It is for us now to make the effort, to take their causes as our causes, and to enlist them in our own, to lend to their vision and daring the insight and wisdom of our experience.

Every generation has its central concern, whether to end war, erase racial injustice, or improve the condition of the working man. Today's young people appear to have chosen for their concern the dignity of the individual human being. They demand a limitation upon excessive power. They demand a political system that preserves the sense of community among men. They demand a government that speaks directly and honestly to its citizens. We can win their commitment only by demonstrating that these goals are possible through

personal effort. The possibilities are too great, the
stakes too high, to bequeath to the coming generation
only the prophetic lament of Tennyson:

> Ah, what shall I be at fifty,
> Should nature keep me alive,
> If I find the world so bitter
> When I am but twenty-five?

Race and the City:
The Slums and Community

[EDITOR'S NOTE: Five months after this book was first published, the National Advisory Commission On Civil Disorders presented its Report. The report parallels in many respects the analysis and recommendations made by Senator Kennedy in the following chapter.]

WITHIN A FEW YEARS, four-fifths of all Americans will live in cities.* The cities are centers of culture, fashion, finance, and industry, of sports and communications, for us all: and thus the center of the possibilities of American life. They are also the center of the problems of American life: poverty and race hatred, scanty education and stunted lives, and other ills of the new urban nation—congestion and filth, danger and purposelessness—which afflict all but the very lucky, and some of the very rich.

Urban problems stretch far beyond the center city. Sheer growth has sent suburbs tumbling across the

* This statistic is in a sense misleading; the Census Bureau classifies as "urban" all places of over 2500 population, and the great gains in "urban" population are being made in suburbs of the large cities, not within the city limits themselves. In the wider sense, however, it is accurate to count most of the residents of these suburbs as residents of the cities, which have grown, in effect, to include thousands of smaller towns and villages around them. Almost all the characteristics we associate with residence—where a man works, the newspapers he reads, the teams he roots for, and the way he identifies himself to others—all these tell us that the residents of these suburbs, and thus most of the eighty percent of Americans who will shortly be classified as "urban," are in fact citizens of the metropolis around which their lives revolve.

countryside, overburdening our systems of transportation and water supply, education and medical care, antiquating the means of raising money to finance these vital services. Growth has polluted our water and poisoned our air, and stripped us of contact with sunlight, trees, and lakes. Government has floundered as new agencies have proliferated, splitting tasks and energies among dozens of distant and unconnected bureaus. Individuals have lost touch with the institutions of society, even with one another; and thus have become more and more both perpetrators and victims of coldness, cruelty, and violence.

In the next forty years our population will double, and our problems will double as well. We will have to build as many homes and hospitals and schools as we have built since the country began. More than this, we will have to find space for ourselves: to plan together where we will live and work and play, and where and how we can begin to rebuild our community, a place where each man finds importance and significance in his individual life, and in his contributions to the life of others. This is a large task. But it is the least we can do if our cities are to be places of dignity and safety, of rich excitement and achievement; if our society is to gain the name of civilization.

THE INNER CITY

But of all our problems, the most immediate and pressing, the one that threatens to paralyze our capacity to act, to obliterate our vision of the future, is the plight of the people of the ghetto, and the violence that has exploded as its product—jumping and spreading across the country, sending fear and anger before it, leaving death and devastation behind. We are now, as we may well be for some time to come, in the midst of what is rapidly becoming the most terrible and urgent domestic crisis to face this nation since the Civil War. Its consequences reach into every home, bringing the sure knowledge that failure to deal with this problem could mean failure in dealing with all the other elements of our urban crisis.

For the riots that have taken place—and the riots that we know may all too easily take place in the future—are an intolerable threat to every American, black or white: to the mind's peace, the body's safety, and the community's order, to all that makes life worthwhile. A violent few cannot be permitted to threaten the well-being of the many, and the hopes of their fellows for progress. Those who lead others to burn and loot must feel the full force of the law. The full force of the law means just that: the swift apprehension and punishment of law breakers. Rap Brown to the contrary, the streets of America are not the jungles of Vietnam. The full force of the law, however, does not mean senseless and unnecessary killing by those who act in the name of government.

Effective law enforcement, moreover, is just the beginning. We should not delude ourselves. Punishment is not prevention. History offers cold comfort to those who think grievance and despair can be subdued by force. To understand is not to permit; but to fail to understand is the surest guarantee of failure. The riots are not crises that can be resolved as suddenly as they arose. They are a condition that has been with us for 300 years, now worsened and intensified under the strains of modern life.

Nor will the problem go away. Twenty million Negro Americans, five million Mexican-Americans, nearly three million Puerto Ricans, and a half a million Indians are a reality. The slums are a reality, as are idleness and poverty, lack of education and dilapidated housing. Frustrated expectations and disappointed hopes are realities. Above all, the awareness of injustice and the passion to end it are inescapable realities. Thus, we can face our difficulties and strive to overcome them, with imagination and dedication, wisdom and courage. Or we can turn away—bringing repression, steadily increasing human pain and civil strife, and leaving a problem of far more terrible and threatening proportions to our children.

And we are already in grave danger: the danger of a deepening division between white and black America, the danger that fear will breed resentment, and resentment hostility, and increasing hostility again feed mounting fear. For we live in different worlds and gaze out over a different landscape. Through the eyes of the white majority, of a man of decent impulse and moral purpose, the Negro world is one of steady and continuous progress. In a few years, he has seen the entire structure of discriminatory legislation torn down. He had heard Presidents become spokesmen for racial justice, while Negro Americans enter the Cabinet and the Senate and the Supreme Court. The white American has paid taxes for poverty and education programs, and watched his children risk their lives to register voters in Mississippi. Seeing this, he asks, what cause can there be for dissatisfaction with present progress?

But if we look through the eyes of the young slum dweller—the Negro, the Puerto Rican, the Mexican-American—there is a different view, and the world is a hopeless place indeed. The chances are that he was born into a family without a father—often as a result of welfare laws that require a broken home as a condition of help. His chance of dying in the first year of life is twice that of children born outside the ghetto; and because his mother rarely saw a doctor, his chances of being mentally retarded are seven times the community average. He may spend his childhood crowded with adults into one or two rooms, without adequate plumbing or heat, with rats his companions of the night. He goes to a school which teaches little that can help him in an alien world. His chances of graduating from high school are three out of ten; and if he does graduate, there is only a fifty-fifty chance that he will have even the equivalent of an eighth-grade education. A young college graduate who taught in a slum school sums it up thus: "The books are junk, the paint peels, the cellar stinks, the teachers call you nigger, the window falls in on your head." *

Life later is no better: Stores charge inflated prices for shoddy goods; forty-three percent of ghetto housing

* At one high school, which I have visited a number of times and which is not atypical—located in the wealthiest city, in the wealthiest state, in the wealthiest nation in the world—twenty-five percent of the ninth-graders read at fourth-grade level or below; half cannot read above sixth-grade level.

is substandard and overcrowded; and although there are a quarter of a million Puerto Rican schoolchildren in New York City, only thirty-seven of them went on to college in a typical recent year.

Worst of all, the people of the ghetto and the barrio live today with an unemployment rate far worse than the rest of the nation knew during the depth of the Great Depression. If the unemployment of the Depression was a national emergency—and it was—our cities today therefore envelop dozens of more severe emergencies. The measure of the crisis of joblessness is not to be found in traditional unemployment figures, although these tell of crisis enough. The official statistics tell us that unemployment in the ghettos of poverty—among Negroes in Hough, Mexican-Americans in East Los Angeles, Appalachian whites in Chicago, Puerto Ricans in East Harlem, Indians on reservations *—is over three times the national rate. But these figures do

---

* This discussion focuses upon urban poverty. But over a third of the nation's poor live in rural areas, where the revolution in agricultural technology and the lack of industrial development have already combined to force thousands to the city in search of a decent life. Still thousands remain—white people in Appalachia, Negroes in cotton country, Spanish-Americans in northern New Mexico, Eskimos in Alaska. Just in the Mississippi Delta, which I visited in April 1967 with the Senate Poverty Subcommittee, there are now forty to sixty thousand people who literally have no cash income, who lack even $1 a month to buy Federal food stamps to avoid starvation. Migrant farm workers have been left out of the economic mainstream, earning an average of $1200 a year from farm work and $600 from odd jobs. The camps in which I have seen them living, and their conditions of work, can only be described as shocking. On Indian reservations, unemployment ranges up to eighty percent, and the average man dies at forty-two. In recent years, government policy has encouraged Indians to go to the city to live, without preparing them for its complexities. The resulting problems are immense. Any program for the city must include all of these Americans; not just because they deserve a better life—which is reason enough—but also because opportunity for these rural residents in their own communities will make it easier for the city to help those who have migrated and will choose to migrate in the future. Indeed, I believe our urban problems have been aggravated by an imbalance in our policies. Our farm subsidies have enriched the large producer, and driven the family farmer off the land; we have paid cotton growers not to produce but have made no provision for those who lost their jobs as a consequence. If we are to redress this imbalance and enable people to remain in their own homes if they choose, we will have to devote as much attention to rural community development as we do to our cities.

not count the full extent of the problem, because the whole apparatus of government cannot even find from one-fifth to one-third of the adult men of the ghetto. These men are unknown, have no fixed address, no job. They drift about the city, separated from their families, as if they were of no greater concern to their fellows than so many sparrows or spent matches. A recent study indicates that the last Census may have "lost" a full ten percent of all Negroes. When these lost battalions are taken into account, as well as those men who have lost hope and stopped looking for work, the true unemployment rate in the typical ghetto is not ten percent, or fifteen percent, but over forty percent. If that were the rate of unemployment nationwide, there would be 30 million people out of work today instead of 3 million. And of those men of the ghetto who do have jobs, over a fourth earn less than $60 a week —earn less, that is, than is required for each member of a family of four to eat 70 cents worth of food a day; less than what a family of that size receives on welfare in many cities.*

Moreover, the Department of Labor, in its 1967 Manpower Report, states flatly that "economic and social conditions are getting worse, not better, in slum areas," telling us, for example, that in a heavily Mexican-American area of Los Angeles, real family income —already a third lower than the national median—

---

* Consider the following Labor Department and Census figures. In a "typical" ghetto of 200,000 people, Census estimates are that a quarter, or 50,000, of the population are adult men. As noted above, one-fifth to one-third, an average of twenty-six percent, are uncounted by the Census. Therefore, of the 50,000 adult men, approximately 13,000 are simply drifting. Another 4000 can be found who have stopped looking for work, and for whom no work exists. Hence 17,000, over a third of the adult men in the ghetto, are outside the labor force. About 3500 are counted by the Labor Department as unemployed by traditional measures. Thus 20,500, or forty-one percent, have no work at all. Two thousand more have only part-time work; 5500 earn less than $60 a week, less than subsistence. Thus, of 50,000 adult men in a typical slum area, only 29,500, or fifty-nine percent, work at all, and only 22,000, or forty-four percent, have full-time employment paying more than $60 a week.

Another measure of the extent of the problem was developed by the Labor Department in a recent special "sub-employment" survey. It included the unemployed as traditionally measured, people who work part time, people who work but do not earn a subsistence dropped by eight percent from 1959 to 1965, while real family income nationwide was increasing by fourteen percent. From June 1965 to June 1966, 950,000 new jobs were created for young men; but only 33,000, about 3.5 percent, went to Negroes. A Labor Department spokesman explained that Negro youths "just don't have the connections."

There are, of course, connections they can make. For a few blocks away or on his television set, the young man can watch the multiplying marvels of white America: new cars and new homes, air conditioners and outdoor barbecues. Every day television commercials tell him that life is impossible without the latest products of our consumer society. But he cannot buy them. He is told that the Negro is making progress. But what does that mean to him? He cannot experience the progress of others, nor should we seriously expect him to feel grateful because he is no longer a slave, or because he can vote or eat at some lunch counters. For he compares his condition not with the past, but with the life of other Americans. He and his brothers, as Daniel O'Connell said of the Irish, "have been made more thirsty for liberty by the drop that has fallen on their parched lips." Now as ever, it is when submission gives way to expectation, when despair is touched with the awareness of possibility, that the

---

wage, half of the men who have left the labor force, and a conservative estimate of those uncounted by the Census. Ten slum areas were surveyed, and the following percentages of "sub-employment" were found:

Area	Sub-Employment Rate
Boston	24.2%
New Orleans	45.3%
New York: Harlem	28.6%
E. Harlem	33.1%
Bedford-Stuyvesant	27.6%
Philadelphia	34.2%
Phoenix	41.7%
St. Louis	38.9%
San Antonio	47.4%
San Francisco	24.6%

These figures probably understate the problem, since they include only a portion of the men not in the labor force and none of the women, as well as only a portion of those thought to be uncounted by the Census.

forces of human desire and the passion for justice are unloosed.

How overwhelming must be the frustration of this young man—this young American—who, desperately wanting to believe and half believing, finds himself locked in the slums, his education second-rate, unable to get a job, confronted by the open prejudice and subtle hostilities of a white world, and seemingly powerless to change his conditions or shape his future. Others tell him to work his way up as other minorities have done; and so he must. For he knows, and we know, that only by his own efforts and his own labor will he come to full equality. But how is he to work? The jobs have fled to the suburbs, or been replaced by machines, or have moved beyond the reach of those with limited education and skills.

He feels denied membership in that American society to which by birth and natural allegiance he belongs. And it is precisely among the most vital and determined young men that frustration is greatest. Here, and not in the frantic charade of revolutionary oratory, is the breeding ground of black nationalism and "reverse racism." The violent youth of the ghetto is not simply protesting his condition, but trying to assert his worth and dignity as a human being—to tell us that though we may scorn his contribution, we must still respect his power.

But this is the most destructive and self-defeating of attempts. This is no revolution. The word means to seize power, but the advocates of violence are not going to overthrow the American government; when Rap Brown threatens "to burn America down," he is not a revolutionary, he is an anarchist. The end is not a better life for Negroes, but a devastated America: as William Pfaff has said, "a program for death, not life." So it has already proven, all over the face of America.

We cannot abandon the young Negro to this kind of leadership, or let the voice of his protest turn into such despair. For history has placed us all, black and white, within a common border and under a common law. All of us, from the wealthiest and most powerful of men to the weakest and hungriest of children, share one precious possession: the name "American." It is not easy to know what that means. But in part to be an American means to have been an outcast and a stranger, to have come to the exiles' country, and to know that he who denies the outcast and stranger among us at that moment also denies America.

UNDERSTANDING OUR PAST MISTAKES

As we act, all of our policies must be shaped to a two-fold purpose: to make the inner cities places where men can raise their families and live a decent life, and to give the men of the ghetto the opportunity to develop their own talents and realize their own potentialities. Before we can achieve this purpose, however, we must understand the mistakes that all of us have made in the past. This is not to dismiss the dedicated men and women who have worked for thirty years to create our present social programs. These programs have saved countless lives and made this a better country; and they are all we have, for state and local governments could not, or would not, meet the needs. But it is equally true that these programs have not been enough, and sometimes have created problems that we did not anticipate. We must be aware of the real effectiveness of these programs, and of the problems we did not foresee, so that we can plan for the future. For as one contemporary historian observed, "there is no courage or discipline involved in following failure down the road to disaster. Tragedy is a tool for the living to gain wisdom, not a guide by which to live."

Our policies have been aimed at particular aspects of our problems, and have often ignored and sometimes even harmed our larger purposes. Federal housing and highway programs have accelerated the move of middle-income families and business to the suburbs, while virtually ignoring the cities' loss of revenue and their declining tax base.

More important, the system of social welfare services we have provided for the poor consists of a series of handouts: a separate economy, almost a separate nation, a screen of government agencies keeping the poor apart from the rest of us.

We once thought public housing was the answer. But as one woman in the Pruitt-Igoe project in St. Louis said, "They were trying to better poor people. They tore down one slum and built another." The projects were built without asking what would become of the people who would live in them—where or even whether they would work, where their children would go to school, what they would do when they were sick, even how they would travel downtown—in short, without asking how to solve the problems that caused them to need assistance in the first place. Too many of the projects, as a result, became places of despair and danger for their residents: plagued by high vacancy rates, stealing, mugging, and public drinking. Many projects have been preserved from this fate only by screening, such as is practiced in New York City, to keep the "problem" families—who of course are most in need of help—out of public housing projects, while families with incomes as high as $9000 a year may live there. It is not accidental that only 639,000 units of public housing have been built in thirty years, and that eighty percent of these are in cities of under 25,000 people. Nor is it accidental that the present maximum authorized by Congress is only about 60,000 public housing units each year. And it should be no more than a momentary surprise that less than half of those authorized have actually been built.*

---

* Urban renewal brought related problems. For we rarely asked those whose homes we leveled whether they liked the plan, and we thought too little about what would become of them after their homes were gone. Even today, urban renewal projects, Federal highway projects, and new government buildings force people out of homes and businesses without paying them enough to replace what they are losing. A man may have struggled for years to pay off a mortgage, only to be offered $3000 for his home when it will cost him $15,000 to buy a comparable one, if indeed he can find one in a neighborhood where he is welcome. A neighborhood barber or grocer may have carefully nurtured his clientele and built up a large reservoir of good will, only to have his compensation limited to his building itself, or even just his fixtures if he merely rents. To locate elsewhere and build his business again will likely cost him far more than he was paid. And all efforts to change these unjust laws have been unavailing.

In recent years, education has come to be regarded as the answer; and in 1965, Congress enacted an historic program of education for the disadvantaged. But past efforts to improve life-conditions simply by the expenditure of more money on education have not been notably successful: A recent Brookings Institution study finds only a five percent correlation between increased expenditure on education in the ghetto and better jobs later in life. Certainly much of this is due to discrimination in employment: The average Negro college graduate earns, in his lifetime, no more than a white man whose education ended at the eighth grade.

But the schools are also at fault, and money alone is not the answer. Columnist Murray Kempton wrote recently of a functional illiterate who had graduated from high school without anyone ever pointing out that he could not read. A young Washington Negro said, "They graduated me but I didn't know anything. I had lousy grades but I guess they wanted to get rid of me." The New York City vocational schools in one recent year were spending nearly $1500 annually per pupil, but their average graduate was three years below grade level in reading; the outstanding plumbing student from one school could not pass an eighth-grade equivalent test for admission to the Plumbers' Union apprentice program. Yet different results are possible: A remedial project conducted by Professor Kenneth Clark of City College in New York prepared young men for the apprenticeship test, and they passed with the highest block of scores ever attained.

The schools, bluntly, too often do not teach. The average Harlem child loses ten points in his IQ between the third and the sixth grade; and he is farther behind his white counterpart now than he was thirty years ago. Children are tested and placed in special classes for slow learners, where they remain, often the victims of self-fulfilling prophecies about their performance. In a recent experiment, teachers were told at the beginning of a school year that certain of their children had higher IQs than others; in fact, they were practically equal. At the end of the year, the IQs were no longer equal: those whom the teachers had been told were superior now were so; those whom the teachers were told could not learn as much, in fact did learn less. That fulfillment of often ungrounded expectations goes on in the ghetto schools every day.

Seldom are the schools held to some simple minimum standard of performance. For example, we might reasonably expect that all children at the end of their schooling would be able to pass the Armed Forces Qualification Test—an eighth grade equivalent examination which measures a most basic level of educational achievement. With all the money we now spend in our schools, one-half of all poor children—two-thirds of all Negroes—are classed as unfit for the Army, most of them because they fail this simple achievement test. When the children have not learned, we have blamed the children; the ways and standards of the educational system were assumed to be immutable. But what would we think of a doctor who, when his treatment fails, blames the patient? When penicillin fails, he tries another drug, or an operation, or any one of the other weapons at his command. He assumes an obligation—that the patient should get well—and works till that is accomplished. The schools should be given the resources—and the obligation—to do the same, trying experiments and testing their results until the best approach is found.*

To the government agencies that screen the poor from the community at large must be added also those that dispense medical care. For we have provided health services, to the extent we have provided them at

* It was for these reasons that I proposed an amendment to the Elementary and Secondary Education Act of 1965, requiring that the results of all local programs funded under the Act be measured by objective tests of pupil performance before and after the programs. With the cooperation of Francis Keppel, then Commissioner of Education, the amendment was adopted. The purpose was to test the operation of programs in comparable schools—slum schools against slum schools, suburban schools against suburban schools—to see which were teaching more, and which less, to see whether the children were any better off after the funds were provided than before. However, school administrators around the country resisted the implementation of this amendment. Therefore no comprehensive testing has yet occurred, and the purpose of the amendment has not been fulfilled. We do not yet know how much educational improvement our billions of dollars have bought, if any.

all, in huge, forbidding municipal hospitals, through emergency rooms and out-patient clinics where people wait for hours to see a doctor they have never seen before and are likely never to see again. Service is sometimes discourteous; it is always delayed. At D.C. General Hospital, emergency-room waits of eight hours are not uncommon; nor is the situation very different across the country, at Kings County in Brooklyn, Cook County in Chicago, or Los Angeles County. The result is needless sickness, mental retardation, and often permanent disability—all at great cost, not only in the wasted lives, but also in the welfare and hospital costs that serious illness and disability bring. There are, of course, few family doctors; and partly as a result, the ideas of preventive care and regular checkups, prenatal and well-baby care, are foreign to the poor.

Still, of all the programs and services that have stripped the poor of their dignity and treated them as a nation apart, public assistance is foremost. It is, to begin with, wholly inadequate, both in what it provides and the number of people it helps. In most states, welfare payments are not enough for bare subsistence: $55 to $60 for a family of four in Mississippi; $170 a month for a similar family in urban and industrial Ohio, over half of which is usually taken up by rent, leaving little for food, clothing, and other needs. Over all, welfare aids less than a fourth of those who are poor; less than half the poor are eligible for its assistance.

To obtain welfare aid, the price is too often a broken home and illegitimacy. In most states children can receive help only if there is no man in the house. There is no Federal program, and there are few local programs, to help families where the father is working but not earning enough to support his family. If welfare is to help his children, he has to leave home for them to get it. And few states help families where the father is unemployed and living at home. Because of the lack of jobs and the necessities imposed by welfare, a woman is better able to feed her children if she does not marry. She can have illegitimate children and obtain welfare. But if she does marry, and her husband has no work, he must stay away from home if assistance is to be available to the children.

We know the importance of strong families to development; we know that financial security is important for family stability, and that there is strength in the father's earning power. But in dealing with the poor, we have nevertheless said that for them it will be different—for them the price of aid will too often be the stable family life we value so highly. Then, for good measure, we berate them for failing to have stable families like the rest of us.

Those seeking welfare also find it restrictive and bureaucratic: not just the long and complicated forms that come before, but the intensive and degrading investigation to which they are subject afterward. Many are discouraged from ever applying. And if a mother receiving aid for her children should obtain work, she loses a dollar of welfare assistance for every dollar she earns—a slight incentive indeed to bother to look for work. What one mother in Cleveland told the U. S. Civil Rights Commission is typical. She said some mothers on Aid to Dependent Children sneak out and do daywork to supplement welfare "because what would be the point of them [openly] going out to try to work . . . to buy food if they were going to take the money from them at the end of the month?" It is not surprising, then, that welfare has created a cycle of dependency that is distasteful to giver and recipient alike.

Of all our failures in dealing with the problems of the poor, the greatest is the failure to provide jobs. Here is an aspect of our cities' problems almost untouched by Federal action. No government program now operating gives any substantial promise of meeting the problem of unemployment in the inner city, and thus of any way to avoid the inefficient, wastefully expensive, degrading and self-defeating system of welfare. The Manpower Development and Training Act, the Vocational Education Act, the Elementary and Secondary Education Act—these and similar efforts have been going on for years with little impact in the slum. More recent programs developed under the Economic Opportunity Act have some promise, but unemployment in poverty areas is still rising.

The reasons why Federal manpower programs have not worked well in poverty areas are not hard to find. Most significantly, we have again and again trained people for jobs that did not exist. For there have been few jobs available in low-income areas, and most of what is available is dead-end work, with no possibility of promotion or advancement. Moreover, many in the slums are unequipped to seek jobs away from the areas in which they live. Secretary of Labor Willard Wirtz told Congress that "most of the unemployed in the slums" are so "conditioned by a century of insecurity" that even distances of "more than six or eight blocks away from where they live" create a severe problem. Yet most new job openings are much more than a few blocks outside poverty areas. Even if we could induce the urban poor to commute to jobs far outside their areas, most cities lack the mass transportation facilities to take them there at a price they can afford to pay. Nor is inexpensive housing available, now or in the foreseeable future, near the new job openings that do exist.

Some manpower-training administrators concentrate on the candidates who already have some skill, thus avoiding a heavy dropout problem so that they can produce impressive statistics when the program comes up for refunding. Moreover, the U. S. Employment Service has been slow to reach into poverty areas to find men who want jobs, and to seek employers who would have them. Rather it has by and large functioned too much like a private employment agency, filling employers' job orders as they come along.

I have not offered these observations as much to criticize as to suggest that what we have been doing and what we intend to do in the future must be carefully examined. Too often in the past we have been enmeshed in the traditional debate between liberals and conservatives over whether we should or should not spend more government funds on programs. What we have failed to examine with any thoroughness is the impact of these programs on those we sought to assist, indeed whether they have had any impact at all. We need to chart new directions and find new solutions. The war on poverty, Model Cities, the partnership in health legislation, are efforts to do this. But we need a more fundamental re-examination of what we have done in the past and what we intend for the future.

THE KEY: EMPLOYMENT
IN THE GHETTO

The crisis in employment is the most critical of our failures. It is both measure and cause of the extent to which the poor man is alienated from the general community. More than segregation in housing and schools, more than differences in attitude or life style, it is unemployment that sets the urban poor apart. Unemployment is having nothing to do—which means having nothing to do with the rest of us.

We earn our livings, support our families, and purchase the comforts and ease of life with work. More important, to be without it, to be without use to one's fellow citizens, is to be in truth the "invisible man" of whom Ralph Ellison wrote so eloquently. As John Adams said a century and a half ago, "The poor man's conscience is clear; yet he is ashamed. . . . He feels himself out of the sight of others, groping in the dark. Mankind takes no notice of him. He rambles and wanders unheeded. In the midst of a crowd, at church, in the market . . . he is in as much obscurity as he would be in a garret or a cellar. He is not disapproved, censured, or reproached; he is only not seen. . . . To be wholly overlooked, and to know it, is intolerable. If Crusoe on his island had the library of Alexandria, and a certainty that he should never again see the face of man, would he ever open a volume?"

Every board and commission that has examined urban poverty has concluded that unemployment is our gravest problem. The McCone Commission looked at Los Angeles—and said that the most serious problem in Watts is unemployment. Kenneth Clark's pioneering study looked at Harlem—and said that Harlem's key problem is unemployment. The Urban Coalition looked to all the cities—and said that the first problem is employment.

If we are to deal most directly with the deficiencies in our social programs, we will place the highest priority on making sure men have jobs. For there is no real alternative. There is no way to make the present system truly successful, no way to end the false efficiencies by patch and plaster—by a massive further extension of welfare services or a new profusion of guidance counselors and psychiatrists, whether on a block, neighborhood, or other basis. All these have a role to play. But welfare workers, or higher welfare payments, cannot confer self-respect or self-confidence in men without work: in the United States, you are what you do. Cecil Moore, a militant Philadelphia Negro leader, once described welfare as the worst thing that could have happened to the Negro. Even for such an extreme position, there is factual support.*

Employment is the goal, but not a program in itself. A serious program must attack the fundamental pathology of the ghetto within a framework of development that coordinates action on employment with three other central elements: education, housing, and a sense of community. Other problems and programs are, of course, important: questions of police relations, recreation, health, and other services. Yet these other questions are answerable only in connection with action on the major problems. A police force, for example, can exert every possible effort of imagination and

---

* Contrary to the assumptions of some, the provision of jobs will reduce the cost of welfare. Of the 7.3 million people now on the welfare rolls, 850,000 are female heads of families, and 2.6 million are minor children from these same female-headed families. Thus over fifty percent of the Federal welfare rolls are made up of families with absent fathers. Every study of poverty and its pathology shows that the vast majority of those men are absent precisely because they are unemployed and unable to support their families and because leaving was the only way to qualify their children for welfare. Providing real job opportunities—for the absent fathers and husbands, and for the fathers and husbands of the future—will enable many of these families to reunite and others to remain together, thus helping to reduce welfare and dependency—and their costs, both financial and personal.

will to better relations with the community. But it still must enforce the law. And if poverty produces stealing, for which people must be arrested, or non-payment of rent, for which people must be evicted, even if they have no place to go, then the police will inevitably bear the brunt of the resentment that follows. For another example, recreation is good and necessary for all of us. But a donated swimming pool will not replace an absent father; nor will it produce income for that father's son, who may have to steal a pair of swimming trunks to use the pool. It was not a poor man, but Winston Churchill, the grandson of a duke, who said, "To have freedom, one requires a little money."

A realistic plan must also begin with a perspective: that the building of self-sufficiency and self-determination within the communities of poverty themselves is critical. As a matter of right, all Americans must have complete freedom to choose where they will live, in whatever fashion their budget permits. But realistically, that freedom depends on having financial and social security first. The immediate problem before us, therefore, is to enable the vast majority of the poor to achieve basic financial and social security where they live now. And it is crucial that they do so as Negroes, as Puerto Ricans, as Mexican-Americans—in short, as a community.

This need is most sharply etched in the case of the Negro. While tens of thousands of individual Negroes have carved out places of security, achievement, and prominence within the larger American society, what has been lacking is community achievement, which is more than the sum of individual achievements. For most have remained in their ghettos; and those who seek to escape, even those who have escaped, must every day confront, however subtly, the prejudice that judges them as members of their racial or national group. We are all identified, we all identify ourselves, as members of some group within the wider American nation. Even for earlier minorities, prejudice and the stigma of identification with a disrespected group have often been overwhelming—as witness the many shortened names, or changed religions. But the Negro carries his color for life; he can never be judged solely, by all, on just his individual worth or demeanor. From birth, he carries an armband that cannot be taken off.

If it cannot be taken off, then it must be made a badge of pride and honor. While some use "black power" to preach violence and hate, and thus have made of it a slogan of fear, there are others to whom it means a sense of Negro self-reliance and solidarity, of that group achievement—whether in politics, business, or labor—which has been the base on which earlier minorities achieved full integration into American life.

It was Floyd McKissick, one of the most militant Negro leaders, who said that "total reliance on integration—which amounts to reliance on acceptance by the white man—is at direct odds with that sense of control over one's destiny that . . . correlates so directly with achievement." That statement may be somewhat overdrawn. But it should alert us to the desperate need for action, to help the people of the ghetto to gain self-sufficiency, control over their own destiny. We must act to help them equal or even surpass the achievements of the general society, to build communities of security and achievement and dignity. When that is done—when to carry a dark skin and come from Harlem or Hough is to say to the world, "I share in a great creative enterprise in the life of this nation"—only then will America's promise of equality be fulfilled.

It should be obvious, however, that we can only help; if such communities are to be built, the primary effort must be the labor and sacrifice of Negroes themselves. However, too many of those Negroes who have climbed the ladder of achievement and education have given little thought and less attention to the problems of their fellows on the rungs below them. Only now are many Negro organizations beginning to turn their attention to the young Negro of the ghetto, and for some it may be too late. As the leaders of major Negro organizations frankly told the Congress, they had no contact, no rapport, with these frustrated and sometimes violent young men. In any case the effort must continue. The elimination of poverty and want is a responsibility we all share. But if it is to be met, Negroes themselves must take the leadership among their own people, in the building of their own communities.

The process of community development must begin on an economic base: a foundation of individual and community self-support, at last escaping from degrading and imprisoning dependency. In many ways, the ghettos of poverty face problems analogous to those of an underdeveloped nation in Africa or Asia. They are, for all practical purposes, outside the great chain of investment, production, and consumption. It is this chain that must be extended to include the inner city: investment to create productive jobs, which will afford the jobholders the income they need to consume.

To have a maximum impact on the problems of the poor, the new enterprises must be established, the new jobs must be created, in the ghetto itself.

The development of new jobs within urban poverty areas will have an important multiplier effect in creating other jobs. New retail and service enterprises—restaurants and drugstores, barbershops, dry cleaners, and clothing stores—will be required to satisfy the demands of the new wage-earners. Experience under the Area Redevelopment Act indicates that for every three jobs created in a new industrial facility, from two to three additional jobs may be created in nearby secondary and service facilities.

Above all, however, location of investment and jobs within slums is important for its own sake. Principally, this will advance group achievement, stability of family, and growth of community pride. But it is also important to end the isolation of these areas—to bring not just individual residents, but the entire community, into the mainstream of American life. And it is vital that children and young people see change and development take place through the work of their own fathers and brothers—providing concrete hope through living example.

There are two major categories of employment to be developed: the performance of tasks and works that the community needs, and the development of jobs in private industry.

There is an enormous potential for work on the needs of the community. Our cities are in dire need of rebuilding, especially at the core. In most major cities, the great supplies of housing built to accommodate the influx of migrants, from rural areas and abroad, in the early part of this century are long overdue for rehabilitation or replacement. Our public facilities are in similar need of repair. Center-city hospitals, schools, and colleges are notorious for the deterioration of their physical plants. Our cities' beaches are polluted and their parklands eroded, the parks and playgrounds inadequate to the minimum demands of their people. In the coming years, these needs will multiply almost beyond measure. If we begin now to repair the decay of the past and meet the needs of the future, we can create hundreds of thousands of new jobs directly, and indirectly, millions more.

We also need large numbers of workers to staff our schools and clinics and neighborhood centers when they are built. Even now we face serious shortages of nurses and teachers, of policemen and welfare workers, that could be alleviated by employing people from the communities they serve to aid them, and by giving these aides the opportunity to move up the career ladder as they are trained. The President's Automation Commission, for example—a body of distinguished businessmen, academic experts, and labor leaders—reported that there is a potential of 5,300,000 jobs in the public-service field: in health and welfare, in schools and police stations, in recreation and sanitation.

And if there are great community needs, there is enormous potential in the private sector as well. We can—and must—make the ghettos into centers of profitable and productive private industry, creating dignified jobs, not welfare handouts, for the men and youth who now languish in idleness.

Creating these jobs, both public and private, would say to the residents of all our Harlems that there is hope—that there is a future—that all of us are truly determined to change the conditions under which they live.*

A Program For The Inner City

What then is the content of the program? One guiding principle must be that no program can succeed if it rests solely on massive continuing government appropriations, which depend in turn on annual congressional action. Government at all levels—Federal, state and local—will have to play key roles in any such program. But total reliance on government would be a mistake. It would not only be astronomically costly to the taxpayer; more important, it would make the program, the people of the ghetto, totally dependent on politics—on year-to-year appropriations, and the favor of others. Rather the projects must be self-sustaining, generate income for the community, and have a multiplier effect in improving its economic health.

That is why it is imperative that we enlist the energies, resources and talents of private enterprise in this most urgent national effort. Nearly all our major programs have been designed in Washington. Their funds have been voted by appropriation. They have been run by government agencies. I have supported these efforts, and called for their expansion. I have believed, and continue to believe, they are worthwhile and necessary, and deserve far greater support than they now receive. But their strongest advocate must admit that they are not enough.

To rely exclusively, even primarily, on governmental efforts is to ignore the shaping traditions of American life and politics. To ignore the potential contribution of private enterprise is to fight the war on poverty with a single platoon, while great armies are left to stand aside. For private enterprise is not just another part of

---

* The crisis in employment was the basis for an Emergency Employment Act proposal, which I co-sponsored and which the Senate Labor Committee attached to the 1967 poverty amendments. This proposal was for a $2.8 billion program to create 200,000 jobs immediately across the country, and 250,000 more in 1968—jobs involving the tasks and works I have mentioned above. Although not more than a partial answer to the employment crisis, the program, if finally enacted, will have an immediate impact of critical importance.

America; in a significant sense, it is the very sinew and strength of America. The entire intricate chain of the economy—the means by which we join with our fellows to produce goods and roads, to bring food to our tables and clothes to our backs—all this is private enterprise. Private enterprise has created jobs for dozens of millions of Americans now at work. In my judgment, the lack of private enterprise participation is the principal cause of our failure to solve the problem of employment in urban poverty areas.

It is not for want of a sense of responsibility, nor out of willful ignorance, that private enterprise has not played its full role. There are many businessmen aware of the challenge and eager to meet it. But private corporations, after all, are responsible to their stockholders. Large-scale investment in poverty areas will certainly be more costly and difficult than investment elsewhere, which is why investment has not taken place in these areas in the past. Land, transportation, insurance against fire and vandalism, training of workers, extra supervision, all these are so costly in poverty areas as to make investment there uneconomical under present conditions. If private enterprise is to play its full part in poverty areas, therefore, it must have the support of government to help make up for the increased costs.

The most effective way to encourage new enterprise in urban poverty areas is through tax incentives. The concept of government incentives to induce desired investments by private industry is neither new nor radical. Rather it is a concept honored by practice since the founding of the Republic. From 1792 until well into the 1830s, the bulk of Federal expenditure was devoted to creating and inducing internal improvements, particularly the roads and canals that opened up new territory for settlement. Throughout the nineteenth century, the government induced the building of railroads, including the great transcontinental roads, by offering liberal grants of land on either side of the right-of-way; the railroads sold this land to help repay their investment. In this century, similar practices have extended into every corner of our economy. To increase exports, we created an Export-Import Bank, which guarantees and insures foreign sales on credit. To assist in the task of international development, we guarantee American private investment in foreign nations. To induce the maintenance of a strong merchant marine, we subsidize the building and purchasing of ships. It is estimated by the Defense Department that this last subsidy by itself amounts to $700 million annually.

We have used the tax laws as a means of persuading private citizens and enterprises to invest in desired ways, at desired times, and in desired locations. To encourage long-term investment, we tax capital gains at a ceiling of twenty-five percent. To encourage charitable contributions, we allow them to be deducted from current income. To encourage oil and mineral production, we offer depletion allowances. To encourage the building of grain-storage facilities and defense plants, we have offered faster-than-normal depreciation rates. To encourage investment in capital goods, as opposed to inventory or consumption, we have allowed tax credits for such investment; suspended that credit when we wished to slow investment down; and reinstated it in order to speed investment up again.*

In July of 1967, I introduced two bills to provide tax incentives for investment in poverty areas across the country. The first would provide tax credits, accelerated depreciation, and extra deductions against payroll

---

* The principle that the tax code may be used to induce certain investment applies to questions of investment location as well as to the fact of investment. This has been recognized by both President Kennedy and President Johnson. Each has supported tax credits to induce American private enterprise to invest in underdeveloped countries. In the Foreign Investment Credit Act, in treaties with Thailand and Israel, the concept of tax incentives for qualifying businesses has been stressed as the key to helping less-developed nations reach economic stability.

That such tax incentives can prove effective in attracting investment capital is demonstrated by Puerto Rico's Operation Bootstrap. There, a system of tax exemptions, carefully protected by our own Internal Revenue Code, has helped since 1948 to set up over 1100 plants and factories. Manufacturing income has increased by more than 600 percent; per capita income has risen 300 percent; the number of workers engaged in manufacturing has almost tripled. The economy of this little island has grown at an annual rate of over nine percent—a rate that far surpasses the economic growth of the United States as a whole.

for firms willing to locate new industry in or near areas of low income and create at least twenty new jobs, of which two-thirds or more would be filled by residents of the area involved. The second would provide comparable benefits, as well as low-interest loans, for firms constructing low-rent housing in these same areas. The provisions of these bills are complex, but their aim is simple: to give the same kind of benefits to industry locating in areas of poverty as we give to industry locating in foreign countries.*

But the entry of private enterprise must be consonant with the life and spirit of the community. Its role must complement the other efforts being made in the community: Everything that is done must be in direct response to the needs and wishes of the people themselves. To do this, it will be necessary to create new community institutions that local residents control, and through which they can express their wishes. Therefore the heart not only of the private enterprise program, but of nearly all programs aimed at alleviating slum conditions should be the creation of Community Development Corporations. Such corporations might be financed by an initial contribution of capital from the Federal government; but for their ongoing activities, they would need and receive no significantly greater

---

* Under the industrial incentive bill—formally known as the "Urban and Rural Employment Opportunities Development Act"—a business wanting to locate in a low-income area would gain approval from the municipality and from the residents of the area itself. It would agree to hire a minimum of twenty workers, two-thirds of whom would be either poverty-area residents or low-income individuals. These workers would be trained under Labor Department auspices as they work.

In return for participating, a business would gain the following economic benefits:

• A ten percent credit on machinery and equipment, instead of the normal seven percent maximum;

• A seven percent credit on costs of construction or leasing of facilities;

• A credit carryback of three taxable years and a carryover of ten taxable years;

• A useful life, for purposes of depreciation, of 66⅔ percent of the normal useful life applicable to real and personal property;

• A net operating loss carryover of ten taxable years;

• And a special deduction of an additional twenty-five percent of salaries paid to poverty residents and low-income individuals.

subsidy than is ordinarily available to nonprofit corporations under present law.

The community corporations would ensure that what is done to create jobs and build homes builds the community as well, and builds new and continuing opportunities for its residents. They would ensure that what is done involves not just the physical development of the community, but the development of its educational system, its health services—in short, all the services its residents need. They would be the source of technical assistance to local businessmen. And they would be the main channel through which outside aid —government or private—enters the community. They would have the opportunity to make every government program, and many private efforts, more effective than ever before.

Such corporations, each devoted to improving the conditions of a single community, could go far to changing our techniques for meeting urban needs. For example, there was in the entire area of Watts at the time of the riots in 1965 not one movie theater; and the lack of public transportation between Watts and the rest of the city made theaters elsewhere virtually unavailable to most of the area's residents. A construction corporation with minimal capital could build a

---

Under the housing bill—formally known as the "Urban Housing Development Act"—an applicant would first gain approval of a project for new or rehabilitated housing from the Department of Housing and Urban Development, from the local government and from the residents of the area involved. In return for a low-interest, long-term loan, he would agree to build or rehabilitate a certain number of units, to be rented to low-income families. The investor would gain a three percent return on his base equity—but he would also receive a tax credit and accelerated depreciation, both geared to the size of his initial investment, and thus he would have a return of twelve to fifteen percent on his initial investment. The investor must hold his property for a minimum period, to prevent "windfall" gains. If he sells the property to the tenants at any time after two years, or if he constructs more low-income housing with the proceeds of the sale, he receives further tax benefits.

The cost of the housing bill would be approximately $50 million a year for fifty years. This would build 300,000 to 400,000 units. This is considerably less than the expense of the 221(d) (3) and rent supplement programs now in existence. The industrial development bill would result in a net return to the government and thus, in addition to its other advantages, has a self-regenerating character that our present programs do not have.

theater and either lease it out or operate it as a community venture, with revenues paying off the mortgage, and thus create both employment and recreation for the community. Medical care is a pressing need in many slums, and a Community Development Corporation could build, and carry the cost of, physicians' group-practice facilities in a housing project, and rent the completely furnished offices to young, active practitioners.

The critical element in the structure, financial and otherwise, of these community corporations should be the full and dominant participation by the residents of the community concerned. There are a variety of means by which they could at once contribute to the betterment of their immediate conditions, and build a base for full participation in the economy—through purchase of cooperative and condominium apartments with money earned from new employment and money that formerly went for rent; through subscription to equity shares in enterprises spawned by the community corporation; and through receiving part of their pay from work on community projects in equity shares, by analogy to what has been done in farsighted private enterprises.

These Community Development Corporations, I believe, would form a fruitful partnership with industry; many firms, of which U. S. Gypsum is perhaps the most outstanding example, have actively undertaken the search for ways to bring the slum into the national economic market. And we must enlist resources thus far unavailable to slum areas—sufficient to mount a real attack on the intertwined problems of housing and jobs, education and income. This will require loans and technical cooperation from industry and commerce, trained manpower and organization from labor unions, academic and educational partnership with the universities, funds for education and training such as those provided under many present Federal programs.

The corporations would make special efforts in the field of on-the-job training. Not only will job training be needed to make initial employment possible for many of the slum's residents; just as important, the availability of jobs will make many of our training programs more meaningful than they have been before. Construction work particularly, but all industrial jobs to some extent, are taught through a system of apprenticeship—which means a one-to-one teacher-student ratio, a system of learning by doing, a system in which learning has immediate rewards and the relationship of skill to increased earning power is clear. In a very real sense, these projects could be a vast new educational institution—teaching skills, but teaching pride of self and pride of craft as well.

Our conventional educational system should be directly integrated with the rebuilding effort. For there is real hope of solving many of our most serious educational problems within such a program. The central problem of motivation, for example, would be directly confronted. Any high-school student who so desired—whether for financial or other reasons—could be allowed to leave school to work on community projects. The schools would maintain jurisdiction over these students; and they would, as a condition of employment, be required to continue schooling at least part time until the requirements for graduation were met. In fact, all jobs on these projects should require part-time study to remedy educational deficiencies, and advancement on the job should be directly related to school credits gained, just as it is in the Armed Forces. Without the need to discipline unmotivated students, the schools would find it far easier to educate students who wish to learn. And the young men who work on these projects will learn that the ability to read a blueprint or a specification is worth returning to school to acquire. The school curricula should be revised and directed accordingly, directly heading toward the new opportunities being opened: not just in the immediate program, but in the new fields of public-service employment, city and community administration, and in the new industries being established.

Indeed, it would be possible to open up new opportunities at every level of education. A young man showing supervisory abilities, for example, should be encouraged to study business or public administration at the college level, either part time or full time. Strawbosses should be able to become superintendents, and perhaps receive engineering training. Appropriate branches of city and state universities could be established in the immediate neighborhood to allow maximum participation in this process.

Present social-service programs, particularly welfare, should also be integrated with the rebuilding effort. The program I envision would make it possible for families to turn dependency into self-sufficiency. But we must work to make possibilities into fact—for example, by using a man's new employment as an aid to reuniting him with his family—though this is no substitute for reform of the welfare laws to make the father's absence from the home no longer a condition of help.*

---

* As should be clear by now, no welfare system can take the place of a serious program of employment and economic development in the ghetto. Nor can we allow extension of welfare benefits to be substituted for such a program. However, it is also true that there will always be people in need through no fault of their own, and for these people we should provide a dignified, humane system of assistance. In this perspective, the following reforms are needed, in addition to a welfare policy based on keeping families together, mentioned above: First, social security retirement benefits must be raised substantially, especially for the poorest of the elderly, to relieve them of the necessity of seeking Old Age Assistance. The minimum benefit should be $100 a month, $150 for couples. Second, it should be possible to qualify for aid by filing an affidavit, subject to a spot check. Third, a realistic work incentive—insuring that no welfare payments are lost until combined income from work and welfare reaches the poverty line—should be adopted. Fourth, services should be decentralized to the neighborhood level. Fifth, caseworkers' work should be confined to social service and not include investigation. Sixth, neighborhood residents should be hired to assist in casework and outreach. Seventh, the right to hearing on denial or cut-off of benefits should be extended and uniformly enforced. Eighth, client participation in the making of policy should be afforded. Ninth, states should be required to meet their own definitions of minimum need in calculating assistance. Finally, every effort should be made to break down the present categorical system of providing aid, and instead provide it based on a sole criterion—need.

It should be noted that these reforms have a major attribute in common with concepts now being widely discussed. The negative income tax, the family or children's allowance, the income supplement, and the guaranteed annual income—all of these share with the reforms I have mentioned the fundamental aim of developing a system based on need, and not on artificial barriers of any kind. If we make jobs available and thereby give people the opportunity to work, the cost of welfare would be greatly reduced and it would be far more feasible to institute these reforms.

Using the building program as a base, occupational opportunities and training would be opened up in all related ways. As building takes place, for example, some would be trained and stimulated to operate building-supplies businesses, small furniture-manufacturing establishments, and other neighborhood shops. As health clinics are established, young people would be trained as medical aides. Buildings would be decorated and embellished by art students; housing would contain facilities in which the students of music and drama could put on entertainments.*

It should be clear that the possibilities of such a program are limited only by our imagination and daring. For it does no more, and no less, than apply to the people of the ghetto the same entrepreneurial vision that has brought the rest of us to our present state of comfort and strength. It does no more, and no less, than apply to the needs of the slum the principle that the power to act is the power to decide—and to command resources and energy in the service of decision.

That power—the power to act—is what the Community Action Program of the war on poverty has lacked. Without the resources to change the lives of the poor, the Community Action Programs have too often been limited, or limited themselves, to protest: what the CAPs could not give, they could at least help their constituents to demand from others, particularly from City Hall. One difficulty with this has been that City Hall has not had the money or programs to give. Another more subtle, and yet more pernicious, result is the tendency to perpetuate dependency. It is the difference between giving your son enough money and education to set himself up in business, and giving him

---

* What such a corporation could do for the people of the ghetto would also apply to migrants to the city, orienting them to the special problems of the city and helping them to obtain jobs or job training—much as we did for the Cuban refugees who fled the Castro regime. There should be a major organized effort to aid the readjustment of those coming from rural America to the city—a journey in many ways even more difficult than the journey from Central Europe to the United States fifty years ago. That earlier journey was immeasurably eased by the Immigrant Aid and similar societies. That tradition, in which each group of immigrants helped and counseled those who came after, should be revived today.

just enough to call you long-distance each week to demand an allowance. The work of organizing and energizing the community has been important. But if protest and organization are not to degenerate into futile recrimination, it is past time to act: to use the energies and concern now awakened in a constructive effort, shaping and developing the lives of people and their community.

To provide the war on poverty with the needed resources, turning toward programs that would aid development and self-sufficiency, I sponsored with Senator Jacob Javits a "Special Impact Program" as an amendment to the Economic Opportunity Act in 1966. This program provides assistance, to Community Development and private business corporations, for comprehensive regeneration of depressed neighborhoods: Though all programs are directed to concentrate on employment and economic development, funds are also available for related programs of housing, education, and training. Should a system of tax incentives for private industry be enacted, the Special Impact Program would still be available to fund the community-based efforts that are the necessary complement to industrial investment. As of now, however, the Special Impact Program, with a 1966 budget of $25 million, is the only Federal program that provides flexible incentives to business to locate in urban poverty areas and hire local residents. It is obviously adequate only for the support of a very few pilot programs. But we hope that these programs can establish the principles of community development, along a broad front, with the cooperation of private industry, local government, and private institutions—and with the resources that are essential to success.

THE BEDFORD-STUYVESANT
EXPERIMENT

An experiment to test these principles is now underway in the Bedford-Stuyvesant community in Brooklyn, New York. Bedford-Stuyvesant is the second largest Negro ghetto in the nation: Within its borders, most narrowly defined, are 4000 acres and 400,000 people. Bedford-Stuyvesant was abandoned by the white middle class with almost incredible speed: As late as 1950, only fifty percent of the residents of Bedford-Stuyvesant were Negro; by 1960 eighty percent were Negro, with half of the remaining twenty percent Puerto Rican.

By any standard, Bedford-Stuyvesant is a poor community. The problems of housing, employment, health, education, and economic development common to every urban poverty area are more pronounced, and more urgent, because of its long neglect by government. It received almost nothing out of the hundreds of millions of dollars the Federal government gave to the city over two decades; it was unable to secure a single urban-renewal grant in ten years of effort.

The proposals I have just discussed were mentioned originally in a series of three speeches that I made in January of 1966. Shortly after, at a meeting in Bedford-Stuyvesant, a group of community leaders called for just such a program. These community leaders and I began to explore the possibilities, initially with my staff, then with a widening group of business and labor leaders, academic experts, foundation administrators, and government officials, including Senator Javits and Mayor Lindsay.

The first initial requirement was a program built on the community's strengths and tailored to meet its particular needs. This community of 400,000, with more people than live in Vermont or Wyoming, almost as many as live in Delaware, has only one high school, so deteriorated that the Board of Education wanted to close it. It has no single major source of employment. It has no hospital or clinic within its boundaries; its infant mortality rate is far higher even than that in other poverty areas in the same city. At the same time, Bedford-Stuyvesant has unique strengths, such as a fifteen percent home-ownership rate (as compared with two percent in New York's Harlem).

The second initial requirement was an organization to do the work. It is relatively easy to pass laws and devise programs, announce goals and create government agencies. Carrying the plans out is much harder. The question is always, who will accept responsibility to ensure that the job is done, and who will actually do it? The ambitious goals of this project, moreover, would require that the organization include men of unusual ability to get things done. If, for example, it would want major banks and insurance companies to form a great mortgage pool, to make hundreds of millions of dollars available for physical reconstruction, it would be well to have representatives of those institutions actively involved in all plans and decisions.

The organization was announced in December 1966. Two corporations were formed. One, formed by the community itself under the Chairmanship of Judge Thomas Jones, with former Deputy Police Commissioner Franklin Thomas as Executive Director, would be responsible for establishment of goals and priorities, and daily management of all projects: housing, education, training, health, and other community development activities. The other, made up of outstanding business leaders under the Chairmanship of former Treasury Secretary Douglas Dillon, and guided day to day by Eli Jacobs, a young investment banker,* would advise on economic development activity and seek private investment, a supply of funds, and job creation. Generous grants were made by the Astor and Ford Foundations, and by the Department of Labor, under the leadership of Secretary Wirtz, in cooperation with the City of New York.

---

* Some of the other Board members are David Lilienthal, former head of the Atomic Energy Commission and now of the Development and Resources Corp.; André Meyer, of Lazard Frères & Cie; George Moore of the First National City Bank; James Oates, of the Equitable Life Assurance Society; William Paley, of the Columbia Broadcasting System; Benno Schmidt of J. H. Whitney & Co.; Thomas Watson, of International Business Machines Corp.; Senator Jacob Javits, my senior colleague in the Senate; and Roswell Gilpatric, former Under-Secretary of Defense, who serves as General Counsel as well. I should add that this effort could not have gone forward without the interest and support of Raymond Corbett, President of the New York State AFL-CIO, Peter Brennan, President of the New York State Building Trades, and Harry van Arsdale, President of the New York City Central Labor Council.

By the summer of 1967, these organizations had begun to function effectively. Though it is far too early to claim significant achievement or great accomplishment, the directions of initial effort are worth noting.

First, planning is comprehensive and long-range, involving the local group, the business group, the city, and the Federal government. Urban renewal designation is being sought for the entire area, not as a device to clear it of its present occupants, but to give the community control over the land-use pattern and the location of facilities. Economic planning is aimed at the creation of a self-supporting, viable community, with jobs for all residents who can work. Light manufacturing, local services, and facilities to serve the wider community of downtown Brooklyn are being developed.

Second, of equal importance, planning is involving the community itself: more, it is growing out of the community. Architect I. M. Pei, for example, studied the traffic flow of Bedford-Stuyvesant and concluded that there was a great deal of street space that could be made available for other purposes. As a result, the Corporation is developing plans for a series of superblocks, in which some interior streets in groups of residential blocks will be closed off, making space available for parks and play areas and community facilities. Assisted by a grant from the Astor Foundation, it would have been possible simply to buy two or three blocks as pilot projects and carry out the scheme. Instead, the Corporation is laboriously acquiring the consent and participation of each resident of the blocks affected.

Third, all programs are directed at the creation of jobs. Thus the Corporation was able to buy the largest building in the community, an old bottling plant, for a headquarters and community center. Renovation is awaiting the training of local residents to do the work themselves. Plans for a major shopping center are being integrated, not only with needed community facilities, but with training programs to assure that residents will fill almost all the clerical and sales jobs and eventually many management positions. In this effort the Corporation has had the cooperation of the labor movement, and even now young Negroes are being trained as carpenters and bricklayers and mechanics with the help and assistance of the labor unions.

Fourth, new and innovative approaches are being tried in all fields. Work is underway to try to develop a "University of the Streets," with college level courses being offered throughout the community on a part-time basis; also on the agenda is a Community Antenna Television system to provide communication and a forum for debate within the community.

Fifth, and in some ways most important, all programs are being developed, so far as possible, on a self-sustaining basis: to be independent of the need for public funding or charitable grants as soon as is practicable. This will be a long process; it is nevertheless necessary. The community plans, for example, to acquire title to most of the land that is redeveloped, in turn leasing it to business or residential users. Ownership will assure a steady community revenue: growing as the value of the properties increases, independent of congressional appropriation and foundation generosity alike, available for the support of any activity the community decides to undertake—perhaps a private school to establish a yardstick for judging the public schools, a summer camp for children; or new cooperative business enterprise, a community theater, sports arena, or art gallery. Coupled with the increased personal independence that comes from steady employment and improving skills, such community income would leave Bedford-Stuyvesant on its own feet, in control of its destiny. It will engage in active partnership with the institutions of private industry and government, but be dependent on none. That, if it can be achieved, might be a first step—not more, but also not less—toward cure for many of our urban ills. Even as to this particular effort there is much to be done, much that remains to be seen, before we will know whether it has made a difference. But, with the cooperation of many people and institutions, a beginning has been made.

The City Beyond

Bedford-Stuyvesant is more than an experiment in economic and social development. It is an experiment in politics, an experiment in self-government. Indeed, it is above all a chance to bring government back to the people of the neighborhood. For the loss of the sense of community is not just a problem of the ghetto; it affects all of us. Housing developments spring up, but there is no real place for people to walk, for women and their children to meet, for common activities. The place of work is far away through blackened tunnels or over congested highways. The doctor and lawyer and government official are often somewhere else and hardly known. In far too many places—in pleasant suburbs as well as city streets—the home is a place to sleep and eat and watch television; but where it is located is not a community. We live in too many places and so we live nowhere. Long ago De Tocqueville foresaw the fate of people without community: "Each of them living apart is a stranger to the fate of all the rest—his children and his private friends constitute to him the whole of mankind; as for the rest of his fellow citizens, he is close to them, but he seeks them not; he touches them but he feels them not . . . he may be said at any rate to have lost his country."

Lewis Mumford observed recently that "democracy, in any active sense, begins and ends in communities small enough for their members to meet face to face." One may argue about the ideal size, but certainly there are strong arguments to support the decentralization of some municipal functions and some aspects of government into smaller units, no matter what the race or economic status of the governed, no matter whether they live in center city or suburb.

Of course, there is nothing unique or novel in these observations. By 1825, just three decades after the nation's founding, Jefferson was writing that no less than the "salvation of the republic" depended on the regeneration and spread of the principles of the New England townships—already being overshadowed by the growing state governments. Throughout the century and a half since, we have periodically lamented the passing of local initiative and local control over the condition of our daily lives. But the question now assumes even greater urgency, as the growth of cities propels us toward the "mass society"—that frightening vision of people as interchangeable units, the middle class as powerless as the poor to affect the decisions of government.

To meet the problem, Jefferson urged the division of the nation, within each state and community, into what he called "republics of the wards"—areas perhaps a fourth the size of a (nineteenth-century) county—that would provide for their own elementary schools, a company of militia, their own lower courts, police, and welfare services. "Each ward would thus be a small republic within itself," he said, "and every man in the State would thus become an acting member of the common government, transacting in person a great portion of its rights and duties, subordinate indeed, yet important, and entirely within his competence." "The wit of man," he concluded, "cannot devise a more solid basis for a free, durable and well-administered republic."

We are far removed from Jefferson's time. Still, nearly a century and a half of history has also brought us new assets to help us toward his vision of participating democracy. Our population is better educated, our communications are vastly improved, and we are richer. The vitality and effectiveness of hundreds of voluntary organizations—political clubs, PTAs, antipoverty groups—all these attest to the energy and intelligence of the American people: not in scattered, isolated instances, but throughout a broad spectrum of all economic and educational classes in every community and neighborhood. The very municipal functions that Jefferson saw as most appropriate for ward government, the substance of daily life in the city—the elementary school, or the time of garbage collections, or the setting of local traffic patterns—all these might today be better controlled and administered by neighborhood or community bodies. A few experiments in

RETURNS IN GRIEF—Mrs. John F. Kennedy, with Atty. Gen. Robert Kennedy holding her hand, sees the casket of her slain husband placed in an ambulance at Andrews Air Force Base Friday evening. At right are Kenneth O'Donnell and Evelyn Lincoln of the White House staff.

such decentralization have begun: as in Columbus, Ohio, for example, where the East Central Citizens Organization (ECCO), sparked by an outstanding Lutheran minister, Pastor Bernhard, took over administration of welfare services from a church settlement house—and building on this base, evolved a sophisticated and effective democratic assembly of citizens in the neighborhood.

And there has been widespread discussion about the decentralization of education. Our schools, like other municipal services, are, in the supposed interest of efficiency, run only on a city-wide basis: using the same kind of organizational structure whether the city has two thousand people, or two million. The traditional school board is a means of assuring democratic control over education: a citizen board oversees the professional school administrators, ensuring that broad policy guidelines, if not the details of implementation, will be determined by the community and its parents. A city-wide school board can perform this function very well in a small town, where its members are known and accessible, and a meeting can encompass a significant segment of the community. But in a city like New York or Chicago, the Board of Education, however dedicated and intelligent its members, must be as remote and anonymous from the community as is any part of the permanent bureaucracy.

The very size of the system, the huge budgets and staggering problems, draw the board away from broad considerations of policy into the mass of detailed problems. More dangerously, the board is separated from the parents and citizens of the community, and drawn toward identification with the permanent bureaucracy that it was created to oversee, or with only a part of the community it is supposed to represent. A further consequence of size is that the responsibilities of the board are too varied and numerous for effective action. Slum neighborhoods with special educational problems may have as many as 350,000 residents—equal in population to, say, Fort Worth, which in 1960 was the thirty-fourth largest city in the United States. But in the midst of millions of others, even hundreds of thousands of people often cannot compel the attention of a city-wide authority to their particular problems.

Some communities, particularly in low-income areas, have already demanded greater local control over neighborhood schools; and in New York City, experiments in such decentralization are underway. It can and should occur, regardless of the economic status of the neighborhoods involved. New local institutions like the Bedford-Stuyvesant experiment would facilitate such decentralization. Indeed, the development of such new institutions could place some responsibility for the control of many services—not just education, but also welfare and recreation, health and sanitation—back in the hands of the people they are supposed to serve, whether they live in city or suburb.

These new institutions have another potential role as well—to help in accelerating action, in seeing that people's views are heard on problems that can only be solved ultimately on a city-wide, metropolitan, or even interstate basis: air and water pollution, traffic and transportation, zoning and local finance.*

The struggle against crime presents possibilities for the neighborhood corporation both for new efforts at the neighborhood level and for expressing people's views about the need for more effective law enforcement generally. There is hardly an issue of greater concern around the country, and much more can and must be done at all levels of government to deal with it. Within the neighborhood itself the corporation might undertake activities in aid of normal police efforts. The corporation might enlist some of the young men of the community on an auxiliary basis to assure the safety of

---

* Take, for example, the pollution of our air. Everyone who has spent any time in our major cities in recent years has had personal experience with air pollution—all one had to do was look and breathe. And most know of the startling rises in death and disability due to air pollution. What most do not know is that in many cities —New York is the outstanding example—air pollution could be drastically reduced by a simple step now within our control: if utilities were to burn a higher grade of fuel oil, the sulfur content of the air could be reduced by nearly fifty percent at little cost to the consumer. If more people knew of this and were organized more effectively to press for the necessary action, this simple step might have been taken long ago.

the streets, much as occurred this past summer with the "White Hats" in Tampa, PRIDE, Inc. in Washington, D.C., and with similar groups in Dayton, Ohio and Brooklyn. I find that insufficient police protection —rather than police brutality—is a major concern of slum residents; a community undertaking to provide some of the needed protection would help meet this concern.

At the same time the neighborhood corporation could serve as a focal point to press for more vigorous efforts against organized crime. The life of the ghetto is scarred daily by the force of organized crime—by the peddling of narcotics, by prostitution, by loan-sharking, by racketeer domination of some local unions in low-wage occupations. I saw the difference that a new commitment to fight organized crime can make when I was Attorney General. In 1961 some twenty-five different Federal agencies had some responsibility to deal with organized crime. We set up a special unit in the Department of Justice, thus centralizing investigations and prosecutions for the first time. We began prosecuting some of the major figures in the syndicate; convictions rose by 1400 percent. In addition, we set up a clearing house of information about organized crime to aid state and local law enforcement officials, and local prosecutions in some areas increased markedly as a result. But as I also saw in those years, law enforcement is in large part a matter of public commitment. The necessary work of officials and leaders—including their willingness to seek and commit sufficient resources— depends in turn on the concern and support of the community. Mobilizing the community, organizing it into groups that can both stimulate and show that concern, is a vital part of the law-enforcement process. Once concern is mobilized, there is much one can do.*

* We should ensure, for example, that police training methods are improved, adequate salaries are paid to recruit enough competent personnel, courts are reorganized to handle cases faster, prisoners and reformatories offer education and job training to help prisoners get jobs when they get out, and probation is improved to help meaningfully in the process of readjustment. The new community institutions I have discussed could express effectively the common interest in all these reforms, which are badly needed if law enforcement is to be improved and crime reduced.

Bedford-Stuyvesant, then, is far more than an experiment in slum self-regeneration. It is a demonstration in political change that could enhance the power, the sense of community of all of us. Its effects will not be felt overnight; to do what I have outlined will take time. And the idea of new community institutions is no guaranteed panacea. It must be part of a program that involves government at all levels, together with other private institutions in the society.

Nor will the formation of these new institutions be easy. Neighborhood leadership will be required, but progressive city-wide leadership that recognizes the need for smaller bodies in which local citizens can express themselves will also be essential. City council members represent neighborhoods, but they do not —they cannot—have the awareness of people's needs and interests that an ongoing neighborhood entity would express. Federal incentives to encourage these new community bodies may be needed as well.

This is obviously not the only program that is worthwhile for the city as a whole and the ghetto in particular. Many other suggestions have been made that should be carefully examined. We will have to act to improve the quality of the institutions we now have —our Federal-city relationships, our schools, our hospitals, our housing authorities. We will have to deal with those problems that the whole society has created for itself—the pollution of our environment, the crime in our streets, the very quality of our lives. We will have to act to develop rural areas, so that people who now migrate to the city can stay in their homes, if they so wish, and our cities will not be unnecessarily crowded by new waves of migration.

But all our great cooperative efforts will come to little if they do not succeed in restoring importance to the lives of individual men. Long ago the Greeks defined happiness as "the exercise of vital powers along lines of excellence in a life affording them scope." The fulfillment of that objective is increasingly difficult in the face of the giant organizations and massive bureaucracies of the age. Still it is what we must seek, helping men and communities to mark off a corner of the world in which to move, to stretch mind and body in the effort, "not only to equal or resemble, but to excel," which John Adams told us would forever be "the great spring of human action"—and which was our goal for ourselves and one another in our compact two short centuries ago.

The Alliance for Progress

THE ALLIANCE FOR PROGRESS was one of our most hopeful foreign-policy initiatives, offering the possibility of a new and deeper partnership among all the American nations. On a trip I made in 1965, I saw much progress and much retrogression as well. Military coups, stagnating economies, unchecked population growth, tiny islands of enormous privilege in the midst of awful poverty: These, and the smarting wound caused by the U.S. intervention in the Dominican Republic, posed serious threats to the Alliance's bold hope. Some of the difficulties could be traced to the United States; far more to the Latin Americans themselves.

For in Latin America, development depends not on money, but to a unique degree on spirit. Justice and a sense of participation in the life of one's country are essential preconditions to any material progress. The dispossessed and the landless will not work to improve land they do not own, in whose proceeds they do not share. Parents will not sacrifice to ensure education for their children, the children themselves will not study, if the schools to which they go end in the third grade, and if they are considered "unfit" for admission to higher grades. Individual entrepreneurs will not flourish in a closed society, which reserves wealth, power and privilege for the same classes, the same families, that have held that wealth and power for the last three hundred years.

So the building of the Alliance is for Latin Americans. We can help them; but only by a renewed consciousness and dedication to our own heritage, our own oldest dreams. Without this spirit, the Alliance for Progress, the Peace Corps, all our efforts will be useless. With this spirit, no matter what the obstacles, any material poverty can be overcome.

THE CHARTER AND ITS ROOTS

In the spring of 1961, President Kennedy called on all the people of the hemisphere to join in a new Alliance for Progress, "a vast cooperative effort, unparalleled in magnitude and nobility of purpose, to satisfy the basic needs of the American people for homes, work and land, health and schools—*techo, trabajo y tierra, salud y escuela.*" He proposed "a vast new ten-year plan for the Americas, a plan to transform the 1960s into an historic decade of democratic progress."

The proposal was accepted by all the Latin American nations except Cuba. In August of 1961, at Punta del Este in Uruguay, twenty nations signed the charter of an Alliance established on the basic principle that free men working through the institution of representative democracy can best satisfy the common aspirations of man. The charter pledged efforts at development, setting a target of at least 2.5 percent per year growth in income per person. But it was far more than a promise of economic development. In addition it pledged a comprehensive program of reform and restructuring throughout the hemisphere.* The United

* The specific elements of the Alliance pledge were: a more equitable distribution of national incomes, raising more rapidly the income and standard of living of the needier sectors of the population; diversification of national economic structures, to reduce dependence on a limited number of primary products; acceleration of industrialization, particularly of capital goods, to increase productivity, storage, transport, and marketing; comprehensive agrarian reform, with a view to replacing latifundia and dwarf holdings by an equitable system of land tenure, so that, with credit, technical assistance, and improved marketing, the land would become for the man who works it the basis of his economic stability, the founda-

States pledged at least a billion dollars a year of assistance of all kinds to help make these changes possible.

This Alliance for Progress was a response to the demands of the 1960s; yet its roots run deeper and farther in time. In the past the United States had acted as "protector" of hemisphere stability, intervening militarily in Latin American nations twenty-one times in the period 1898 to 1924 alone. Too often our great strength was used not to advance the freedom and aspirations of the Latin American people but, in the name of stability, to protect our short-range economic interests. Military intervention ended with the Good Neighbor policy; the last Marines left the Caribbean in the 1930s; and relations improved through inter-American cooperation in World War II. But in the years following World War II our attention, energies, and resources were largely concentrated on the great and urgent task of rebuilding Europe and working for the containment of, and then a just and stable peace with, Soviet power. Latin America was neglected and ignored. In the fifteen years after the war we provided $30 billion to Europe, $15 billion to Asia, but only $2.5 billion to our own hemisphere, to help the declining economies of an entire underdeveloped continent. We were content to accept, and even support, whatever governments were in power, asking only that they not disturb the surface calm of the hemisphere. We gave medals to dictators, praised backward regimes, and became steadily identified with institutions and men who held their land in poverty and fear.

In the late 1950s the failures of this policy, or lack of policy, erupted into anti-Americanism and the growth of Communism. Vice President Nixon was mobbed and stoned in Caracas. Communist revolution—a

---

tion of his increasing welfare, and the guarantee of his freedom and dignity; the elimination of illiteracy with a sixth-grade education for all school-age children; improved health, including new water supply and sewage services for seventy percent of the urban and fifty percent of the rural population; expanded housing and public services for urban and rural population centers; stable price levels, but without forgetting the necessity of maintaining an adequate rate of economic growth; and cooperative programs designed to prevent the harmful effects of excessive fluctuations in foreign exchange earnings derived from exports.

product less of Castro and his band in the Sierra Maestra than of the bloody and corrupt tyranny of Batista, which we supported to the moment of its collapse—took power in Cuba; and Castro's defiance of the United States aroused the secret admiration of many who hated Communism, but rejoiced to see the discomfort of the huge and seemingly callous giant to the north.

Thus were we awakened from what Roberto Campos called "the perilous lull." Latin American leaders seized the opportunity to press for change: President Kubitschek of Brazil proposed a great Operation Pan America; progressive statesmen like Romulo Betancourt in Venezuela received new strength in their own countries and new recognition from the United States. In August of 1958 we had agreed to the creation of the Inter-American Development Bank and, in the Act of Bogotá, committed ourselves to take some tentative steps toward social reform. Then, in 1960, Congress authorized $500 million for a Social Progress Trust Fund to be administered by the new Development Bank.

The stage was set for the great adventure—the Alliance for Progress—an Alliance whose goal was nothing less than to lift an entire continent into the modern age. There was a great difference between the Alliance and all our previous relationships with Latin America. The Alliance assumed that what was important was not the statistics of economic development but the human and spiritual reality behind them. It would matter little that a nation's economy grew by some millions of dollars, if those dollars were not used to improve the lot of the dispossessed and hungry poor. No material improvement would bring dignity to the lives of men unless other men treated them with the honor and respect that are due the citizens of a just and democratic state. And there could be no lasting peace in the Americas unless relations between all the American nations were rooted in a deep and genuine understanding of the hopes and rights and future of the people in every part of the hemisphere. Therefore, the Alliance was not and could not be a program of U.S. assistance, but must be a cooperative effort among all the nations of the Americas. For an attack that went beyond poverty, to eliminate the oppression and exploitation of man by man which had too long been the ruling pattern in the hemisphere, could only be mounted by the Latin American nations themselves.

This was a pledge of revolutionary change, for Latin America as well as for the United States. But the need for change was not universally accepted, either in Latin America or in the United States; nor is it universally accepted today. There are still those who believe that stability can be maintained, and Communism defeated, by force of arms; or, a counterpart belief, that the economic machinery of the twentieth century can be developed and managed by social structures that were outmoded in the eighteenth. But there can be no preservation of the status quo in Latin America. The central question is not whether we can prevent change, but whether when change comes, it will lead to progress and justice, achieved by free men within a framework of democratic institutions; and for us, whether change will advance or injure the national interest of the United States.

To appreciate the force of that question, and the meaning of the choices ahead, it is first necessary to look at what is in Latin America—at its geography and resources, the legacy of the past, and the stirring currents of the future.

BACKGROUND FOR CHANGE

Latin America is in large part an abstraction, covering a vast and complex variety of nations and peoples. Each nation has its own institutions, its own history, its own dream of the future. Income standards, education, numbers and composition of population, the quality of life and living—all vary greatly within and among nations.

Still they share many characteristics in common. Foremost among these is the feeling of respect and deep affection that their people arouse in the visitor, not least for their perseverance in the face of continuous adversity. In the words of the Mexican economist Victor Urquidi: "These people have endured three centuries of colonial rule, a hundred years of civil war, invasion and various forms of organized bloodshed, a good deal of exploitation by domestic landowners and foreign investors, the effects of the world economic depression of the thirties, and, more recently, the hot and cold wars of the great world powers—and, throughout it all, an almost intolerable amount of corruption and repression."

Even today they cling to life with a precarious hold; it is as if they were not *of* the land but only *on* it. Life is short and the works of man impermanent; it is for some as if Pizarro came only an instant before. Governments sometimes seem to come and go almost at random, and the dynamics of change may seem entirely arbitrary. A civilian government may infringe on army privileges; or the navy may come into conflict with the army, or two branches of the army with each other; or a popularly elected president may go mad, or the army remove another for alcoholism.

Political labels, to the eye of a North American, are confusing and make uninformed judgments dangerous. Latin Americans themselves are sometimes bedeviled by the overlap and contradictions between parties or factions. There is a "right" of the past, of the old landed oligarchy, and a "right" of the present, of business and commerce. There are popular forces of reaction; there are popular forces of democratic progress; and there are popular forces of Marxist socialism or Communism. The divisions and antagonisms may be as great between the two kinds of right-wing forces as they are between left and right. There are similar antagonisms between the popular forces; and the former dictators Odría in Peru and Perón in Argentina got the votes of the poor slum dwellers through programs for their benefit (Perón also had an alliance with the trade-union movement), though neither one was either democratic or progressive, and each repressed even mildly socialist parties of the left. Many political factions, in this many-faceted politics, have their own military allies, ready to seek by force a predominance not conferred by the electorate. Underlying all politics is the subtle working of social class: an upper-class Communist revolutionary may receive more lenient treatment from the authorities than does a middle- or lower-class moderate reformer.

Inflation, the cruelist of taxes on the tenant farmer and the unorganized worker, is in some countries endemic, and the savings of millions may be almost wiped out in a year. Yet even such harrowing uncertainty does not touch the millions of Latin Americans who live entirely outside the money economy.

Hazards of Geography

The continent has not been physically conquered. The distances between places are immense: 745 miles from Guayaquil in Ecuador to Lima, Peru; then 1600 miles more down the west coast to Santiago; to Buenos Aires another 706 miles; to Rio de Janeiro 1200 more; and from there to Caracas another 2810. Between many of these places lies almost nothing—nothing but mountains and desert and vast plains or jungles. Chile is 2630 miles long; just over eight million people live there, nearly three million in and around the single city of Santiago. It is as if the population of New York City were strung out from Goose Bay, in Labrador, to Key West, with the Rocky Mountains less than one hundred miles from the Atlantic. Capital cities, which may hold one-third or even one-half of their countries' populations, often sit like islands in mid-ocean, cut off by a hostile nature from contact with each other or with the world outside. Communications are primitive, often better with Washington than with neighboring capitals.

This is true among countries. Peru and Chile are neighbors; they are separated by a great desert on which few men live. Between Chile and Argentina rises the great cordillera of the Andes; between the cities of Brazil and those of Venezuela or Peru are the largely unexplored jungles of the Amazon. But isolation and insularity are the rule even within nations. Peru, for example, is a seacoast nation, with an advancing export economy based on marine products. It is also a mountain nation, a place of scattered, inaccessible villages where the word "Peru" has no meaning. And it is a nation of Amazon jungle beyond the mountains, a jungle that is little closer to the thoughts of Lima than to the thoughts of Washington or Indianapolis.

As Walter Lippmann has incisively noted, this geography has severely limited progress in the past, and still does today. Economic integration is handicapped because it is cheaper to ship goods from Europe than across the Andes. The Indians of the *altiplano,* the high plain of Peru and Bolivia, live almost as if the conquistadores had never left, or even come, in part because from their village it may take weeks of lonely journey to reach the capital city. Millions of peasants are apathetic because their miserable poverty is the only way of life they have ever seen. The aimlessness of much of Latin American politics must result in part from the severe limits the land places on the possibilities of action upon which a meaningful political life must focus. The extent to which Latin American governing classes have lacked concern for the welfare of their people also probably results in part from the fact that people and places of misery have seldom seemed like parts of the same country in which the more fortunate lived.

The Legacyo fthe Past

The people of the Latin America struggle with more than the hazards of geography. They live also with the inheritance of history: a history of conquerors, as Teodoro Moscoso has written, "who sought above all the gold and the many other riches of the new world. . . . They established in their new world," he says, "the authoritarian rule of the elite which was the mode of government at home. . . . Indians in the Western countries and Negroes on the shores of the Caribbean and the Atlantic were serving as workhorses on plantations and rocky farms while the landlords enjoyed the finer things in life. . . . They produced bananas, sugar, wheat, meat, metals, and other food and raw materials that industrializing nations in Europe and North America were eager to buy. In short, economically they were very much like the African and Asian possessions of the European powers."

There are many legacies of this colonial period. One is the basic economy of much of Latin America—dependence on single-commodity exports, relative lack of industry, absence of a mass market, prevalence of government monopolies. The past lives, more importantly, throughout the social structure: in educational systems designed for a social elite; in concentrated land ownership; in constitutions that in some areas may effectively disenfranchise eighty percent of the electorate; in a feudal disdain for productive investment and for the hard work that is the lot of the majority.

Poverty

The final legacy of this pattern of development is poverty and degradation and want, the statistics of which have become almost a litany. Income per person is often less than $100 yearly; the average for all Brazil is at most $300 and may well be less; sixty percent of the people of El Salvador have incomes of less than $55 a year. Education is wanting in nearly all countries. In Colombia, for example, only sixty percent of all children enter the first grade, and ninety percent of these have dropped out by the fourth grade. Fifty percent of all Latin Americans are illiterate. Disease and malnutrition are almost everywhere; half of all the people buried in Latin America never reached their fourth year. To travel in Latin America, to see the terrible reality of human misery, is to feel these statistics with stunning force. In Recife, in the Brazilian Northeast, there are people who live in shacks by the water in which they dump their refuse and garbage; the crabs that feed on that garbage are the staple of their diet. In fields nearby, men cut cane in the broiling sun from dawn to dusk, six days a week, and take home $1.50 for their week's labor; children under sixteen make half as much; the minimum wage of sixty cents a day is not enforced. In some of their villages, seven out of ten children die before their first birthday, and there are primary schools for only one-quarter of those who survive. In other villages nearby, a new factory has contaminated the water supply, and the mortality rate for children and adults is catastrophic.

In Peru, outside Cuzco, we met men working their landlord's fields for forty-five cents a day, a good wage in an area where others must work three days with no pay beyond the right to cultivate a small mountainside plot for themselves. They had never heard of President Kennedy or President Johnson; they had never heard of the United States; they did not know the name of the President of Peru; and they spoke no Spanish, only the Quechua tongue of their Indian ancestors. In one village I was introduced as the President of Peru; according to our Peace Corps guides, the mayor had dreamed shortly before that the President of Peru was coming to his village.

Everywhere, in and around every major city, are the slums; incredible masses of tin or tar-paper or mud huts, one room to each, with what seemed like dozens of children coming out of every doorway. They are *barriadas* in Lima, *callampas* in Santiago, *villas miserias* in Buenos Aires, *favelas* in Rio de Janeiro and *ranchitos* in Caracas. They are all the same: vast numbers of peasants who have come to the cities in search of a better life, but find no work, no schools, no housing, no sanitary facilities, no doctors, and all too little hope —their life bearable only because the countryside is so much worse. And in Peru, Bolivia, Brazil, and other nations are the Indians, sometimes more than half the population, cut off not only from the outside world but frequently from their own political structures.

These are some of the obstacles that confront the people of Latin America. Yet they have endured. They have sustained a faith in a democracy that most of them have never known, and in a concept of man's individual value that is never applied to most of them.

They have kept a great fund of friendship and admiration for the people of the United States. They have produced some of the finest artists and poets of our time. They have preserved a spirit of spontaneous gaiety and humor, even in the midst of their adversity.

Greatness is also part of the legacy of Latin America: in the civilizations, Mayan and Aztec and Inca, built before the conquistadores came, whose buildings and treasures still thrill the eye; in the proud and audacious men who came to conquer a continent, not with great armies but with bands of a few hundreds; in Hidalgo and O'Higgins and San Martín and Bolivar, liberators who caught the fire of our own revolution and sought liberty and equality for all men in the Western Hemisphere.

New Winds Blowing

These legacies, this spirit, are alive today, perhaps more than ever before. Everywhere we traveled, the ideals of independence and freedom and justice are a moving, active force. Everywhere it is this legacy that is thrusting forward, the future seen plainly on the faces of the people. Latin America is poor. But Venezuela's gross income is already on a par with Southern European levels of a few years ago, and is rising every year. Latin America is short of trained people. But in Brazil and Chile and Peru the "new men," economists and engineers and administrators, are stretching their considerable talents in the cause of progress. Latin American politics have too often been a ballet in which only the upper classes could dance. But in Chile and Venezuela we saw democratic parties speaking for the majority of the people and acting in response to their interests; in every country there are men and parties dedicated to new progress and to ancient ideals of justice.

For the legacies of the past, the states of rest, are under assault by the forces of change. In the *ranchitos* of Caracas, Peace Corps-styled projects of community organization and self-help are being carried on by an

Acción force made up primarily of Venezuelans. In the countryside of Chile, agricultural workers are organizing unions to better their wages and working conditions, and ultimately to secure land for themselves. In São Paulo, Brazil, new industries and new prosperity have built a boom city as contemporary as anything in the United States. In remote villages in Peru, students are working with poor peasants to build schools and housing and public facilities. In Bolivia, 400,000 people have come down off the high plain, following a new road into the jungle to clear and cultivate new lands. In Minas Gerais in Brazil, other thousands are following the new roads to Brasília; at the mouth of the Orinoco in Venezuela, a new Pittsburgh is rising.

Still for most Latin Americans there has been little progress, little fulfillment. Old dreams have received new form and new life in the charter of the Alliance, but the obstacles to progress have not been overcome. Overcoming those obstacles, fulfilling those dreams, demands revolutionary changes in the economic, social, and political systems of every Latin American nation. And these changes the people of Latin America are determined to have. The coal miners in Concepción, Chile, laboring five miles out under the sea for $1.50 a day; the mothers in Andean villages, where schoolteachers tell the children that their parents' tongue is the speech of animals; the cane cutters and laborers watching their children die; the priests who see the teachings of their church violated by the lords of the land—these are the engines of change. Therefore a revolution is coming—a revolution that will be peaceful if we are wise enough, compassionate if we care enough, successful if we are fortunate enough, but a revolution that is coming whether we will it or not. We can affect its character; we cannot alter its inevitability. The question is how the revolution is to be made and guided.

At the heart of the revolution, underlying all hope for economic progress and social justice, are two great and resistant problems: education and land reform. These are desirable and necessary in themselves. They are also essential to economic growth. No amount of capital, no purely economic measures, can bring progress unless each nation has the trained and skilled people to do the work of modernization and change. Nor can any industrial economy be built on a failing, inadequate, and obsolete system of agricultural production.

LAND REFORM

The Need

Unproductive agriculture is probably the major factor in Latin American poverty. As a continent, Latin America does not feed itself. Sorely needed foreign exchange is spent to import food—$140 million for eight million Chileans alone. Insufficient nutrition saps the strength and productivity of many of the hemisphere's workers.

Over half the population of the continent is engaged primarily in farming. Much of the labor of the subsistence farmers of Latin America is relatively wasted; often they cannot feed themselves decently, let alone produce surpluses. By contrast, farmers are one-fifteenth of the United States' labor force. Yet they have provided the greater part of increases in our own productivity and wealth; our agricultural productivity has risen six percent yearly, as against about two to three percent in manufacturing.

The lack of productive employment on the land reverberates throughout Latin America. Children drop out of school because of their poverty. Manufacturing languishes because there is no mass market. The cities receive great new influxes of people since poverty in the city is at any rate more exciting than poverty in the countryside. In short, no solution to Latin problems is possible without great progress in agriculture. This was recognized by the charter of the Alliance, which called for comprehensive agrarian reform; and it is recognized throughout the nations of Latin America, where land reform is in the forefront of public attention. But still the Inter-American Bank tells us that the fundamental pattern of the agrarian structure has not changed in the past few years; and food output per person is just where it was five years ago.

The Elements of a Program

True land reform requires much effort, of many different kinds. First, land must be redistributed. Many Latin American farmers are really laborers who own no land at all; they have neither the incentive nor the means to increase production. Of those who do own land, the great majority farm less than ten acres, which are likely to be of poor quality. Throughout Latin America it is estimated that more than seventy percent of the landowners control less than four percent of the land. Ninety percent of all land is controlled by less than ten percent of the landholders, and there are nations in which less than one percent of all landholders control nearly seventy percent of the land. Thus one family in Peru owned over 741,000 acres, an area nearly as great as the State of Rhode Island.

The smallest plots, the dwarf holdings, can build up no capital—for fertilizer, for machinery, for better seeds; their poor and unschooled owners are largely ignorant of better farming methods. But the great latifundia, the huge estates employing tenant or low-wage labor, often have been no more productive per acre than the smaller holdings. Most owners are absent. Their workers are uneducated and underpaid, with little incentive. The very size of the estates has allowed their owners to become wealthy without substantial capital investment to increase productivity. In Peru, for example, haciendas of over 6175 acres are one-tenth of one percent of all farms, and hold sixty percent of all the acreage; yet they cultivate less than five percent of their land, compared with the smaller farms that cultivate half or two-thirds of their area.

For these reasons the charter of the Alliance called for the replacement of latifundia and dwarf holdings by an equitable system of land tenure; it recognized that redistribution of land, to create adequate family-size farms and cooperatives, must be the basis of a productive, efficient agriculture.

Land redistribution is a complex and difficult task. Efficient use of land must be rewarded and inefficient use penalized; complicated formulas may have to be devised to take account of such factors as whether land is irrigated. The method of compensation for land that is taken for redistribution will present serious difficulties. The lack of a basic system of recording land titles, or even determining who actually owns land, can delay distribution for years. Therefore, redistribution may well result, in the short run, in lowered agricultural productivity and lowered food shipments to the cities, creating additional hardships for city dwellers and additional obstacles to economic development, such as inflation. Further, many of the farmers of the hemisphere are unprepared for independent ownership.

Yet for all the problems, all the difficulties, land must be redistributed. Over the long run, it is an essential step toward a productive agriculture. But land reform is also the essence of human dignity and democracy in Latin America. To give land to the man who works it is to give him, for the first time, a degree of security, something more than subsistence living, a place to stand for his rights as a citizen, a share and a stake in the society around him. As our own Daniel Webster said in 1820: "The freest government, if it could exist, would not be long acceptable, if the tendency of the laws was to create a rapid accumulation of property in a few hands, and to render the great mass of the population dependent and penniless. . . . Universal suffrage, for example, could not long exist in a community where there was great inequality of property."

The question then becomes what else must be done to make redistribution work. Fences, seed, fertilizer, machinery, livestock—these are as important to farm output as the land itself. But Latin American smallholders have neither these things nor, as a rule, access to agricultural credit with which to buy them. Farmers must be instructed in the use of their land and tools, but there are no land-grant colleges, no extension agents or advisers, to help the new farmer to make his land more productive. When he produces more, the farmer will have to send it to market. But agricultural marketing is also in a rudimentary state; only the relatively few cash-crop plantations have convenient and direct access to markets; grades, prices, and quality must be standardized, a structure of middlemen created between farmers and consumers that can assure a fair price to the farmer. Thus land reform requires the creation of a new institutional structure: agricultural credit, training for farmers, extension services, new networks for transportation and distribution.

Next, the geography of Latin America must be overcome. There is simply not enough acreage under cultivation. In Peru, for example, there is under cultivation about one-half an acre per person. President Belaunde has set an average of three-quarters of an acre per person as a target. But even this is far from the U.S. average of over two acres per person. Given the low productivity of land in Latin America, Peru would need to more than quadruple its present acreage under cultivation in order to match our food output per person.

Increases of anywhere near this magnitude will require a great colonization effort east of the Andean Mountains, in that part of Peru, three-fifths of its territory, which is part of the Amazon Basin. This in turn will require efforts of many different kinds. Roads are the first priority, but schools and housing and other facilities will also have to be built for any new settlers. More basically, we do not yet know how to raise many crops in the Amazon Basin; temperature and rainfall levels have so far prevented systematic colonization. Thus major efforts at research in tropical agriculture are necessary; and even after new techniques are developed, it will be necessary to instruct tens of thousands of farmers in their use.

In summary, then, land reform must be far more than an attractive slogan. Real improvement in Latin American agriculture, and in the lives of those who till the soil, requires decades of effort—economic, educational, and social.

The Politics of Land Reform

Land reform requires a great political effort; for it is at the root a political question. Land is the principal form of wealth in Latin America. Its possessors, while by no means all-powerful, still are highly influential everywhere, and naturally resistant to reform. Large-scale land redistribution necessarily implies major changes in the internal political balance of many Latin American countries, away from oligarchy and privilege, toward more popular government.

Improvements in the educational system, vital to comprehensive land reform, would also work great changes in the political balance. Representation of any area in the Brazilian Congress, for example, is based on total population. But illiterates are ineligible to vote, and in some areas, dominated by large landowners, up to eighty percent of the people are illiterate. This illiteracy gives to the established groups in these areas great leverage in the Congress; there is a vested interest against educational improvement. Establishment of agricultural credit institutions for farmers may threaten local rural moneylenders or established urban banking interests. Channeling higher-education resources into agricultural service and improvement would mean denying to middle- and upper-class students some of their present monopoly on university study and limiting their opportunity to take liberal arts and law courses.

All these changes, the essential components of a serious land reform program, thus raise social and political conflicts as basic, and as difficult to resolve, as were comparable issues within our own country—states' rights, slavery, tariffs, and economic reform. All require the creation of new institutions and patterns of behavior. All give rise to the simplest and most important of questions: "Who governs?"

There is no such thing as "pure" economic development in Latin America. Development depends on change—on new balances of wealth and power between men. Economic development requires hard political decisions; it depends on political leadership, political development, political change. For many years, debate has focused on whether the primary thrust of U.S. assistance policy should be toward economic growth or social change. In concrete terms, this comes down to the question of whether our aid should be based on measures of conventional economic "soundness" like control of inflation and a favorable balance of payments, or whether it should be based on land and educational reform, or progress toward democracy. Advocates of emphasis on economic development have argued that social reform is inefficient and economically disruptive—the classic example is the contention that land reform depresses agricultural production—and that, like other luxuries, it must await the achievement of economic success. But that view, in my judgment, ignores the fundamental connection between development and reform: that revolutionary social and political change is the necessary base for economic development.

What We Can Do

There are two ways in which the United States can help accelerate comprehensive land reform in Latin America.

First, we can help with material assistance, in money and technology—for the training, schools, personnel, equipment, and roads that are necessary. Agriculture, like any other industry, requires investment. All but a few Latin American nations are desperately short of investment capital; this we can help to supply.

We can also help with technical assistance. In Venezuela, for example, one year's work by agricultural technicians taught farmers to increase their corn yields from 1000 to 2300 kilograms per hectare; they expect to reach 4000 kilograms per hectare. This experiment required a ratio of one technician to thirty farmers; its duplication throughout the hemisphere would require a million agricultural technicians. Clearly, we do not have this many trained people. But we do have far greater resources than we now are using.

Our agriculture has been built not directly by government, but through the work of the land-grant colleges, the state extension services, and voluntary associations such as the Grange, 4-H Clubs, the Farm Bureau, and the Farmers Union. We made a first step toward using these state and private skills in a partnership between Chile and California.* But these institutions and individuals could be more directly involved in the work of development—for example, by subcontracting our agricultural development program in a specific country to a single state or group of states, managing our AID funds through their own extension services and volunteer groups. Without creating great new bureaucracies, this could secure the service, the energy and devotion and skills, of tens of thousands of Americans on less than a career basis. In the long run these jobs should be done by Latin American technicians, and we should help to train as many as are required. But in the shorter run, the help of Americans is possible, needed, and, I believe, available.

Second, we can help Latin Americans meet the political challenges involved; above all, by clearly associating ourselves with the forces of reform and social justice. In nearly every Latin American nation elections are fought on the basis of the Alliance and its ideals; the opinions and judgments of other men and governments in the hemisphere have substantial weight in nearly every nation. Strong association of the United States with reform will help its supporters and make others more reluctant to oppose it. This is not, we should understand, a matter of embracing particular politicians as our "representatives" in these countries. Such embraces will only smother the recipients, with no corresponding benefit to the Alliance. The most forceful and effective means of furthering Latin American reform, rather, will be through the firm enunciation of sound principles, coupled with generous sup-

---

* This partnership was promoted by President Kennedy over the objections of many within the government bureaucracy, who it seemed to me, never accepted the principle of shared responsibility.

port of reform activities for which our support is requested. And we can help, above all, by not extending our material and moral support to governments that actively oppose necessary political, economic, and social change, including the comprehensive land reform that is at the heart of development efforts.

EDUCATION

The Need

Education is not only important to understanding the world and each other; it is the foundation of progress in the modern world. No nation, not one, has entered the ranks of modern economic society without trained and educated people to run the factories, manage institutions, guide government and draw plans. Without them all the money and loans are worthless.

Education is also the key to progress of another kind: Like land reform, it is a passport to citizenship. As Horace Mann put it, "A human being is not, in any proper sense, a human being until he is educated." Men without education are condemned to live as outsiders—outside political life, outside the twentieth century, foreigners in their own land. Men who are illiterate cannot read newspapers, or instruction manuals, or even the road signs by which we guide our footsteps. Even for those who can read, further education is the key to social and economic mobility and freedom; there can be no career open to the talents without the education that develops talent.

Education is sadly lacking in Latin America. There are not nearly enough trained and educated people to run the machinery of modern society at the top, and the illiteracy of fifty percent of all Latin Americans holds back progress of all kinds. Popular education, in the sense in which we understand it in the United States, is only beginning in most countries. Although enrollment in primary schools has increased by six percent yearly since 1961, and secondary enrollment by more than ten percent a year, the statistics of improvement can be misleading. The school-age population is also mush-rooming, so that in some countries there are more il-literates now than there were five years ago. In rural Peru many primary schools do not go beyond the first grade; in none of the five countries we visited were there schools available for all children above the third grade; and opportunity decreases rapidly thereafter. Of 1400 Brazilian children, for example, 1000 enter the first grade and 396 the second. Of these, 169 finish the fourth grade, 20 complete high school, 7 enter some form of higher-education institution, and perhaps 1 of the original 1000 who entered the first grade will finally graduate from the university: 1 out of 1400 Brazilian children. Even in Argentina, where ten per-cent of the college-age population are enrolled in uni-versities, only 4.9 percent of those who do enter the university leave it as graduates.

Quality standards are often low. In Peru less than one-third of elementary-school teachers have any professional training, and fifteen percent are them-selves only elementary-school graduates. Even in the universities throughout the hemisphere, professors can teach only part time, and must hold outside jobs to live. In Buenos Aires, at the best medical school in Latin America, one microscope and one cadaver must be shared by forty students.

And the educational resources available are not suf-ficiently directed toward the task of development. Fully twenty percent of university students study law; an equal number study medicine; more pursue a classical liberal-arts curriculum. Less than one-twentieth of the students are preparing for work in the critical field of agriculture, and too few prepare for work as engineers or teachers. Secondary schooling is academic, directed at university entrance—though only a small fraction of those who attend secondary schools ever enter college —and does not provide the skilled and semitechnical manpower that is needed in the factories and work-shops of the continent.

The product of the educational system, in sum, is a very small group of professionals at the top; all too few middle-level workers, without vocational training;

a great mass of the semieducated and semiliterate; and tens of millions, adults and children, without any education at all.

Programs for Educational Reform

Improving educational levels is by its nature a gradual process: There is no short cut. To teach more children, more teachers are needed; to get more teachers demands more college and high school graduates; to have more graduates, more children must be taught.

We now help this process, with money and people. Peace Corps volunteers teach thousands of children and help many local communities to build schools. Many U.S. universities aid universities in Latin America; some have established branch campuses there. U.S.-donated food enables hundreds of thousands of students to stay in school, and U.S. assistance has built thousands of new schoolrooms throughout the hemisphere. All these efforts can and should be intensified. Other kinds of educational assistance, not generally made available to Latin America, should be. For example, teaching machines and educational television, which, whatever their shortcomings, can make a major contribution to learning where teachers are in short supply and poorly trained. Educational television has been used with great success by the Peace Corps in teacher-training in Colombia. Important educational resources can also be found outside universities. Thus Latin America's pressing need for subprofessional medical personnel to work in the remote rural areas might best be met by an extension of our experiences with Medical Corpsmen of the Armed Services.

Beyond all this, however, is once again the primary need for Latin American action. We can help build more schools; but schools themselves will not erase the poverty that is largely responsible for the overwhelming drop-out rates. Thus keeping more children in school in turn requires major improvements in the lot of the poor: land reform in the countryside, and increased employment in the cities. Nor can United

States assistance make, for the Latin Americans, the political decision for wider educational opportunity— such as a reversal of the fantastic Brazilian policy under which secondary schooling is mostly private, and universities are supported by the state: so that those who can afford to pay for high school are given free higher education, but most of those who cannot pay for secondary schooling do not get even that.

Above all, improving education will require that those now receiving an education contribute their time and work to the education of their countrymen. This elite, the university students, are the key to better general education, as they are to every other hope for progress in their society. But this is another problem.

University Students

Part of the problem is politics. The University of Caracas has for some years been the center and command post of Communist terrorism in Venezuela; other universities elsewhere are also centers of extremist politics. Fidel Castro was not the first Latin American revolutionary to come out of student politics, nor will he be the last. Not all student activists are so violent or irresponsible. Many Latin American students have in the past given their lives for independence and freedom. Many others have come to lead their nations toward reform and progress, such as Presidents Betancourt of Venezuela and Frei of Chile. Student activists are today building schools and roads, clinics and houses, the first generation of Latin American students to soil their hands and bend their backs. Peruvian students are working in the slums of Lima and in Andean villages; Chilean students are the backbone of the Peace Corps-type programs in their own country; Venezuelan students work in community-action programs in the *ranchitos* of Caracas.

Those who are radical and not active, however, are far more numerous than those who are active in support of any belief, whether extremist or constructive. In this combination of extreme speech and little action is great danger for their countries, and difficulty for the United States. The dangers are that the real problems of Latin America, which in large part depend for their solution on these very students, will go unsolved; that extreme speech will contribute to further political and social instability; and that the social problems aggravated by inaction will be blamed upon the United States.

I saw this again and again during my trip. Students in Peru blamed the United States for the military coup in Brazil. Students in Venezuela blamed the United States for the weakness of the Organization of American States. Students in Chile blamed the United States for their border quarrel with Argentina. And students everywhere blamed the United States for poverty and stagnation in their own countries, though most of them were doing little or nothing themselves.*

What are the roots of extremism among the sons of a class that has been privileged for three hundred years? Partly, it is simple nationalism. For most of their history, the upper classes of Latin America have neglected their own nations, preferring to enjoy the benefits of a cosmopolitan European culture. But the post-World War II period has seen a resurgence of national feeling all over the globe, and the birth of dozens of new nations from the former colonies of the great powers. It is not easy, now, to be without a nation in which to take pride. The Latin American countries are weak and poor and not "modern"; they suffer badly, in the eyes of their young men, by comparison with the United States, or even with newer nations that defy our power. To demand sweeping change is to be modern; to be anti-United States is not only modern,

---

* In Brazil, when a group of college students were attacking the United States for conditions in their own *favelas,* I asked how many had done any work in the *favelas;* no hands went up. Few, it developed, had ever been in a *favela.* Of course, the reluctance to enter areas of poverty is not confined to Latin America; but in few places is it so pronounced. At one point in my tour, an official of one country we were visiting complained indignantly to American newsmen about the *barriada* we were visiting: "He's been here for three days and seen a dozen of them, but I've lived here all my life and never been in one."

but brave; to be Marxist is to be at once anti-United States and intellectual.

A second source is the obvious demand of justice. No man is insensitive, and young people are particularly sensitive, to injustice, the cruelties of poverty, disease, and repression. The manifestoes of left-wing students in Latin America, in fact, are often less advanced in many respects than the platforms of the Democratic Party in the United States, or the Conservative Party in England. It is often a measure not of themselves but of their societies that these students are cast in the role of extremists.

But more than anything else, I think, these students are what they are out of the simple desire to stand out. Those I saw and talked with seem to have sensed that their societies have not enough room for achievement; that they have inadequate opportunity to establish themselves on the great stage of public affairs, to dare and to achieve for their countries and for their posterity.

Students: What We Can Do

We can help the students of Latin America, and help ourselves through these students: The two are not separate. We can begin by extending all possible help to the improvement of their education generally. But much more is possible.

We could begin by learning how to talk to them. We tell them, for example, that we have a "capitalist" economy and that they would do well to follow our example. But this does not mean to them what it means to us; to them, "capitalism" stands for the rapacious and irresponsible colonial economy of their history, and nine out of ten of them say they are opposed to it. We should find a better way of describing our own society, one that more accurately conveys to them what the facts are here. To do this, however, we must be clear in our own minds about what our society represents, what we personally believe about America, and what we stand for: an effort, in any case, more than worthwhile for its own sake.*

Any words and messages, however, will work no magic changes. I know that ever since the onset of the Cold War, we have been urged to develop a concise, exciting American manifesto: a platform that would compete with the simple rousing calls of the Communists. But what matters about this country cannot be put into slogans; it is a process, a way of doing things and dealing with people, a way of life. There are only two ways of telling these students what this country is really about: to bring them here, or to send Americans there.

Bringing students to the United States, however, is more than a matter of opening places in universities. Too often, students who do come here have little contact with the substance of our life. Programs to help them understand us, to meet not just with other students, but with government officials, labor and business and community leaders, and ordinary citizens, are too often scattered and fragmentary, or even non-existent. These exchange programs should be built up and encouraged: not in a spirit of salesmanship or propaganda, but in an honest effort to help these students see our own blemishes along with our assets, and the ways in which we are dealing with our problems.

The opportunity for exchange should be extended to all those—students, professors, writers, and others— who wish to come to this country, regardless of whether their political or economic views are in agreement with our own. Too often, entry is denied to distinguished

---

* We might begin with Lord Tweedsmuir: "Democracy, the essential thing as distinguished from this or that democratic government—was primarily an attitude of mind, a spiritual testament, and not an economic structure or a political machine. The testament involved certain basic beliefs—that the personality was sacrosanct, which was the meaning of liberty; that policy should be settled by free discussion; that normally a minority should be ready to yield to a majority, which in turn should respect a minority's sacred things. It seemed to me that democracy had been in the past too narrowly defined and had been identified illogically with some particular economic or political system such as laissez-faire or British parliamentarism. I could imagine a democracy which economically was largely socialist and which had not our constitutional pattern."

Latin American scholars, even those working with U.S. universities, because their political views are at variance with our own, or are thought "dangerous." But we need not fear the presence of dissenting voices, whether of our own citizens, of Latin Americans, or others. Rather, our willingness to listen, and to let our most severe critics see our strengths and our weaknesses, will be a clear demonstration of our own basic faith; and it will, in my judgment, make a distinct impression on the students and young intellectuals of Latin America.

Beyond talking to these students is action. They want and deserve a full chance to participate in the building of their continent. That chance is available to some; but the students of Argentina, for example, have no organized opportunity to serve in Peace Corps-type work, though many have expressed a desire to do so. I proposed, in Brazil, that more Latin American nations form their own peace corps; Brazil did take this step, a form of which had already been taken in Peru, Chile, and Venezuela. We should consider also the formation of a multi-national hemispheric peace corps in which Americans from both North and South could join for work in their own or other American countries, as well as in the United States. The benefits of such participation would be as great for the United States as for Latin America. It could add to the efforts of our Peace Corps, and to the work of such groups as the International Volunteer Service and the Papal Volunteers, thousands of eager workers, thoroughly knowledgeable about Latin America. If our young people joined in this effort, they could give to their Latin American compatriots a far-improved knowledge of the United States. Such a corps might one day become the nucleus of a true hemispheric community.

Finally, let us preserve perspective and balance in our judgments. There is, on the extreme left, a highly disciplined, highly motivated minority. But even these students are not necessarily dangerous to us, and we should neither unduly bemoan their victories nor gloat over their defeats. When I was in Indonesia in 1962, the mass of students were, if anything, more vocal in their anti-Americanism and Marxism than the students I saw in Latin America. Yet the same Indonesian student organizations, perhaps many of the same individual students, led anti-Chinese and anti-Communist demonstrations in 1965 and 1966, and helped install the nationalist-neutralist army in power. The students had not suddenly become pro-American or even anti-Communist; but they saw foreign-supported Communism as a threat to their national independence, and reacted as strongly as they would have if the United States had tried to dominate their country.*

Among those students who are bitterly critical of the United States, even among those who call themselves Communists, we should not abandon our efforts. During my Latin American tour I spoke to the students of the University of Santiago. The only students opposed to my speaking were not the orthodox Communists but the militant Chinese-oriented group; they threw eggs and tried to shout me down for twenty-five minutes. Other students tossed them bodily out of the hall. Many of the students who remained, indeed many of those who fought the Communists, were highly critical of the United States. But they would fight to listen to one of its representatives speak, answer their questions, and defend it against their accusations.†

Thus we should not become discouraged because of

---

* It should go without saying that there was nothing to cheer about when these students joined in the slaughter of 500,000 alleged Communists, of whom most were probably innocent victims of mass hysteria. The point is only that anti-American sentiments are not necessarily the same as pro-Communism or subservience to our enemies.

† The next night, at Concepción, a hundred extremists, better organized, were able to prevent me from speaking. But they did so at the cost of alienating most of the rest of the students and exposing the weakness of their position. At a meeting before my appearance, I told the extremist students I would admit that the United States had made mistakes, challenged them to debate their case before their fellow students and asked whether they would admit their wing of the Communist Party had ever made a mistake. Their answer was "no" to the debate and "yes" to the question; they said their mistake was in not making a revolution in Chile. These replies had a profound effect on the other students present—although I am afraid only temporarily, as the extremists were much better organized and thus recovered rapidly.

these incidents; that is what those who create them wish to accomplish. They realize that rudeness, disorder, and violence receive considerable publicity in the United States, that Americans become disturbed and concerned, and wonder whether our efforts of friendship are worthwhile. But our efforts are productive. In Concepción, where a minor riot had taken place as I was attempting to speak, tens of thousands of people poured out into the streets of the city in a demonstration of friendship for the United States.

The students of Latin America are the future leaders of their countries. They do have a great reservoir of patriotism and idealism, and a basic belief in the importance of the individual. They are worth listening to, and worth talking to with patience and candor; they are worth all the time and effort we can spare. It is easier to talk to government officials, or to businessmen, or to other North Americans; and too often, only one or two members of an entire embassy staff ever meet with students. It would be better for our understanding and our policies if more senior members of our embassies, as well as the many U.S. officials and citizens who travel in Latin America, would try to achieve some personal contact, some dialogue, with individual students and student groups.

Universities and Intelligence Agencies

It should be apparent that the universities of the United States have a great contribution to make—to Latin American education, agriculture, and public administration, to the Alliance for Progress, and thus to the national interest of the United States. But recent revelations show that the sincerity and prestige of our universities have been seriously compromised by arrangements with agencies of the U. S. Government.

The first of these with special relevance to Latin America was a study named "Camelot," commissioned by the Department of the Army from a group at an American university. The Army, with intelligent foresight, was attempting to find out what social, economic, and political factors might influence the growth or decline of insurgent movements. But the Army was not the proper agency to do the study; and the study itself, designed by the university, seems to have been so clumsily drawn as to antagonize any self-respecting Latin American. The study was to have been conducted in secret; when the news inevitably leaked, U.S. university studies throughout Latin America came under hostile suspicion as tools of the Pentagon.

The embarrassment of "Camelot" has now been compounded and overshadowed by the public revelations of Central Intelligence Agency penetration of a host of universities, student groups, and private organizations. These activities were approved by representatives of the White House, the State Department, and other agencies under four Presidents, for reasons that in their judgment were appropriate and necessary at the time. During my service as Attorney General, I was myself aware of some of them. In any case, the result is that U.S. university missions all over the world are now suspect—impairing to a degree we cannot measure their ability to function as scholars and teachers, forcing the cancellation of dozens of important and worthwhile projects, even the innocent. How long the effects will last is impossible to know. Whatever benefits or costs the policy has had in the past, it is now clear that universities cannot and should not be used for this purpose in the future. Our universities have a potentially great role in the economic and social development of Latin America. It is this end to which they should now apply themselves.

ECONOMIC DEVELOPMENT

I have said that land reform and education, the major components of social justice and development in the hemisphere, rest on the people of Latin America. They must make the reforms, elect the leaders, and provide most of the resources needed. The Alliance is their revolution. It cannot be imposed from Washington or by citizens of other lands. If they are willing to work and sacrifice, to yield up old privileges and shape new institutions, our help can be of decisive importance. If they are not willing to do these things, then all our effort and money will be as sand cast into the sea.

Yet, understanding this, we must also understand that the acts and attitudes of the United States, the wealthy and omnipresent giant of the hemisphere, are of vital importance. Nowhere is this more true than in the effort of the Alliance for economic development and in its pledge to eliminate the material misery of Latin America. That effort embraces our own program of assistance, the need to assure consistent and sufficient export earnings, the stimulation of responsible private enterprise, and the need to meet the danger of the unchecked growth of population, as well as the greatly increased efforts for education and land reform.

It is clear that our own program of aid, resting as it does on the unparalleled generosity of the American people, is still far too small to meet the commitments of the Alliance. We now authorize about $1 billion of public funds for aid to Latin America each year. Of this, only $400 million represents development loans on liberal terms; the balance consists of surplus-food shipments and businesslike project loans from the Export-Import Bank.

Latin America's greatest economic need, however, is foreign exchange. In all but a few nations, foreign exchange shortages restrict industrialization and agricultural investment, help to cause inflation, and involve governments in tortuous manipulation of the financial system. George Woods, President of the World Bank, has said that the underdeveloped world has a foreign exchange shortage of $3 to $4 billion annually. CIAP, the Inter-American Committee for the Alliance for Progress, has estimated Latin America's share of this shortage at $1 billion yearly, after all assistance and private enterprise investment are counted. Our present direct assistance meets less than one-half of Latin America's foreign-exchange assistance needs.

And our worldwide economic assistance program of which it is a part is only one-third the effort, in proportion to our wealth, that the American people made fifteen years ago. In these fifteen years the income and wealth of the United States have risen far faster than income in the developing nations. Fifteen years ago, we contributed to economic development ten percent of our federal budget, nearly two percent of our gross national product. Today, to meet the greatly increased needs of the 1960s, we contribute only three percent of our federal budget, only one-half of one percent of our gross national product: a much smaller proportional effort than is made by France, West Germany, or Great Britain.

I believe the American people will support a greatly increased aid effort, an effort equal in sacrifice to what we were willing to do fifteen years ago. We are ready to recognize, I believe, that foreign aid is not a "give-away"; rather that it is both a moral obligation to fellow human beings and a sound and necessary investment in the future. We are incomparably richer than any other nation, now or in the history of mankind; our wealth is as great as that of all the rest of the non-Communist world put together. Moreover we know that millions saved now can mean billions lost five or ten or twenty years from now, and that the human cost of delay is incalculable. Time after time, in these uncertain and dangerous years, we have reaped the consequences of neglect and delay, of misery and disease and hunger left too long to fester unremedied—Cuba and the Dominican Republic are two outstanding Latin American examples. As President Kennedy said, "If a free society cannot help the many who are poor, it cannot save the few who are rich."

If the Alliance is to succeed, it will probably require that we commit ourselves to a major increase in the development effort, perhaps doubling the amount of capital aid over the next few years. We cannot spend additional large sums at the moment, but we could pledge now to assist in a realistic way in meeting the needs in the years ahead.* One worthwhile recent step

* It might be well to remember that the most this suggests is the annual equivalent, for all Latin America, of the cost of approximately two weeks of the war in Vietnam.

was President Johnson's pledge of 1966 that the United States would continue its assistance to the Alliance through the decade of the 1970s.

Export Earnings

Yet even greatly increased assistance will be inadequate if ways are not found to assure to the Latin American economies sound and expanding export earnings. No modern economy is sufficient unto itself; all, even the highly developed nations of Europe, must export to live. The exports of Latin American nations have traditionally been dominated by single commodities and thus have been highly vulnerable to shifts in a few world prices. In Brazil, for example, fifty-four percent of export earnings come from coffee. Petroleum products are eighty-seven percent of Venezuelan exports. Uruguay's livestock industry—beef, wool, and hides—accounts for eighty-nine percent of its exports. Bananas are fifty-six percent of Ecuadorian exports, thirty-four percent of Honduran.

This dependence on single products has led to unhealthy boom-and-bust cycles in many Latin American economies. Bolivia has risen and fallen with the price of tin, Chile with that of copper, Brazil and others with that of coffee, Venezuela with that of oil. To take a single example: Venezuelan growth was 1.7 percent in 1961, 6.3 percent in 1962, 4.1 percent in 1963, 8 percent in 1964—largely as a consequence of the ups and downs of the world petroleum market.

Efforts to reduce such fluctuations have led in recent years to calls for stabilization of world commodity prices through international marketing and production controls; one agreement on coffee in which the United States joined did check a steady decline in prices which had occurred from 1960 to 1963. However, efforts to extend this principle to other commodities have not been successful, and even the Coffee Agreement may be subject to heavy pressure from unchecked overproduction.

Commodity agreements are, and can be, only a part

of a comprehensive program to insulate the Latin American economies from short-run fluctuations in export earnings. While many individual Latin American nations depend heavily on a single commodity, most depend on different commodities, so that a dozen or more agreements, shared in by many nations on other continents, might be necessary to protect them all. Some commodities, like bananas, are highly perishable and cannot be protected by ordinary agreements. In addition, these agreements, whatever their immediate benefits, still encourage continued reliance on a single commodity and subsidize the continuance of the old economic and social order. Nor can they protect against long-term declines in the world prices of raw material.

More effective and lasting solutions are necessary, including improvements in the machinery of the International Monetary Fund for making up foreign exchange shortages caused by short-term fluctuations in export earnings, and perhaps the creation of special inter-American machinery to meet emergencies. It is also necessary to diversify exports; thus Peru's rapid growth can be traced in large part to its newly diversified foreign trade: its exports are twenty-five percent fish meal, fifteen percent copper, fourteen percent cotton, ten percent sugar. Diversification requires new investment capital, which in turn requires increased foreign assistance.

But here again, the most significant part of the task is for Latin Americans themselves. This is the creation of an internal market, a market for their products within their own countries, that both affords them economies rising out of increased production and lessens the dependence of production and employment on foreign demand over which they have no control. A wider "internal" market can come in part from integration of the Latin American economies; but as important as the lowering of trade barriers between countries, however, is the lowering of class barriers within countries: Small internal markets are the inevitable result of systems in which wealth is concentrated in the hands of the few, in which investment is made only in the cities and not in the countryside, and where the great majority live at a level of bare subsistence.

For most Latin American countries the creation of an internal market is a necessary but not sufficient condition for achieving high rates of economic growth. Few have populations large enough, even with important changes in income distribution and market participation, to support efficient large-scale industry. For industries to be built without unduly taxing their people, Latin nations must be able to export their manufactured products, primarily to their neighbors. Such trade would lead, through a lowering of trade and tariff barriers, to a specialization of production, the use of modern technology, and lower prices for Latin American consumers. Thus economic integration could benefit all the people of Latin America.

Industrialization has become more and more inward-looking in the last forty years; imports as a percent of gross national product have fallen steadily, from twenty-three percent in 1929 to ten percent in 1963. Trade among Latin American nations is less than ten percent of their total trade. The result has been highly protected, inefficient industrial production, lack of competition, national monopolies, and products priced too high for most of their people or for competition in world markets.

It was the United States' hope, at the Punta del Este conference of 1967, to urge the Latin American nations closer to integration as a solution to these ills. Unfortunately, we seemed out of touch with one another. We sought guarantees for U.S. investment and lower tariffs on U.S. sales to Latin America; they sought more favorable treatment for Latin American exports, both of commodities and manufactured goods, to the United States, and had no further desire to protect our economic interests in their countries.* The result was an agreement to reach integration, excluding the United States, in 1980, but with no institutional

---

* As Secretary of State Rusk testified in March, "the United States will only support a common market that is commercially outward looking and receptive to foreign investment on reasonable terms."

framework for its achievement. Nor did we reach or progress toward agreement on better trade relations between the United States and Latin America; though if we want more rapid economic development in Latin America or wider opportunities for U.S. business there, we will have to reciprocate by lowering barriers to the sale of their goods in the United States.

Development: Private Enterprise, The United States and Latin America

Government alone—whether through aid or improved trade patterns—cannot meet the desperate need of impoverished lands for capital and skills and technology. Private enterprise, both that conducted by Latin Americans and that created by foreign investment, can provide an important and even critical stimulus to growth and increasing human welfare. This was recognized by all the American nations in the Charter of Punta del Este. For private industry is the primary source of investment capital and technological skill in all the developed nations; without sustained private investment from abroad, the aims of the Alliance will be far more difficult—perhaps even impossible—to achieve.

Investment there, in recent years, has lagged; and the reasons for this lagging investment are not difficult to discover. In 1961–62 there was widespread fear of Castroite action throughout the hemisphere. Then and now, instability, from right-wing coups and their aftermath as much as from the left, has plagued many countries. Government regulation of prices and profits, particularly in the extractive industries and in public utilities, has become more stringent, sometimes unreasonable, while repatriation of capital and profits has often been restricted. All this has taken place while Europe and the United States have offered investment opportunities greater than ever before.*

---

* Of the $2 billion annual inflow of capital that the framers of the Alliance projected would come from abroad, direct private investment from the United States was to contribute $300 million. Considering that U.S. investment during the 1950s had averaged

Each nation must decide how much foreign investment it wishes, and on what terms it will be admitted to do business. This is not just a matter of national sovereignty, nor of Latin American sensitivity to foreign investment. Rather, it is the best basis for an expanded inflow of foreign capital in the future. It is when a nation and its citizens are confident that they have full control over their own economies that they will be free to deal with foreign investment reasonably and equitably. So long as that control is in doubt, they will be forced by every principle of nationhood to test it: by harassment, by threats of expropriation, by denying price or rate increases, however justified. But the greater their control, the greater will be the freedom and thus the participation of foreign capital.

The proof of this paradox is in Mexico, which over the last thirty years has established firm control over all foreign investment. Under the "Mexicanization" laws, foreigners are discouraged by heavy tax burdens from owning more than small minority interests in the sensitive extractive industries, and effective inducements are offered to all businesses that are fifty-one percent Mexican-owned. Ever since 1940 the Mexicans have known that they were masters in their own house. The result is that private foreign investment is sounder and safer in Mexico than perhaps anywhere else in the hemisphere; its participation in the Mexican economy continues to grow; and both the companies and the government have prospered.

Business can also do much to protect itself and improve the general investment climate: selling equity shares in the local market, hiring and upgrading local employees, and providing clinics and housing and other services to the one million workers employed by American firms in Latin America. And it might also draw up a Uniform Code for Foreign Investment in Latin America, laying down voluntary guidelines for U.S. firms on such matters as recognition of labor

---

about $400 million annually, this was not an overambitious aim. But it has not yet been reached; in fact, in 1962, U.S. business liquidated $32 million more than it invested, and by 1964 our investment was still only half the $300 million target.

unions, opportunities for local capital participation, training of Latin Americans for executive positions, equalization of pay for equal work performed by U.S. and Latin American citizens, fair return rates, and repatriation of capital.

Foreign Investment: The Problems of Expropriation

The most difficult problem regarding U.S. business is expropriation or other action that threatens its interests. To us, expropriation seems a dangerous and self-defeating course for Latin Americans to pursue. Where it is carried out without adequate compensation, it directly injures foreign investors, usually a U.S. corporation and its stockholders, and is contrary to generally accepted international law. By discouraging private foreign investment, it makes economic development more difficult. Where, as often happens, the government undertakes the management of the expropriated industry, the result is frequently great inefficiency, overloaded payrolls, artificial price structures, and a general loss to the economy of the nation; this has been the case, for example, with Bolivian tin, and Argentinian and Brazilian railways.

For these reasons, Congress has taken the position that U.S. aid must be withdrawn when expropriation is not accompanied by compensation that is prompt, adequate, and effective. And the Department of State has, in certain cases, curtailed aid even before expropriation took place—as, for example, in the midst of negotiations over compensation.

From the viewpoint of Latin Americans, however, things are very different. They often feel that most foreign companies have long since recouped their original investments: that the companies would be ahead without compensation of any kind. This is particularly their feeling with regard to foreign owners in the extractive industries—oil, minerals, metals—which are also criticized as depleting resources essential to their future. Few Latin Americans can fail to be sensitive to their history, to the centuries in which their mineral wealth was taken by a small privileged minority, to be sent abroad to the coffers of Spanish kings and then to the banks of Europe.

For most of the sins and crimes of foreign companies in the past, we do not regard ourselves as responsible, nor should we. In Argentina, for example, Great Britain was the dominant foreign economic power until twenty years ago. Yet we have succeeded to all the hostility and resentment once directed at British private investment; just as elsewhere in the continent, we have succeeded to historic grievances against the Spanish, or against the privileged class within Latin America.

Given such disparate views of right and reality, which almost guarantee disagreement, it is necessary to clearly define our goals. The United States wants to protect the interests of U.S. firms and shareholders, to encourage Latin Americans to look favorably on further private investment, both domestic and foreign, to aid Latin America's economic, political, and social development, and to further friendship and cooperation with the Latin American nations.

These aims, however, may conflict with each other; and dogged pursuit of one may make the achievement of others impossible. In one dispute over the expropriation of an American property, for example, certain aid funds were held up, including those for a project for Peace Corps-type work by Peruvian students in the depressed rural areas of Peru; the aim was to make the Peruvians more "reasonable." The programs that were held up were potential sources of great democratic reform, strength, and stability—the essence of the Alliance and of our own national interest. The pressure, moreover, made expropriation a more serious nationalist issue, which was used to criticize President Belaunde for not standing up to the United States more vigorously; much of the criticism was from the right. Most significantly, in the same year that aid to Cooperación Popular was held up, our military assistance deliveries to Peru nearly doubled: from $5.2 million to $10 million, more than to any other Latin American nation. Our policymakers may not have intended this result, but I am sure that many Peruvians thought we favored arms over social reform. And future private investment may have been seriously prejudiced by further identification with foreigners and with domination by the United States.

This case should be contrasted with the results of a different policy in Mexico. Toward the end of the continuing Mexican revolution in 1938, Mexico nationalized all foreign oil companies. For a time, the use of economic sanctions, perhaps even force, was considered to compel full compensation. As the dispute dragged on into 1940, when we were concerned with possible Axis penetration of the hemisphere, President Roosevelt settled it on terms quite favorable to Mexico. One result was to help secure our southern flank throughout World War II. A second result was that the Mexican revolution came to terms with the United States, and our relations have been consistently good. Now, a generation later, not only is Mexican private industry expanding in importance, but U.S. firms, paying due respect to Mexican political supremacy, operate there without serious economic hindrance.

Another example of a more realistic policy—in this case not government policy, but that of American business—can be seen in Chile. There President Frei reached a settlement with U.S. copper companies, under which the Chilean Government is to become a major partner in their operations, the companies are to establish plants for fabrication of finished products, and output is to be expanded with substantial tax concessions. What is important about this settlement is that it was reached by the companies themselves, without the cutting off of aid or other pressure from the U.S. Government.

These examples demonstrate that expropriation should be handled just as are other questions of private U.S. investment. The essential need is for U.S. business to reach its own accommodations with Latin American governments, paying full respect to their sovereignty and national independence, as creative U.S. enterprises and businessmen have shown it is possible to do. Aid, however, should not be withheld to force special advantages for U.S. business. Even where business is expropriated without compensation satisfactory to the owners, the President should have the means to set policy, in the context of our entire relationship with the nation concerned. In my judgment, the absolute requirement of present law that aid be cut off deprives our relationships and negotiations of needed flexibility, and is harmful. In the last analysis, withdrawing aid is not a policy, but the failure of policy; the aim of creative business and creative diplomacy is to ensure that withdrawal in retaliation for expropriation never becomes necessary.

Population: Growth and Control

All our efforts to stimulate economic growth must be informed by an awareness that population growth threatens to eat up our gains as fast as they are made. Latin America is growing faster than any other part of the world. In the continent as a whole, population is rising by 3 percent yearly; in several countries it is rising by 3.5 percent. At present rates of growth, the United Nations estimates that Latin America will have a population of 363 million in 1980, an increase of more than 50 percent over 1965. Although food production has increased 10 percent in the last five years, this increase was directly matched by population growth. Each person has no more to eat than he did five years ago, and the level of nutrition is totally inadequate. And the same population growth that negates progress in agriculture dilutes progress in gross income.*

Some Latin Americans, nevertheless, do not regard

* Venezuela's gross income, for example, grew by 5 percent annually between 1960 and 1964, but its population grew by 3.7 percent yearly, and per-person income growth was less than 1.5 percent. Peru, where income rose by an average of 7.7 percent annually in 1960–64, had a per-person growth rate of only 4.5 percent. Chile's population grew slowly for the hemisphere, at 2.3 percent yearly, but even this cut a 4.4 percent gross-product rise to one of 1.9 percent per person. In rural areas of Guatemala, with population growth of 3.1 percent in recent years, per-person income actually declined by almost 5 percent from 1950 to 1964.

their burgeoning populations as a danger. "Most of the countries," says a United Nations report, "look on the prospect of population much larger than the present as a challenge but not as a burden." After all, they say, Latin America has a population density only one-half as great as the United States, one-tenth as great as Europe; surely more hands are needed for the work of development and for the colonization of the interior.

The rapid increases in population, however, are not colonizing the interior, but swelling the numbers of the urban poor. Moreover, the population increase seriously handicaps efforts to improve educational levels, to provide decent housing, to raise Latin American living standards in dozens of other ways. Just as among poor people in our own country, large poor families have a far more difficult time raising children. After development there would be more force to underpopulation arguments, but the problem of Latin America now is not that its people are too few.

These facts have been recognized by many Latin Americans. Polls have shown that most women want only three or four children; we know that in some Latin American cities one out of four women has had an induced abortion; and many Latin American governments are showing active interest and purpose in population control.

I believe we should provide assistance to any nation that decides family planning and population control are in its national interest, as well as accelerate our research into population control devices and techniques. Every effort should be made to inform the Latin American governments and people about what assistance is available, how to plan sound population control policies and programs, and what the consequences can be of various courses of action or inaction.

But we cannot force Latin Americans to adopt birth control. There are already deep suspicions in Latin America that, as a typical view has it, "The rich nations who worry about population growth are concerned about reducing the number of Puerto Ricans, Hindus, Negroes, Chinese, and Mexicans; or else of certain classes and social groups, like the poor, the working class, or the Catholics. But they do not worry, for example, about the increase of Aryans, or Protestants, or Rotarians."

In fact, of course, it is individuals in the advanced and fortunate nations who now practice the most active population-control policies. But the quotation does illustrate the barrier of suspicion facing our efforts to limit the growth of population. Any attempt to compel Latin Americans to practice birth control would only inflame these suspicions. But we should stand ready to help; we should encourage any efforts they undertake to make themselves more aware of their problem; and, while recognizing that the decisions must be made freely by Latin Americans themselves, we should help them make the decision that is truly in the interest of their people and serves the goals of the Alliance.

THE POLITICS OF THE ALLIANCE

Capital resources, investment, education, land reform, and all the rest are essential to the creation of a modern state. They will be the program of any developing country, anywhere in the world, that is engaged in the painful and arduous search for economic progress and social justice. In Latin America, however, those achievements are sought within a framework of political democracy and individual freedom. The Latin American nations are Western nations. Unlike many others, they share values and traditions, history and religion, with the countries of Europe and with the United States. Their intellectuals, leaders, and peoples have been nourished on a belief in freedom.

That freedom has often been denied. They have suffered more than their share of despots, dictators, and oligarchical rule. But from Bolivar to the present, democracy and freedom have been a goal, a rallying cry, and a belief. Of course, the choice and struggle are for the Latin Americans themselves. But we must also realize that our acts can have an enormous influence on the third great pillar of the Alliance: the politics of democratic development.

The Problem of Power: The United States
Through Latin American Eyes

The United States can never seem neutral to Latin Americans. Partly this is because the United States is so powerful; most Latin Americans sincerely believe that we ordain most of what happens in the hemisphere. The United States looms over the continent in a way that is difficult to appreciate from the North. The Dominican Republic was for us only one of many crises, its memory now almost erased by Vietnam; yet long after the fighting, it was the one issue raised with an American visitor by Latins of all political persuasions. We saw it as an isolated incident, an *ad hoc* response to a unique threat; for them it was a reminder of the past and a harbinger of the future, a threat to every principle of national independence and self-determination; just as in the past the Bay of Pigs invasion seemed to many to signal a new type of threat from the North. We seldom think of overseas oil operations as important factors in our economy; but in Peru an impasse in negotiations between the government and a U.S. oil company brought a slowdown of our development assistance; the same was true in Argentina; and the Venezuelan economy depends in large part on oil company decisions on whether to sell from their fields there or from the Middle East. The price our housewives pay for coffee is perhaps a matter for a few minutes' casual conversation, but a small drop in the price we pay would cancel out much of the benefit of our development aid to Brazil each year; and our allocation of sugar quotas can shake economies in several nations. These are but examples of the many ways in which Latin America is directly dependent on events and decisions made in the United States; circumstances of the greatest importance to them, which they feel powerless to affect or alter.

Because these actions are of great importance to Latin Americans, they assume that we realize and intend every consequence of our acts. They often try to read far too much into a particular policy or decision. If we recognize a government, they assume that we approve it. If we give assistance to a nation's army, many assume that we desire a military takeover. Latin Americans, whose governments are deeply intertwined with business, do not distinguish between private acts—decisions about investment or market prices—and the decisions of government. So, in their eyes, the U.S. Government is directly responsible for every facet of Latin American economic relations with the United States.

We know that the United States is not omnipotent, that we often act, or fail to act, by mistake or inadvertence, that we may recognize or deal with a government simply because it is there, and assist it because it is the best of alternatives, none of which is wholly satisfactory. We know too that most economic decisions in the United States are made by private parties, not by the government. But Latin Americans see us in their terms, just as we see them in ours. And the essence of a foreign policy is results, which means that we should be concerned not just with our own judgment of our motives and actions but as much with the judgments of those with whom we deal.

This is not to say that popularity should be the judge of our actions. Indeed, there have been many occasions in the past, and there will be others in the future, when our judgment of national interest, or even the best interests of others, will be decidedly unpopular; on those occasions, we will simply have to stand unpopularity. But the standard for our actions should be the "decent respect for the opinions of mankind" that the Declaration of Independence professed; moreover, we owe the deepest solicitude for the views of our partners in the unique experiment of the Alliance for Progress.

Every decision we make that affects Latin America, therefore, should receive close and knowledgeable attention at the highest levels of government. We must learn to deal with our hemispheric colleagues in a manner that at least accepts their definition of an issue's importance. We will not thereby come to agree with them on every decision, nor will we thus solve our problems in Latin America. But we will at least not fail to do so through carelessness and lack of effort. Some years ago, John Foster Dulles went on a mission to Latin America. His hosts said to him, "Good to have you here, Mr. Secretary." "You shouldn't feel that way," Dulles replied, "for I go only where there is trouble." If the policy of paying attention only to trouble were ever to return, then there would be trouble enough for generations to come.

The United States and the Internal Politics of Latin America

With these considerations in mind, what should be our role in political and social change in Latin America? To what extent can the United States influence social and political change in Latin America? To what extent is it legitimate for us to do so—or fail to do so? Should we deal with people only through established governments? Most difficult of all, what should be our attitude and policy toward undemocratic governments, or those which resist necessary reform? In the last decade, as earlier in Latin American history, many governments have been overturned in military coups. Since the inauguration of the Alliance in 1961, elected or other constitutional governments have been overthrown, or prevented from taking office in Honduras, Peru, Argentina, the Dominican Republic, Brazil, Guatemala, Ecuador, and Bolivia. Almost every Latin American government lives under threat of such military action; only Mexico has avoided it in the last thirty years, though other governments have contained the power of the military.

Our stated position is that the United States "reserves its special friendship" for progressive, democratic governments and that "despots are not welcome in this hemisphere." To say that the United States must reserve its special friendship for the forces of democratic progress does not, of course, answer all questions. It is easy, in Venezuela or Chile, to support a bona fide democratic government, with the purpose and promise of effective reform; but this is not the case in every country. Each country presents a unique situation which must be confronted on its own facts. But in those confrontations, we could do with a much stronger bias against the military.

In 1966, when I first reported to the Senate on my trip to Latin America, I attempted to deal with this question by analyzing our policy choices in Brazil, the victim of a military coup in 1964. The previous government had been ineffective and corrupt: Inflation was growing by 100 percent yearly, and the President and his circle had become some of the largest landowners and richest men in the country. The coup had been supported by large numbers of the urban middle classes and many civilian politicians; no one bothered to defend the old government. The new government of General Humberto Castelo Branco instituted repressive controls over politics and the press; but it moved toward significant reforms and promised new elections in 1966.

For this government, in Latin American eyes, rightly or wrongly, we bore a heavy responsibility. Less than three weeks before the coup, it was reported in the press that, in private Administration councils, our Assistant Secretary of State for Latin American Affairs said that the United States would not automatically oppose every military takeover in the hemisphere. We recognized the new government within three days of the coup, three months later gave it a special loan of $50 million, and by the end of 1966 had provided $1 billion in aid. We became heavily identified with the new government and its program: the Brazilian joke about our ambassador there was "elect Gordon—eliminate the middleman."

I said in 1966 that aid to Brazil should not be cut off: that cutting off aid would harm, not benefit, the people of Brazil; that it would be sharply resented by the many Brazilians who supported the government, indeed by many who did not. It was then my view that continued assistance, coupled with clear support for a return to democracy—expressed through diplomatic channels and in public opinion—was the most hopeful course. In retrospect my view was much too hopeful. Our continued heavy assistance seems only to have confirmed the military in their power, encouraged them to harden their repression and to write their continued rule into the Constitution. It certainly encouraged, to some unknown degree, the Argentine military in their coup of 1966; there were even reports that the Brazilians met with the Argentine military before the Argentines moved, to advise them on how to "handle" the problem of U.S. recognition and assistance.

The Alliance for Progress was not meant to be—and could not be—a means for the United States to determine the government of every American nation. The governments of Latin America are for the people of each Latin American nation to determine; their struggles and their political conflicts must be their own. Independence and responsibility are not given or taught; they can only be learned by practice—including the practice of making mistakes. But when power is seized by the military, or a constitutional government overthrown, our assistance should be reduced to the minimum consistent with humanitarian concern for the people of the country. As a practical matter, we should support, at the most, specific projects that directly contribute to reform—for example, rural schools or health clinics or land reform programs—and avoid providing general "program loans," which tend to identify us with the government. Latin American nations, in the future as in the past, may temporarily acquiesce in their domination by military force. But assistance and identification of the kind and magnitude we have provided in Brazil since 1964 can help neither this nation nor Latin America, and could deal a fatal stroke to the ideals of the Alliance.

There is precedent for more drastic action. After a military coup in Peru in 1962 we suspended all assistance programs and refused recognition until definite commitments to free elections and respect for civil liberties were made by the military government. Those commitments were made and kept, and led to the election of the progressive Peruvian Government of President Belaunde in 1963. This policy was attempted elsewhere, with less success; more often, it was briefly attempted only to be abandoned. Conversations with representatives of the State Department, however, suggest that this practice will no longer be followed in any circumstances. For the benefit of Latin America, and for the United States, I hope they are not correctly stating our policy. For if they are, they violate the spirit if not the letter of the Alliance for Progress—they attack its basic philosophy, which made the Alliance more than a United States aid program, and rather a mutual assistance program built around social and political reform and development.

Aid as a Weapon: Foreign Policy

Self-determination was central to the Alliance. It was matched by the counterpart principle that only governments and nations moving toward development and reform could fruitfully participate in its programs and thereby qualify for assistance. Judgments of who qualified and who did not would be determined, not unilaterally by the United States, but in a collective consensus of all the American nations. Otherwise would be to make true the accusation of Che Guevara at Punta del Este that it was "an alliance of one millionaire and twenty beggars." Least of all was it intended that the Alliance should be a crude device for the United States to dominate particular aspects of the foreign policy of the Latin American nations.

Yet there is a temptation, and one to which we have sometimes given in, to use our great power and our aid in this way. At times, we have tried to force agreement from other nations or to punish them for their disagreement: on such matters as whether a country voted in the Organization of American States to approve our action in the Dominican Republic, or whether it recognizes Communist China or votes for its admission to the United Nations. It is perhaps understandable that officials in the Executive Branch or members of Congress would feel that nations that fail to stand with us on such questions are not reliable allies, and should not receive U.S. assistance. But this feeling, so understandable in the passions and excitement of the moment, can only be harmful over the long run. We expect our government to reflect the feelings of our people. Latin Americans expect the same from their governments, and deeply resent any government that seems less than fully independent in its decisions. One Latin American president told me succinctly: "If you want a government that says always 'yes, yes, yes,' you will soon have to deal with a government that says always 'no, no, no.' "

THREATS FROM LEFT AND RIGHT

The forces of progressive democracy in Latin America have many enemies and obstacles. They are under attack from the right and the left: from those who would sacrifice justice to preserve the past and from those who would heedlessly impose bloodshed and dictatorship to hasten change. Two of the most pervasive obstacles to democracy in Latin American countries are the Communist threat and the interference with constitutional processes by some of the Latin American military establishments.

The Communist Threat

The threat of Communism in Latin America is real. But there are many mistakes made about this threat: of fact, of judgment, and of action. If the threat is not to become reality, we cannot afford mistakes. Communism means different things to Americans on different sides of the Rio Grande. To Latin Americans, the Berlin Wall, Hungary, the liquidation of the kulaks, or the repression of thought that has outlasted the passing of Stalin, all these matters are far away. Our confrontations with the Soviet Union and Communist China are largely irrelevant to their concern. Communism in Latin America, furthermore, is not simply a conspiracy to take power, financed and supported from abroad;

although Cuba, China, and to a lesser extent the Soviet Union are directly helping Communist movements in many places in the hemisphere, seemingly competing with one another for the allegiance of Latin American revolutionaries. Communism also has an appeal for many who seek a nonexistent short cut to economic progress and social justice. As an interpretation of their experience, moreover, Marxism has strong appeal to many Latin Americans. They have, after all, been exploited for generations; capitalism to them means foreign domination, or a system in which their own privileged classes create monopolistic enterprises with which to rob the nation. Since Communism says that capitalism must fall, some see it as the answer to many of their most pressing social problems. For some, this is most true of the more radical orientation of Chinese Communism, which adds to traditional Marxist theory the prediction that the poor southern half of the world will eventually encircle and vanquish the more fortunate north, and offers to all an alliance against the fortunate half in which we live.

This alliance has been accepted by only a small minority: guerrilla bands in Peru and Guatemala, terrorist groups in Venezuela, small groups of intellectuals and students elsewhere. Their small numbers, however, do not make these groups harmless. In Venezuela, for example, the elections of 1963 were carried out with the greatest difficulty in the midst of terrorism; during my visit in November 1965, Caracas still resembled in many ways a city under siege by hostile forces. More significantly, these groups are often more disciplined and active than the forces of democratic reform; and all too often, they are the only group showing apparent concern for improvement in the lot of the landless peasant or the urban slum dweller. There is a village in the Andes where only one person has ever come to say that he believed in land for the peasants. That one man was a Communist, and now many of these villagers call themselves Communists, too, since they are in favor of land reform. Here is the great danger of subversion in Latin America: If we allow Communism to carry the banner and promise of reform, then the ignored and the dispossessed, the insulted and injured, will turn to it as the only way out of their misery.

Some of our actions, and those of some Latin American governments, have helped the Communists to seize reform as their own. For many years the established order in Latin America has referred to all efforts for justice as Communist, thus strengthening the false Communist claim to represent the forces of progress and democracy; and the claim is further strengthened when such leaders as Presidents Frei of Chile and Leoni of Venezuela or the great Brazilian Archbishop Dom Helder Camara are referred to by right-wing Latin American circles as Communists. We must clearly understand that Communism is not a native growth in Latin America. Given any meaningful alternative, its people will reject it and follow the path of democratic reform. But if we allow ourselves to become allied with those to whom the cry of "Communism" is only an excuse for the perpetuation of privilege; if we assist, with military matériel and other aid, governments that use that aid to prevent reform for their people, then we do much to ensure that reform, when it comes, will bear the Communist label.

Communism Armed: Insurgency and Its Counter

Even a government of true reform is not invulnerable to armed force: Bombs and bullets can terrorize and intimidate even citizens who are thoroughly loyal to their government. In the present circumstances of most Latin American nations, tens of millions of people, whatever efforts are made in their behalf, will continue to have substantial grievances for many years to come; some may explode into violence and insurgency. Throughout much of the Latin American countryside, moreover, there is a tradition of freebooting violence and banditry, which organized terrorists may recruit to their own banners.

If governments are to move toward progress and freedom, they must be able to defend themselves against internal attack, as the Venezuelan government did in 1963—when the insurgent challenge was defeated; the election was held; and for the first time in Venezuelan history an elected president succeeded a president who had himself served a full legal term. This outcome was due in large part to the competence of the Venezuelan police, who proved able to contain the terrorists without such use of excessive or indiscriminate force as to alienate the general population.

This result in turn was due in large part to the counterinsurgency training program initiated by Venezuela three years before, in the midst of another crisis. In 1961 terrorist activity, supported from Castro's Cuba, was at a peak. President Betancourt was threatened on two sides: by the terrorists themselves and by the army, which was close to taking over in the name of "public order." A special crash program was then begun by Betancourt and Venezuela to combat the insurgency. Police were trained, among other things, in mob and riot control, in infiltration of subversive organizations, in fast communications. The immediate crisis was surmounted, and the groundwork was laid for the successful election of 1963.

This special effort was needed, even in a country with large and powerful armed forces, because of the special nature of counterinsurgency. Counterinsurgency is not a military problem; a military answer is the failure of counterinsurgency and often the beginning of full-scale civil war. The special problems of revolutionary war will be discussed in more detail in relation to Vietnam. Here we should note only that there is much more to controlling insurgency than the training of police and controlling the military. Insurgency aims not at the conquest of territory but at the allegiance of men. In the Latin American countryside as in other threatened parts of the world, that allegiance can be won only by positive programs: by land reform, by schools, by honest administration, by roads and clinics and labor unions and even-handed justice, and a share for all men in the decisions that shape their lives. Counterinsurgency might best be described as social reform under pressure.

Any effort that disregards the base of social reform,

and becomes preoccupied with gadgets and techniques and force, is doomed to failure and should not be supported by the United States. Counterinsurgency is not a miracle detergent that whisks away Communists from any country. Its techniques are useful and valuable only when government meets its basic responsibilities and the basic needs of its people. However obvious this lesson might appear, there are some within our own government, as well as some leaders of other countries, who have not recognized its teachings. For us, this failure will be costly; for others, around the world and not just in Latin America, this mistake will be their last.

Communism, Intervention, and the Dominican Republic

It is not my purpose to rake over the rights and wrongs of our intervention in the Dominican Republic. Certain things, however, must be said; for there are lessons to be learned, and the Dominican Republic will be a major element in our relations with Latin America for years to come. Everywhere I went in Latin America, this was the first question raised with me, not just by students but by reporters, businessmen, and government officials. That immediate passion has dimmed in the two years since. But it has entered into the fabric of our relations with Latin America, another element of mistrust of the colossus of the north. Its effect will not be readily apparent in good times; but unless it is offset by vigorous positive action, it will be brought up at every difficult period in the future. Most Latin Americans did not believe that the revolt was Communist-inspired or directed. Even if they did, they do not concede any right of the United States to intervene unilaterally.

I was opposed to our intervention at the time, urging that "Our determination to stop Communist revolution in the hemisphere must not be construed as opposition to popular uprisings against injustice and oppression just because the targets of such popular uprisings say they are Communist-inspired or Communist-led, or even because known Communists take part in them." And I said that characterization of the revolt as "Communist" might only alienate the non-Communist democrats who were in the great majority, and indeed strengthen the Communists. But what is now most important is what we do in the future. The efforts of McGeorge Bundy, and the later work of Ambassador Ellsworth Bunker in ensuring that free elections were held and the elected government installed, were a major step forward. It is acknowledged, however, that our times of difficulty are not yet past.

We must realize that we cannot put down disorder everywhere in the hemisphere. If we wish to minimize the damage and danger of revolution, we must concentrate instead on programs of social improvement. It was one thing in 1965 to send 30,000 troops to an island nation of 3.6 million, of whom a few thousand were under arms in a single major city. It would be something else again to do so now, while we are so heavily engaged in Vietnam. It would be even harder to imagine intervention in a country like Brazil, larger in area than the United States, with a population of eighty million; or Argentina, with twenty-four million people and vast expanses of plain; or any of the nations of the Andean *cordillera*.

Further, we should make it clear that we will not take any such action in the future without serious and precise consultation with the Organization of American States. We may wish to explore means to strengthen the machinery of the OAS for dealing with future crises, though with limited expectation of successful action; several nations are convinced that a strengthened OAS might be only a tool for U.S. intervention in their internal affairs. And nations such as Peru, Chile, and Venezuela would rather deal with their subversion problems unaided than subject themselves to multilateral intervention by nations like Argentina and Brazil.

There is another lesson to be drawn from the Dominican Republic. The greatest success for nations, as for individuals, is found in truth to themselves. We did not build the United States on anti-Communism. Our strength comes from positive faith; we need neither to hate nor fear our adversaries. Let our emphasis be, then, less on what the Communists are doing to threaten peace and order in Latin America and more on what we can do to help to build a better life for its people.

The Military

The other principal obstacle to progressive democracy in Latin America is the deeply ingrained habit of intervention in politics by the armed forces of many Latin American countries. At one time such interventions often took the form of military dictatorships, designed to retain political power for an indefinite period. Since the wave of revolutions in the 1950s, which swept most of the generals from office, military intervention has, for the most part, taken a new form. It is used to depose civilian leaders who are distasteful to the military, or, at times, to their allies among the reactionary forces of a particular country. After a period of time, the country is then returned to civilian rule more acceptable to the military.

The military has also changed in its composition in recent years: Once the preserve of the oligarchy, it is now largely made up of sons of the middle class, who see it as an attractive and prestigious career. These new officers have brought new focus to the military's interest in politics; in some countries the army has sought to play a modernizing—if not a democratizing —role.

Still the day and the danger of military dictatorship are not over. Though we should recognize that the military has been an important force for order in some situations, yet many a Latin American leader must live in constant awareness that he is watched from the barracks, that a misstep may bring the tanks to his door. Under such circumstances, the establishment of democratic traditions and constitutional process becomes difficult in the extreme. For whatever its short-run effects, military intervention only creates instability over the long run. Constitutions are obeyed out of practice and habit; every military takeover breaks the structure of consensual obedience, encouraging others to seek change through force rather than by democratic persuasion. Those who would look to the military as the source of long-run stability and friendship for the United States should look instead to history. Military leaders, such as Colonel Juan Perón, have often been as demagogic, and as ready to bid for popular support through anti-U.S. acts, as civilians. And the most stable country in Latin America, with a sound currency and a reasonable policy toward U.S. investment, is Mexico, which virtually abolished its army in the aftermath of revolution thirty years ago.

The military also absorbs resources that would be better used elsewhere. Some of these resources are matériel. While arms expenditures are low, compared to the more developed countries, some countries devote substantial sums to military items for which there is not a real need. The budgets of many Latin American governments contain nearly as much for arms as they do for capital budget investment on the roads, dams, and schools that are essential to development. Argentina, for example, spends 15 percent on arms as against only 17.7 percent for capital investment; the Dominican Republic, before the revolution, 17.8 percent on arms and only 15.7 percent on capital investment.

Further waste is in the young men who go into the army, men whose energies and talents would be far better used in the economic and political life of their countries. More is in the other young men who go neither into the army nor into civilian politics, because they regard their politics as ineffectual.

The question, therefore, is not whether the role of the military should be diminished, but how. Primary responsibility, of course, belongs to the Latin Americans themselves. But we can help them, above all by not hindering, through careless or undue aid to the military, their own efforts to eliminate the military from politics. This will require re-evaluation of the amount and quality of our military assistance. Grant assistance to Latin America is not great; in recent years it has averaged about $40 million a year, fifty percent of it in counterinsurgency equipment: small arms, jeeps, communications. Some of our aid, however, is in forms that only encourage greater expenditure, of little relevance to the problem of subversion, which is the only major threat to these nations' security. For example, we loan warships to several nations. The ships are free, but they must be manned and operated, and sometimes modernized. And the dynamics of interservice rivalry ensure that whatever opportunities for arms spending we offer will be accepted.

Moreover, we should carefully weigh the internal political consequences of any proposed military assistance. It is one thing to aid a Venezuelan army that must combat Castroite terrorism; it is quite another thing to make jet planes available to an air force that has never seen action except against its own government, against other service branches, or against peasants trying to seize land to live on.

Rather, we should lead the way toward cutting down arms sales to Latin America. Our military representatives in each of these countries should clearly understand this to be our policy. Frequently in the past, it would appear that they have not, or if they do, they have ignored it—promoting the purchase of military equipment and the importance of the military establishment itself. Of the needlessly advanced weapons in Latin America, most were purchased—not donated by the United States; it is arms purchases, not grants, that use up valuable foreign exchange. As we are the major supplier of military arms, we should make the major effort to cut down arms sales to Latin America and other countries around the world. This will require cooperation with our European allies; thus we made one recent fighter plane sale largely because the French firm that manufactures the plane under license would have sold the airplane if we had not. But cooperation comes out of leadership, which we must be willing to exercise. We should also exercise our influence in support of efforts for Latin American disarmament. Such efforts would help to eliminate that part of arms expenditure which grows out of national rivalries. It would, over time, help to diminish military intervention in politics; and it could furnish a model and testing-ground for other disarmament efforts—in Africa, in the middle East, eventually perhaps in Europe and Asia.

This is most notably true in the area of nuclear weapons. However, there has been little discernible progress made; and that is tragic, in this most important area. One serious obstacle in the way of agreement is that Cuba has thus far regrettably refused to join any agreement on a nuclear-free zone, and some nations of Latin America are understandably reluctant to sign such an agreement with Cuba outside it.

The spread of nuclear weapons cannot increase the security of any American nation. Those who are concerned with possible nuclear weapons in a Communist Cuba should remember how swiftly and firmly the whole hemisphere acted, through the Organization of American States, to remove a nuclear threat from Cuba in October of 1962. There can be no doubt that the OAS would again act to prevent any nuclear threat from Cuba in the future. We should therefore strive for a nuclear-free zone even if Cuba elects not to join it, even if Cuba remains outside the treaty and outside the inter-American system. For the insecurity and possible destruction that would follow the introduction of nuclear weapons into this continent could be to the advantage of no nation and no cause.

We should attempt to work with the many Latin American military officers who come to the United States for training—to help them acquire the spirit of nonpolitical military service that has been so important to our own political development, and to help them also understand the necessary difference between the patient ways of civilian politics and the direct action of war. We spend nearly twice as much to train foreign military personnel here as we do for all the operations of the Voice of America; yet we do not, apparently, pay enough attention to whether they leave these shores with a proper respect for the constitutional processes which it is our stated purpose to defend. All too many of the young officers who have intervened in politics, in Latin America and elsewhere in the world, have been trained in the United States. We would do better to try to help them move toward a role in the work of economic and social development. In many nations of the developing world, some in Latin America, the army has played a significant role: educating its young recruits, building houses and roads and schools in remote rural areas. We might well seek technical assistance from the most successful of these development-oriented armies, that of Israel.

Finally, and most importantly, we must realize that the solution to the military problem lies in a solution to the basic problems of Latin America. Here, as elsewhere, it is essential that the full influence of the United States be exercised on behalf of basic reforms that improve the life and opportunities of the mass of Latin America's people, which build the power of democratic civilian institutions, in political parties, in labor unions, in rural cooperatives. That, in the end, is the source of true stability.

CONCLUSION

It was to all these problems, to the need for fundamental economic and political and social change, that the Alliance for Progress was addressed. What progress have we made in these six years? Economically, the Alliance is moving, but it is not moving fast enough. Governments are working, but they are not working hard enough. The United States is making a contribution, but in many ways not enough. Francis Bacon said, "Hope is a good breakfast but a lean supper." The ideals of the Alliance stirred men's hearts and minds throughout the continent; not enough has been done to fulfill these hopes and keep the passion, imagination, and commitment alive and growing.

Above all else, in every way, through a broad array of attitudes and policies, which should infuse the acts and decisions of our government and every individual official, we must be associated with the goals of human dignity, social justice, and political democracy toward which economic and material progress is only a means. We must stand with the men and women and parties who themselves stand for these goals. We must increase our stress on the need for basic social reforms as a condition of full participation in the Alliance for Progress.

For the people of Latin America demand dignity and justice for themselves and for their families. We cannot buy them with aid, any more than we can buy the people of any other nation. We may, perhaps, succeed in buying some of them, just as some may be bought in the United States. But in Latin America as in Asia, or in the United States, man's dignity and independence cannot be sold or bought for money. They can be won by respect and generous friendship.

From the beginning of our history we have been aware of the special intimacy and promise of the American republics. In 1822 President Monroe recognized the independence of several Latin American states, proclaiming that "the revolutionary movement in the Spanish provinces excited the sympathy of our fellow citizens from its commencement. The provinces belonging to this hemisphere are our neighbors." Almost half a century later William Seward related Abraham Lincoln's prophecy that foreign powers would not easily be able to dominate Latin America in the century to come, "while," he said, "population is so rapidly increasing, resources so rapidly developing, and society so steadily forming itself upon principles of democratic government."

In the years of that century, now concluded, there have been times of darkness and anger and arrogance, as well as brighter years of goodwill, understanding, and help. Yet the same principles, the same dreams, guide our action that first moved a young America to rejoice at the independence of its neighbors, and a war-torn America to shield those neighbors from hostile forces: respect for independence, the development of resources for the welfare of all the people, and the growth of democracy. In this respect the Alliance for

Progress is rooted in the deepest and most enduring sympathies and experience of the American people.

To accomplish its spacious purpose will require growing programs of assistance and reform, difficult political judgments, painful sacrifices. But it will also require something more. We cannot buy or plan or manage this vision into existence. We must believe it and create and then hold fast to those beliefs and dreams, however strongly the urgencies of the moment tempt us from that path. For economic development, social reform, education, land reform, and all the rest are, like the shadows of Plato's cave, only the material cast of the great realities of human freedom. No matter how brilliantly we build, how generously we pour forth our treasure, how wisely we use our power, if we neglect the reality behind the act, then we will surely fail. Leadership in freedom cannot rest on wealth and power. It depends on fidelity and persistence in those shaping beliefs—democracy, freedom, justice—which men follow from the compulsions of their hearts and not the enslavement of their bodies. We must cope with real dangers, overcome real obstacles, meet real needs, but always in a way that preserves our own allegiance to the principles of the Alliance. Otherwise we will preserve the shadow of progress and security at the expense of the substance of freedom in the New World.

Nuclear Control

Every man, woman, and child lives under a nu-
clear sword of Damocles hanging by the slender-
est of threads, capable of being cut at any mo-
ment by accident or miscalculation or by mad-
ness. The weapons of war must be abolished be-
fore they abolish us.

—President John F. Kennedy

FIVE NATIONS NOW HAVE the capacity to
explode nuclear weapons. This capacity was developed
at great cost, over a period of a generation. At least
ten other nations are now in a position to develop nuclear devices within a few years. Two, Israel and India,
already possess weapons-grade fissionable material,
and could fabricate an atomic device within a few
months. Five others—Canada, Japan, Sweden, Switz-
erland, and West Germany—could do so in less than
two years. These capabilities, moreover, can be developed at a fraction of past costs. In little more than a
decade, the spread of civilian nuclear reactors will
make available to the forty countries possessing them
the explosive material for the manufacture of thousands of atomic bombs each year. And for these countries, an additional investment of a few million dollars,
well within the capacity of virtually any state, will produce nuclear weapons. Once a weapons capability is in

being, the weapons themselves will probably be produced for costs in the hundreds of thousands of dollars each. Similarly, delivery systems are far cheaper than they once were. Jet bombers can be purchased from the great powers for a few million dollars. Our own Minuteman missiles are far less costly than were earlier missiles, or even the B-52s that preceded them.

Thus nuclear capability will soon lie within the grasp of many, and it is all too likely that if events continue on their present course, this technical capability will be used to produce nuclear weapons. Since the explosion of the first Chinese bomb, for example, pressure to develop a counterpart has built steadily in India, mounting with the border conflict and China's hydrogen test. If India does acquire nuclear weapons, Pakistan will not be far behind. In the churning and hate-filled Middle East, deep suspicions of weapons activity have been present for many years, and further Israeli progress would certainly impel the Egyptians to intensify their present efforts. Similar developments are possible all over the world.

Once nuclear war were to start, even between small, remote countries, it would be exceedingly difficult to stop a step-by-step progression of local war into a general conflagration. As many as 160 million Americans, and hundreds of millions of other people, might die within the first twenty-four hours of a full-scale nuclear exchange. And as Nikita Khrushchev once said, the survivors would envy the dead. The proliferation of nuclear weapons immensely increases the chances that the world might stumble into such catastrophe. As President Kennedy said in 1963, "I ask you to stop and think what it would mean to have nuclear weapons in so many hands, in the hands of countries large and small, stable and unstable, responsible and irresponsible, scattered throughout the world. There would be no rest for anyone then, no stability, no real security, and no chance of effective disarmament."

There would be no stability anywhere in the world when nuclear weapons might be used between Greeks and Turks over Cyprus, between Arabs and Israelis over Suez or the Gulf of Aqaba, between India and

Pakistan in the Rann of Cutch. If nuclear weapons spread, it is dangerously likely that they will be so used, for these are matters of the deepest national interest to the countries involved. Between the United States and the Soviet Union, a "balance of terror"—the knowledge that nuclear war between us would destroy us both—is a strong restraint against war. But for countries without such massive nuclear arsenals as we command, there would be no such balance.

There could be no security when a decision to use these weapons might be made by an unstable demagogue, by the head of one of the innumerable two-month governments that plague so many countries, by an irresponsible military commander, or even by an individual pilot. It is far more difficult and expensive to construct an adequate system of control and custody than to develop the weapons themselves. Even the United States, which has the most highly developed of control systems, has accidentally dropped two hydrogen bombs over Spain; fired a missile into Mexico; flown fighter planes over China; and sent a U-2 over Siberia at the height of the Cuban missile crisis. Such human errors may be inevitable. In a world of nuclear weapons, one could be fatal. And there could be little effective disarmament when each nation would want guarantees, not from one or two or five powers, but from a dozen or a score of nations. But if nuclear weapons spread, such guarantees would be necessary.

Think just of the unparalleled opportunities for mischief: a bomb obliterates the capital city of a nation in Latin America, or Africa, or Asia—or even the Soviet Union or the United States. How was it delivered? By plane? By missile? By car, or truck, or ship? There is no evidence. From where did it come? A jealous neighbor? An internal dissident? A great power bent on stirring up trouble, or an anonymous madman? There is only speculation. And what can be the response—what but a reprisal grounded on suspicion, leading in ever-widening circles to the utter destruction of the world we know? If the *Liberty*—clearly marked on a clear day—had been attacked by Egyptian planes rather than by those of Israel, would we have believed the attack was accidental? And considering the strained state of our relations at the time, what would have been our response?

The need to halt the spread of nuclear weapons must be a central priority of American policy, deserving and demanding the greatest additional effort. This is a broad statement, for our interests are broad; and the crises of the moment often pose urgent questions of grave importance for national security. But these immediate problems, and others like them, have been with us constantly for twenty years—and will be with us far into the future. Should nuclear weapons become generally available to the world, however, each crisis of the moment might well become the last crisis for all mankind.

Thus none of the momentary crises are more than small parts of the larger question whether our politics can grow up to our technology. The nuclear weapon, as Henry Stimson said, "constitutes merely a first step in a new control by man over the forces of nature too revolutionary and dangerous to fit into the old concepts—it really caps the climax of the race between man's growing technical power for destructiveness and his psychological power of self-control and group control—his moral power."

The United States took the initiative and made the maximum effort to secure the nuclear test-ban treaty in 1963 because we knew that our security and the future of the world depended on halting the arms race and exerting every possible effort toward peace. We hailed the treaty not principally for its specific benefits, important and necessary as they were, but for its value as the first of many necessary actions: it was "the first step in a journey of a thousand miles." But we have not yet taken the second step. The world has not moved, beyond the limited nuclear test ban itself, to halt the proliferation of nuclear weapons. At the onset of this journey, we cannot allow the demands of day-to-day policy, even on matters of serious importance, to obstruct our efforts to solve the problem of nuclear spread. We cannot wait for lasting peace in Southeast Asia, which will not come until nuclear weapons have spread beyond recall; nor for a general European settlement, which has not existed since 1914; nor until all nations learn to behave, for bad behavior armed with nuclear weapons is the danger we must try to prevent.

Rather, we must begin to move now, on as many fronts as possible, to meet the problem. As time goes by, the likelihood constantly increases that another nation will develop the bomb; and every new possessor will lead others to abandon the restraint that alone keeps them from acquiring a nuclear capability now. William Foster, head of the Arms Control and Disarmament Agency, has pointed out that as long as the problem involved only the United States and the Soviet Union, a delay of a year or more was not fatal to the conclusion of an agreement. But in the multinational problem in which we now find ourselves, "a delay of a year or so, or perhaps even of months . . . could well mean the difference between failure and success." Indeed every day of delay may be the day somewhere in the world, in a secret council or the innermost mind of a single man, that yet another nation may decide to proceed with the development of nuclear weapons and start an irreversible slide toward catastrophe.

A Treaty And After

Time is running out. For two years, the eighteen-nation United Nations Disarmament Committee has struggled at Geneva to reach agreement on a treaty to halt the spread of nuclear weapons. The essential principles of such a "nonproliferation" agreement have been known for many years: The major nuclear powers would pledge not to transfer nuclear weapons or weapons capability to nations not now in possession of them; nations now without nuclear arms, on their part, would pledge not to acquire or develop them in future. This is the substance of the draft nonproliferation treaty proposed at Geneva by the United

States and the Soviet Union. On this simple treaty, however, the Disarmament Committee has not yet been able to reach agreement as I write; though all hope that one will be signed soon.

Whether or not a draft treaty is finally agreed upon, the obstacles that have delayed it so long are worth brief examination. The problems they reflect will remain long after any treaty is concluded. And they will determine whether the treaty effectively prevents nuclear spread—or goes the way of the forgotten Kellogg-Briand Disarmament Pact of 1928.

Acquisition or development of nuclear weapons by any additional nation would now have a serious effect on the possibility of limiting further spread in the future. But each of them will balance the advantages of nuclear armament against its disadvantages to itself; it is a nation's own political and military situation, and not the wishes of other nations, that will determine its decision. Any of the present nuclear powers, including ourselves, would regard it as absurd to abandon its nuclear forces while the other nuclear powers retained theirs. Yet the non-nuclear powers are in fact being asked to forego nuclear armament, while other nations maintain and increase arsenals already capable of destroying life on the planet. It must, therefore, be the aim of our policy to make nuclear armament unnecessary—and to make abstention from its development as attractive as possible—for each of the nations with the capability of nuclear development.

Such a policy of country-by-country political action will clearly be necessary in the absence of a nonproliferation agreement. We are not so much concerned that the Soviet Union will give nuclear weapons to other countries as we are that the lack of an agreement will lead other countries, in the interests of their own security, prestige, and power, to undertake nuclear armament themselves. This is not like the test-ban question, where Soviet refusal to come to an agreement and their massive testing compelled us to resume atmospheric testing ourselves. Whatever course of action the Soviets, the French, the Chinese, or others, take or fail to take on a nonproliferation treaty, it will still be in our deepest national interest to prevent nuclear weapons from spreading beyond their present possessors.

Moreover, this country-by-country approach would be necessary even if we do reach agreement on a treaty at Geneva. Nations with the potential power to develop nuclear weapons capability will not be bound—unless they agree—to a treaty between the United States and the Soviet Union. Their adherence to a U.S.-Soviet treaty, or continued adherence after they sign, will also depend on continual agreement. The present draft includes an escape clause, allowing signers to develop or acquire nuclear weapons for reasons of supreme national interest. Even without such a clause, the treaty would not be a self-executing agreement. For history shows that nations will break treaties —including, we may expect, this agreement—if they think that by doing so they may gain some important advantage in power or security. Even the conclusion of a treaty to prevent the spread of nuclear weapons, then, will still require our attention to each nation with the potential capacity and desire for nuclear capability.

An example of the urgent pressures with which we must deal can be seen in India, menaced on the North by Communist China and on the West by Pakistan, with whom she has struggled over Kashmir for twenty years. India is the non-nuclear nation closest to weapons capability: She has brilliant and well-trained scientists, natural uranium reserves, and nuclear power-plants. She has the reprocessing facilities that are the last step in the production of weapons-grade fissionable material—and bombers capable of carrying an elementary nuclear device. And there are powerful voices in India that would develop and use nuclear weapons to try to awe Pakistan into retreat on Kashmir, or to prevent humiliation by Communist China.

In this situation, there is special urgency to preserving the Tashkent agreement and securing a permanent settlement over Kashmir—urgency far beyond even that which would otherwise follow from the recent memory of American weapons being used on both sides of a dangerous conflict. India has been the leader of the new nations, born since World War II, not aligned with any of the great power blocs. India's leadership, while we do not agree with it in all situations, is still oriented to democratic methods of development. India thus furnishes to other nations an alternative model to that offered by Communist China—and it is in our interest to maintain Indian prestige.

At the same time, for India to preserve her position through the development of nuclear weapons would be a tragic blow to our hopes of containing their spread. She would be the first of the nonaligned powers to develop them; and others would be only too eager to follow her lead. The direct pressure on Pakistan would certainly push that nation also to seek nuclear weapons, possibly by agreement with Communist China. Perhaps most seriously, nuclear weapons in countries like India would almost certainly lead several European nations with far larger industrial capabilities to throw off restraint and acquire full nuclear arsenals. It is, after all, one thing to forego nuclear arms when they are held by five nations, the same five nations whose special world position was recognized in the assignment of permanent seats on the Security Council of the United Nations. But if India, or Israel, or others of the new nations "go nuclear," prestige alone may urge nations that think of themselves as greater states to build these most modern symbols of power and position.

There are steps we can and should take to preserve India's position in Asia and to persuade her that nuclear armament is not to her advantage. The most important of these is a guarantee of protection against nuclear attack or threat from Communist China. President Johnson has indicated the willingness of the United States to defend India against nuclear blackmail. But India, wishing to preserve her nonaligned position, has indicated at Geneva that she will demand parallel guarantees by both the United States and the Soviet Union; a position that may be shared by many nations fearful of Chinese power and intentions. Such a joint or parallel guarantee, perhaps under United Nations auspices, but quite possibly without any explicit U.S.-Soviet cooperation, should be given.*

Beyond direct security measures, we should intensify our aid to India's domestic development. If India can achieve her aim of democratic development, she will not be in the same need of nuclear arms to maintain her prestige and position in relation to China, and there will be far less internal pressure on the government to become involved in the nuclear arms race. There should be no mistake: There is no country, including our own, in which irresponsible elements may not seek to brandish the nuclear sword; England's Henry the Fourth was not the last ruler to seek to submerge domestic quarrels in foreign wars and adventures.† But the pressures for nuclear armament are also in part responsive to legitimate consideration of national security: for India, the threat of a two-front confrontation with Pakistan and China. If we ask India to forego nuclear arms, we must act to help assure her security in other ways.‡

---

* It will be recalled that the Soviet Union, during India's border conflict with China two years ago, continued to send combat aircraft to India at the same time as the United States worked to assist the Indian air-defense system. Not in equal parallel with U.S. efforts, but equally indicative of Soviet strategic interest in maintaining India's position versus China, was Premier Kosygin's mediation in the Kashmir dispute with Pakistan.

† "Therefore, my Harry, be it thy course to busy giddy minds with foreign quarrels."—Henry IV to his son, *Henry IV, Part II,* IV:v.

‡ There are other examples of this situation, which may require other kinds of action by the United States. For example, the continuance of Israel's pledge not to be the first to introduce nuclear weapons into the Middle East may depend on much firmer U.S. support of her rights and conventional military strength.

Country-by-country action to prevent nuclear-weapons spread should not, of course, be restricted to nations that otherwise might acquire them, but extended also to nations with the potential to aid others to become nuclear powers. Thus the few nations capable of fabricating certain special equipment should be induced to prevent its use for the development of nuclear weaponry, just as the United States and Canada seek to prevent uranium which we sell from being used for weapons purposes, through inspection by the International Atomic Energy Agency, or similar safeguards.

The Treaty: Nuclear Spread In Europe

Throughout 1965 and much of 1966, the greatest barrier to agreement was the question of future West German access to nuclear weapons. For the Soviet Union, denying nuclear weapons to West Germany was and remains the principal object of a nonproliferation treaty. The United States, however, was attempting to preserve the option of West German participation in a common NATO nuclear force (of which MLF, the Multilateral Nuclear Force, was one proposed version). The MLF, like other attempts to shore up with gadgets an alliance that required basic readjustments, is now discarded and forgotten. The underlying problem of European security still remains.*

Since the onset of the Cold War, Europe has sheltered under the American nuclear umbrella: the NATO alliance, designed to prevent Soviet penetration into the Western part of Europe, relied in the last analysis on the willingness of the United States to use nuclear force to respond to any Soviet aggression. In the early years, NATO was an unqualified success. Behind the shield of American power, with the generous and far-sighted assistance of the Marshall Plan, a shattered Europe rebuilt its cities and industries, stabilized politics once threatened by internal dissension and large Communist parties, and regained self-confidence.

Time was to prove, however, that history knows no final victories: The problems of success are often as intractable as the problems of failure. NATO set the line dividing Germany as the final boundary of Soviet ex-

---

* The issue has of course been of central importance for many years. The MLF itself was under consideration from 1959 onward, particularly during President Kennedy's administration in 1962–63; although he had personally become disenchanted with the effort by the fall of 1963. In 1964, however, it was resurrected by its State Department advocates and became again a matter of national priority. 1965 and 1966 are mentioned here only as two years in which, active negotiations having begun, the MLF was the principal obstacle.

pansion, and offered West Germany a place in a renascent Western Europe. West Germany took that place, becoming a major military and economic contributor to the Alliance. But the closer West Germany drew to Western Europe, the more it was integrated into the structure of Western defense, the more reunification receded into the future. For growing West German strength—in its own right, and in contrast to the shabby cruelties of East Germany—posed a growing threat to the Soviet Union. The Soviets, with their dependents in the East German regime, hardened in their resistance to reunification, threatened to make the division permanent by signing a separate peace treaty with East Germany, and provoked a series of crises over Berlin. The more Khrushchev blustered, the tighter grew West Germany's bonds with the United States, and so on, until no statesman or leader could offer any real timetable or prospect for reunification. West Germany's defense, and especially the survival of West Berlin, rested on the American nuclear guarantee. But reliance on that guarantee, with its concomitant political and military ties to NATO and the United States, prevented any forward motion. Politically, Germany was frozen: unable to seize the future without jeopardizing the present, or to protect the present without abandoning the future.

France meanwhile had begun her own resurgence. With De Gaulle's accession to power in 1958 came the first steps toward governmental stability, and a gradual recovery from the colonial wars that had, since 1946, drained its energies in Indochina and then in Algeria. De Gaulle brought also a vision of French glory and leadership reborn and an end of dependence on the "Anglo-Saxons." With remarkable prescience and rare political skill, De Gaulle went far toward making the vision reality: Almost by sheer force of will alone, he brought France to a position of leadership on the continent, dominating the Common Market, the focus of debate across a wide range of issues.

One of his principal political tools was the nuclear weapon. Before the easing of Soviet-American tensions, De Gaulle questioned whether the United States would ever risk 150 million casualties in the defense of other nations, the NATO allies; even if the Soviets attacked Europe in force, he contended, the American nuclear guarantee would not be honored.* Therefore France must have her own nuclear deterrent; and he ordered a nuclear program begun. In 1962, after the Cuban missile crisis, De Gaulle argued that the NATO alliance could be drawn into nuclear war without its consent or even consultation, offering as evidence the fact that the United States decided on the blockade and the confrontation with the Soviet Union without first consulting NATO. At the same time, he argued that the missile crisis had proven that the Soviet Union no longer represented as serious a threat to Europe, and the American deterrent was no longer worth its price in "the subordination known as integration which is provided by NATO." As time went on, and the Soviet Union seemed more peaceful, he argued that reliance on NATO and the United States would prevent progress toward *détente* among the European nations and a general European settlement. In 1963, when we reached agreement on the Test-Ban Treaty, De Gaulle refused to sign; this time saying that the nuclear duopoly was a U.S.-Soviet scheme to rule the world together. Ever since, while rejecting all American plans for nuclear sharing within NATO, he has used his nuclear power as evidence that Europe can sever its close ties with the United States, relying on its own nuclear deterrent capability; and that from this independent position, Europe can effect its own reconciliation with Soviet power, eliminate both the Soviet Union and the

---

* President Kennedy had tremendously strengthened our conventional forces in Europe (which had been weak, unprepared, and underarmed), so that a confrontation with the Soviet Union would not automatically result in a nuclear exchange. He wished to avoid, so far as possible, being forced to choose between surrender and all-out war. The conventional buildup, however, aroused suspicions in France, and with Adenauer in Germany, that the United States would be unwilling to use nuclear weapons in any case. It is true that President Kennedy was understandably reluctant to employ nuclear weapons and would have used them only if all other possibilities of defense had been exhausted—and he felt that we should have many possibilities before that fateful step.

United States from Central Europe, and re-establish itself as the major force in the affairs of the world.

The full implications of West Germany's position, or De Gaulle's politics, are too broad and too much in flux for treatment only within the boundaries of the nuclear problem. This brief discussion is intended only to illustrate some of the complexities and dangers of the question of nuclear weapons spread. And from the foregoing, certain things are clear.

First, nuclear weapons are in no sense a solution to the problem of national security or a substitute for policy. They can prevent, as they have prevented in the past, a sudden major assault against our most vital national interests. But they can neither achieve nor prevent major shifts in the politics of nations—shifts that may be as significant and vital as any military confrontation. Nuclear weapons could not achieve the reunification of Germany; indeed West Germany's reliance on the American nuclear shield became, to many Germans, a hindrance to reunification, and therefore a reason for turning instead to France. Nor could our unquestioned nuclear superiority preserve NATO as it was; rather, by increasing French security, it may only have encouraged De Gaulle's capacity for independent action.

Second, there is nevertheless a great and terrible temptation to use nuclear weapons as the foundation of national prestige and independence. National power and position, after all, are measured in relation to those of other nations; and while most elements of prestige are intangible and subject to argument, nuclear weapons are facts: either one possesses them, or one does not. Thus De Gaulle, seeking a position of independence and leadership in Europe, both dramatized and furthered his cause by making France a nuclear power. De Gaulle's steady and constant drive for nuclear capability has been supported by arguments that have shifted with every turn of events. That so many arguments all have led to the same result may raise at least the possibility that the goal, in fact, determined the reasons.

Third, we cannot expect that other nations, even our closest allies, will continue to forego nuclear armaments indefinitely on the promise that we will protect them from the Russians. No matter how often or how loudly we repeat our assurances and pledges of nuclear support—indeed, no matter how seriously we really mean them, or feel them to be in our own interest—other nations will continue to question whether we would invite our own destruction in their defense.

All this points beyond nuclear spread, to the need to lessen our own reliance on nuclear weapons, and to halt the growth of the overwhelming nuclear capabilities of the United States and the Soviet Union. The margin of our power over that of all others is what arouses European fears for their independence. The mutual destructiveness of American and Soviet power is what arouses the fears of some Europeans that we would never risk war in their defense—although, paradoxically, it is our assured capability to destroy any attacker, even after a surprise attack on ourselves, that makes our deterrent credible, and allows Europe to rely on it. Most important of all, it is the prestige associated with nuclear giantism, humbling and infuriating smaller nations, that leads them to think that only a nuclear power is heard in the councils of mankind.

It would be in the direct self-interest of the United States and the Soviet Union if we could cut back our nuclear forces. As Secretary McNamara has shown, though each nation has more than enough to destroy the other, neither can ever acquire enough to prevent its own destruction. Cutbacks might well be possible while still preserving the "second-strike" capability that is at the heart of the balance of terror. And even substantial reductions would not affect our nuclear superiority over China in the foreseeable future. Most of all, it is essential that the two superpowers demonstrate to the world, by concrete example, their determination to turn away from weapons of absolute destruction, toward a world order based on other strengths. In the last two years, President Johnson has taken the initiative, with a slowdown in production of plutonium and uranium-235, with the phasing out of certain bombers, and with his proposal for mutual conversion, by the United States and the Soviet Union, of weapons material to peaceful purposes. Much more, however, remains to be done. For, as *The New York Times* reports from Geneva, the real question "is whether [the treaty] will stand up . . . if, by the time the review conference is held [in five years], the nuclear powers have not started disarming. Britain, Canada, and others have warned that the treaty will not last if it merely seeks to make permanent the gulf between nuclear haves and have-nots." If we are unwilling to put down our club, others are not likely to refrain from picking up clubs of their own.

Of course, progress toward halting the continuing buildup of nuclear armaments depends on direct negotiations with the Soviet Union. Such negotiations would raise issues of the deepest importance for the national security. The Soviet Union is still the one power physically able to endanger our supreme interest—the survival of the United States. And whatever assessments —or guesses—are made about Soviet intentions, the truth is that there is much we still do not know, and more that we do not understand, about the Soviet Union. We would be foolish indeed to stake our future on the "liberalization" of the Soviets, as accused by the Chinese. The present leadership may be more "pragmatic" than Khrushchev. Yet while he himself was regarded as more liberal and pragmatic than Stalin, he pursued a far more dangerous and adventurous foreign policy, including direct confrontations with the United States, over Cuba and Berlin, of a kind that Stalin was usually careful to avoid. Khrushchev's successors have thus far proven relatively cautious and inward-looking. But we have no guarantee of their future policy— whether, for example, they would give greater weight to the Soviet military, as a result of setbacks in the world, continuing tension in Vietnam, or difficulties at home. Nor do we know whether they represent only a transition between the activist Khrushchev and some other leader who might attempt to revive the messianic appeal of the Soviets' more aggressive period. It took a full three years, let us remember, for Khrushchev himself to emerge from the collective leadership that followed the death of Stalin. The Soviet Union remains for us, in many ways, an unknown—and dangerous—adversary.

Caution, however, cannot lead us to inaction. Rather, the appreciation of continuing danger, and the relative moderation of the present rulers, should spur us to greater efforts to control, before it is too late, the awesome destructive capacity of our two nations. But because any arms-control negotiations with the Soviet Union go to the heart of our national security, they can be carried on only at the highest levels of government, by officials with the discretion to act, enjoying the full personal confidence of the President. And they can be entered only in the context of a continuous effort to coordinate policy throughout the government —to ensure that negotiations will neither founder on obstacles raised by other agencies, nor inadvertently injure some other national interest. High-level coordination and direction are also needed to overcome bureaucratic preferences for the *status quo* over active initiatives. The Nuclear Test Ban Treaty could never have been achieved through normal channels. Many high officials within the government felt that such an effort was certain to be unproductive; but as the President's special representative, supported by him and reporting directly to him, Averell Harriman was able to reach an agreement with the Soviet Union, preserving the vital interests of the United States, with full coordination between all departments and agencies of the Government.

All the nations, however, including ourselves, have not devoted the same supreme urgency to the quest for a nonproliferation treaty. The result is serious damage to its prospects of success. We set out to achieve a treaty, and discovered its implications for policies and interests as objections to the treaty were raised. We "discovered" West Germany's unwillingness to rely solely on the American nuclear guarantee, and European desires for an independent deterrent, and attempted to revive the MLF and similar schemes; these caused us to wrangle with our allies and prevented any agreement with the Soviets. Similarly, it was only during the progress of the Geneva talks that we became fully aware of European fears of being cut off from the progress of nuclear technology; again, time was lost searching for a policy response. Most seriously, we conducted the nuclear negotiations while attempting to resist any change in the Western Alliance. Concerned with De Gaulle's effort to alter, if not destroy, NATO, we grew more dependent on West Germany, and West Germany drew closer to us: thus further aggravating that country's already-sharp dilemmas, and limiting our own ability to negotiate on the treaty. Determined to preserve our nuclear duopoly with the Soviet Union, and lacking a systematic policy for the easing of tensions in Europe, we ignored the urgency of concrete steps toward mutual reduction of Soviet and American nuclear forces on the continent.

If nuclear weapons are to be controlled, however, the responsibility cannot rest solely with the United States, or even the United States and the Soviet Union. Many nations have assumed their share, and more: for example Ireland, which first suggested the nonproliferation treaty, and Sweden, which has shown great imagination and persistence in the search for ways to break the deadlock on a comprehensive test-ban treaty. But some others have been far less forthcoming. One instance, as described earlier, is the reluctance of some Latin American countries to create a nuclear-free zone; which, once created, might have important effects in helping to establish similar zones in sub-Saharan Africa, or even eventually in Central Europe. Another important case is the issue of inspection, which has been one of the principal barriers to agreement at Geneva; the joint U.S.-Soviet draft presented in August left the Inspection article blank, so serious was the range of disagreement on this issue.

Inspection is critical to any nonproliferation agreement. Even small research reactors can produce enough weapons-grade plutonium for a bomb in a period of a year or two. Power reactors produce much more, all as a by-product of their normal operation. The United States has always inspected the many reactors throughout the world that are built or maintained with our assistance. But the confidence necessary to agreement on a nonproliferation treaty can only be created by an international inspection agency in which all signatories to the treaty participate. Such a body, the International Atomic Energy Agency (IAEA), now exists. The IAEA, in fact, is the only forum in which the United States, the Soviet Union, and Great Britain have worked without serious friction and without a Soviet veto. We have given it major support, by insisting that all reactors we assist be subject to IAEA inspection, and by opening a few of our own civilian reactors to its inspectors.

The European nations, however, have thus far refused IAEA inspection, contending that their own mutual inspection—carried out under the provisions of the Euratom agreement—was sufficient. They have objected to any treaty provision that would supersede Euratom inspections with IAEA safeguards. But the Soviets, concerned above all with West Germany, insist that Euratom be subject to IAEA; and nations such as India and Japan would certainly object to a privileged position for the Europeans. As a compromise, the United States has proposed a gradual transition from Euratom to IAEA jurisdiction. A possible further compromise would be for Euratom to continue operation under the supervisory jurisdiction of the IAEA. For the Europeans to insist on less, however, would be in my judgment simply unreasonable; a blow to any hope of a treaty unjustified by any danger it poses to Euratom.

In 1965, making my maiden speech to the Senate on the overriding need of a nonproliferation treaty, I urged that any United States assistance to European nuclear development be stopped unless they would agree to international inspection of their civilian reactors. I still hold this position; but we should go beyond it. The major stated reason for the European reluctance to allow IAEA inspection is a fear of industrial espionage: that their nuclear technology will be discovered and copied by others. Their concern is a natural one; progress in nuclear technology will be, in all probability, a major element of competitive economic advantage in the coming decades. But the danger of losing some such advantage is little in comparison to the threat of unrestrained weapons proliferation. This the Europeans must recognize; and we must recognize it also. Probably, then, the only true long-run solution will be for us not only to open all our civilian reactors to equal international inspection, but also to freely share our civilian reactor technology with the Europeans, giving up some commercial advantage in the interest of our ultimate survival.

Western defense, national prestige, commercial advantage, resentment against nuclear giantism—these are some of the factors that have delayed a treaty from 1965 to 1967, and possibly beyond. The responsibility rests with many nations. The consequence is serious for all. For there has been a significant loss in momentum for the treaty. Nations that would have signed without hesitation in 1965—not only India, but also countries like Brazil—expressed reluctance to do so in early 1967, raising objections not thought of two years earlier. Hopefully, the treaty will nevertheless be agreed upon and signed this year. But if we are to prevent the spread of nuclear weapons, we must all make far more serious efforts than we have made in the past: not only to seek out and plan for the contingent problems, but also—when that is unavoidable—to subordinate other goals and interests to the supreme, overriding need: preventing the spread of nuclear weapons.

CHINA AND NUCLEAR WEAPONS

Our most neglected need for initiatives toward control of nuclear weapons is in regard to China. It is difficult to negotiate on any question with the intransigent leaders of that nation, doubly and triply difficult in the midst of the war in Vietnam and the internal chaos of China itself. China, moreover, is profoundly suspicious and hostile toward us, as we are highly and rightly suspicious of her. But China is there. China has nuclear weapons. And without its participation in attempts to solve the nuclear problem, it will be infinitely more difficult, perhaps impossible, to prevent proliferation in the long run. For the specter of Chinese nuclear power, in the hands of men that few outside China trust or know, impels many nations to think of their own need for nuclear weapons—and causes both the United States and the Soviet Union to hesitate before attempting to limit their own nuclear arsenals.

Despite China's hostility, it may be possible to arrive at agreements—definite and limited in nature—that are in the interests of both of us. "World peace," as President Kennedy said in 1963, "does not require that each man love his neighbor." The rulers of China may be persuaded that their long-run interest, like that of the United States and all other nations, lies not in the spread of nuclear weapons but in their strict control. We have engaged, for some years, in regular discussions with the Chinese ambassador in Warsaw. In some of these discussions, I understand that the Chinese have put forward certain arms-control proposals that, whatever their merit or sincerity, showed considerable attention and effort in their preparation. But these talks are too limited a forum. The Chinese, as I urged in 1965, should long ago have been invited to participate in the Geneva disarmament talks. If they accept, the talks will be more meaningful. If they decline, theirs is the only prestige that would be damaged. More serious, perhaps, than the fact of failure to invite China to Geneva, is what the fact implies about our attitude: that the general hostility in our relationship with China can be allowed to interfere with possible agreements that would be in our own national interest.

In May of 1966 China exploded her third nuclear device in the atmosphere. Premier Chou En-lai then stated that China had informed the United States that it would cease atmospheric testing—and thus accept a major restraint on its weapons development—if the United States would pledge not to initiate the use of nuclear weapons between our two countries. This offer, he said, had been refused by the United States. Subsequently the State Department confirmed that the offer had been made and rejected. The explanation was that the Department judged the offer not to be sincere, and that it was "without adequate safeguards."

It would have been in our clear, direct national interest to obtain from China a pledge to cease nuclear testing: The less China's nuclear capability is developed, the safer a world we have. Skepticism of Chinese seriousness in this offer was justified, since they must already have been well on their way toward developing their hydrogen weapon. It is possible, however, that they appreciated how much greater was our nuclear capability and were willing to forego atmospheric testing if that would tend to keep American nuclear attacks off China. At any rate, sincerity in this case would have been subject to proof. If the Chinese broke their pledge and resumed testing, it would at once be detected, and we would be released from ours. No further "safeguards" were necessary. The agreement proposed would not have limited our own nuclear development or affected our arsenal. It would not even have limited our use of nuclear weapons against Chinese troops outside Chinese soil, such as in Vietnam. Rather, it was limited to preventing the use of nuclear weapons against Chinese territory. And if implemented by China, the proposed agreement might have significantly lessened pressure on India to develop nuclear weapons. In short, we had everything to gain and little to lose; yet we refused, thus inviting serious questions from the world as to the seriousness of our intention to control nuclear weapons. A short time after Chou's statement, the State Department reversed its position and announced its intention to explore this question with the Chinese. By then, however, the Chinese had tested their bomb, and the offer—if such it really was —had been withdrawn.*

* Two years earlier, China had publicly proposed that all nuclear powers pledge not to initiate the use of nuclear weapons against one another. The offer disclosed in May 1966, however, was understood to have been put forward in private discussions, and to have concerned only a "no-first-use pledge" between the United States and China.

Why we took this position is part of a larger question, which will be examined in the next chapter. What is of greatest importance here is the need to overcome the complacency that regards the control of nuclear weapons as just another "problem," about which we should certainly do our best, but need not be unduly concerned if we do not solve. This view is fairly common among government officials and commentators; some even profess to welcome nuclear proliferation. Why, they ask, should the United States involve itself in extending security guarantees to other nations that might involve us in nuclear conflict and destruction? Rather, they suggest, let India acquire her own nuclear counterweight to China, and Europe provide her own nuclear umbrella. Mutual fear will ensure that the weapons are not used, or at worst that their use will be confined to local conflicts.

Even in the abstract theory that is sometimes offered as a substitute for thought about world problems, this view is deeply flawed: The Six Days' War in the Middle East was only the latest demonstration of how seriously nations can miscalculate (or conceal from themselves) the likely outcome of conflict. Some view the Cuban missile crisis as evidence that nuclear weapons, in the last analysis, are unlikely to be used between two nuclear powers. But if Khrushchev had not been sensible enough to draw back, that crisis almost surely would have resulted in all-out nuclear war. And the courage to admit a mistake and retreat is not a universal characteristic of national leaders.

Beyond this, those who disparage the threat of nuclear weapons ignore all evidence of the darker side of man, and of the history of the West—our history. Many times the nations of the West have plunged into inexplicable cataclysm, mutual slaughter so terrible and so widespread that it amounted nearly to the suicide of a civilization. The religious wars of the sixteenth century, the Thirty Years' war in the seventeenth, the terrible excesses that followed the French Revolution—these have been equaled and grotesquely outmatched in the modern twentieth century. Twice within the memory of living men, the nations of Europe, the most advanced and cultured societies of the world, have torn themselves and each other apart for causes so slight, in relation to the cost of struggle, that it is impossible to regard them as other than excuses for the expression of some darker impulse. Barbara Tuchman reminds us that the people of Europe were *relieved* at the outbreak of World War I: "Better a horrible ending than a horror without end," said people in Germany. "Is not peace an element of civil corruption," asked the great writer Thomas Mann, and war "a purification, a liberation, an enormous hope?" Englishmen cheered the news of war's outbreak all day and night, and Rupert Brooke wrote:

> Now God be thanked Who has matched us with
>   His hour
> Honour has come back
> And we have come into our heritage

Perhaps only in Germany was similar enthusiasm to greet renewed combat in 1939. But the damage of this second war was greater, especially to noncombatants. The camps and ovens, the murders and mutual inhumanities of the Eastern front, the unrestricted bombing of cities (with deliberate concentration on areas of workers' housing), the first use of atomic bombs—truly this was war virtually without rules or limits. Its most important lesson for us is perhaps that we have no real explanation for it. We can explain how war broke out. We can understand our own response to the Nazi threat. But we have no reason for the fantastic disproportion between the combatants' war aims and the things that were done, none perhaps but the wrath of war described by Achilles in Book XVIII of *The Iliad,*

> "that makes a man go mad for all his
>   goodness of reason,
>   That rage that rises within and swirls like
>   smoke in the heart and becomes in our madness
>   a thing more sweet than the dripping of honey."

The destruction of the two World Wars was limited only by technology. Now nuclear weapons have removed that limit. Who can say that they will not be used, that a rational balance of terror will restrain emotions we do not understand? Of course, we have survived into the third decade of the Atomic Age. Despite many limited wars and crises before 1914, Europe had known substantial peace for a century—and at its end saw war as deliverance. Nuclear war may never come, but it would be the rashest folly and ignorance to think that it will not come because men, being reasonable beings, will realize the destruction it would cause. Yet we have not learned this lesson. On a recent trip to Europe, I asked a high French official if France's nuclear policy, as set out in De Gaulle's speeches, would not surely lead to a similar policy in Germany, and a future German leader (perhaps another in the long succession of strong national leaders there) repeating De Gaulle's speeches and applying them to Germany. "They can't do that," was his reply, "they've caused too much trouble already."

But of course "they" can, and will, in a dozen nations all over the world, unless we now act to control the weapons that have outgrown our politics. This generation has unlocked the mystery of nature; henceforth all men must live with the power of complete self-destruction. This is the power of choice, the tragedy and glory of man. As Pope Paul has said, "The real danger comes from man himself." That is the hardest danger to avert. But it is the one we must face.

Toward a China Policy

"FINALITY," SAID DISRAELI, "IS not the language of politics." Seldom have we been more forcefully reminded of this fact than by the recent course of Chinese history and our relations with her. Seldom have we been more in need of that reminder, as we begin, after fifteen years, the search for a new China policy.

America is beginning to rediscover China—for all the world as if it were a new, strange planet found by our astronauts. For over fifteen years China has not been a significant factor in American political or intellectual life. Once we fought her armies on the Korean battlefield; twice, in the 1950s, by the testimony of our then Secretary of State, we came to the brink of nuclear war; and for a brief moment, two offshore islands became an issue in a Presidential campaign. But for the most part China has been ignored. Partly this is because the main thread of the Cold War was our relationship with the Soviet Union: not only a far more powerful adversary, armed with advanced nuclear weapons, but also the acknowledged leader of the world Communist movement, and hence China's senior partner. A second reason was the isolation of Communist China—refused admittance to the United Nations, unrecognized by us and many other countries of the world—a China, moreover, that deliberately increased its isolation by eliminating foreign influence and excluding foreigners from her territory.

Sufficient unto the day were the challenges thereof: And as we confronted the Soviet Union over Berlin, saw the Cuban challenge in Latin America, and fretted over crises in the Middle East and Africa, China was far from our thoughts. It is hard to believe, but it seems a reasonable measure of our ignorance, that today one-fourth of the American people do not know that China, with one-fourth of the world's people, is ruled by a Communist government.*

Now all this has begun to change. Easing relations with the Soviet Union, the Sino-Soviet split, China's own accession to nuclear power, and the war in Vietnam have forced our attention to the Far East—and to our relations with a nation unlike any other: in its size, its problems, its outlook on the world, and the acerbity of its relations with the United States. It is safe to say that there is no aspect of American foreign policy so important and yet uncertain, no country so seemingly menacing and about which we know so little, as China.

I do not intend to review or assess the full range of our China policy. We know too little, and events are too quickly changing what little we know. For us, therefore, this is a time above all to think: to review the past, to analyze the present, to plan for the future course of relations between our nations. We might start with an effort to recapture history, to remind ourselves of the past roots of present problems: not to re-

---

* Ignorance has not prevented the expression of sentiments like the following, once fairly common in our political dialogue:

With God's help, we are going to lift Shanghai up, up, ever up, until it is just like Kansas City. —Senator Kenneth Wherry, 1940.

Some Chinese are tall, virtually all Japanese are short. Chinese, not as hairy as Japanese, seldom grow an impressive mustache. Most Chinese avoid horn-rimmed spectacles. . . . The Chinese expression is likely to be more placid, kindly, open; the Japanese positive, dogmatic, arrogant. Japanese are hesitant, nervous in conversation, laugh loudly at the wrong time. Japanese walk stiffly, erect, hard-heeled. Chinese, more relaxed, have an easy gait, sometimes shuffle.

"—How to tell your friends from the Japs"
Time, December 22, 1941.

open old wounds; not to find in past injustice to China a present justification for Chinese injustice to others; but simply to understand, to make informed judgments in the service of policy.

Memories of China have faded during these fifteen years of isolation; and perhaps our understanding was never great. China was the greatest of civilizations before the birth of Christ: a mighty empire, exacting tribute and nominal obedience from all on its borders, imitated by its neighbors, especially Japan, in religion, public administration, and ways of making war. We of the West, when we first came into extended contact with China in the nineteenth century, saw only a society of inferior technology, easily dominated by Western military expeditions, defeated in battle, and forced to make trade and territorial concessions. In 1839, Great Britain fought a war to compel China to allow the importation of opium, so that the British could pay for the goods they wished to purchase from China. Defeat in that war began a century of Chinese humiliation. The great powers carved China into spheres of influence, taking railways, coal mines, parts of cities and provinces away from Chinese rule; the gunboats and troops of half a dozen nations patrolled Chinese rivers and ports. From 1844 to 1943, Americans and many other foreigners could not be tried in Chinese courts for crimes committed on Chinese soil. When China sought to reassert her independence, the result was uniform crushing defeat: in the war of 1860, in the T'ai P'ing and Boxer rebellions, in war with Japan in 1894–95, and finally in the Japanese aggression of 1931–45; by 1938, the Japanese had taken virtually all of China's major cities, killed nearly a million Chinese troops in battle, and controlled the major part of China's population.*

What this meant to China is difficult to appreciate; we can see only the outward appearances of what must have been a searing inner conflict. After the Opium

---

* It has been said, with some justice, that China suffered all the disabilities of colonialism without any of its benefits—without the stability, and the organizing and modernizing influence, for example, that the British brought to India.

War, Chinese society was convulsed and disorganized in a series of attempts to adjust to the new reality of impotence and inferiority, aggravated by a progressive decay of its own native institutions. Peasant revolts, traditional in China, now took the form of extravagant attempts to imitate the foreigner and destroy the old China, as in the T'ai P'ing rebellion—or else to exalt Chinese tradition, eliminating all traces of Western ways and Westernized Chinese, as in the Boxer Rebellion. Every Western system—militarism, republicanism, fascism, democracy—was tried, for a few years or a few decades, as an organizing vehicle to rebuild China; only to founder in corruption, inefficiency, and weakness. And through all this lived the peasantry, ninety percent of China's population—squeezed by landlords and corrupt governments, conscripted for the innumerable civil wars that ravaged the countryside, their lands periodically wasted by floods (any one of which might take two million lives), a constant prey to famine and disease. At the last, as Secretary of State Acheson was to say, "the patience of the Chinese people in their misery ended. They did not bother to overthrow this [Nationalist] government. There was simply nothing to overthrow. They simply ignored it throughout the country."

Out of those long years emerged the China we see today: merging the nationalism of three thousand years, and the resentments and humiliations of a century, with the most totalitarian and "modern" of Western revolutionary ideologies; making great sacrifices to achieve the economic development that is the base of power; a nation to which all on its borders—from Japan around a great arc through Southeast Asia and India to the Soviet Union—look with uneasy speculation and concern for the future. This new China has already made strides that few would have predicted when the Nationalist regime collapsed in 1949. Its rate of growth under the first five-year plan was eleven percent, until the serious setbacks of the Great Leap Forward. It demonstrated in Korea that it could at least resist Western offensives with determination. Considerably earlier than predicted, at a far faster pace than

France, it has acquired a rudimentary nuclear and hydrogen capability, and is moving toward the acquisition of significant missile strength. The present internal struggle may seriously damage China's prospects for becoming a unitary, modern nation. But whatever the duration or consequences of that struggle, China has shown that if it can mobilize its formidable population, its people have the skill and drive to become a potential world power.

China, however, blends strength and weakness, limitations and possibilities for the future. In examining China, it is necessary not only to know more, but also to make calm and dispassionate judgments. Yet ever since the Korean war, the American public has heard estimates of China's aggressive potential that were often widely exaggerated. Each new population figure (now something less than 700 million) seemed a further warning of the danger of Chinese hordes sweeping over the world, or into India, or into the fertile valleys of Southeast Asia. But China is, after all, a poor nation, supporting her population only through prodigies of effort and hardship. Her per-person annual income of perhaps $85 (the estimates vary from $75 to $90) is one of the lowest in the world, lower even than India's; her national budget of about $17 billion is about the same as that of France, which has one-fourteenth of China's population, and a far more productive private sector.*

China's menacing nuclear capability will increase, probably rapidly, but she remains without the trans-

* Some sense of the thin edge on which China walks can be glimpsed in Jan Myrdal's recent description of a Chinese village of 212 people. In a year of backbreaking toil, virtually without agricultural machinery or fertilizers, they produced enough to feed themselves and thirty other people. Their "surplus"—the extra thirty people's food—was delivered to the state; together with the equivalent deliveries from other parts of China, it supports "not only the whole Chinese State with armies, atomic weapons, universities, diplomats and national monuments, but also the new industrial development." It also represents the entire surplus available to the village for clothing, shelter, and small necessities. The village gets no aid from the state for welfare, support of the old, etc.; it must take care of its own. Myrdal relates that a family had to kill its tiny dog, because other villagers resented its consumption of table scraps which might have been eaten by human beings.

port and supply capability, the air or naval forces, to engage readily in prolonged aggressive conquest. Once the Soviet Union supplied many of these needs, as in Korea; but that day is gone. Even China's land army is far smaller, in comparison to her population, than is our own, and in fact is little larger than ours in numbers. We both have total forces of about three million, and our firepower is incomparably greater.

If our common understanding of Chinese capabilities has been exaggerated, so has our common understanding of her potential as a source of revolution elsewhere. China's revolutionary experience is unique; and it is clear also that the revolutionary credo that accompanied it is not readily transferable to other nations. In Cuba, in Indonesia, in Algeria, in Africa, men have made clear that they would design and control their own national revolutions. There are sometimes attempts to portray Vietnam as a Chinese-inspired conflict, and China is assisting the North Vietnamese. But Vietnam's Communism is basically a native growth, with its own revolutionary traditions and dynamism. There is always a potential danger to which we must be alert, but as of 1967 there is not one example, anywhere in the world, of Chinese-inspired or directed revolution that has had any lasting success. Only the Malayan revolt had even the most minimal success, before being crushed, and that was carried out not by native Malayans, but by ethnic Chinese. The record of Chinese effort to export revolution has been one of consistent, dramatic failure: as we might have expected from a nation whose principal word for foreigners is the approximate equivalent of "barbarians," and which has a Foreign Minister capable of publicly calling for armed revolution in the presence of the African Head of State who was his host at the time.*

* The Chinese themselves seem to have recognized this, at least for the present. Lin Piao's famous manifesto, calling for revolution in the world's underdeveloped "countryside" to encircle the "cities" of the West, was in fact very clear that each nation must make its own revolution without outside assistance. This doctrinal restraint probably flows from factual weakness, and would be thrown off if adventure promised greater results. The point is not that the Chinese will refrain from exporting revolution where they can; only that they may realistically recognize when they cannot.

All this is not to say that China is helpless—a "paper tiger" as her leaders once called the United States—or that China can be ignored as a force in the world. China's millions, now and in the future, can be expected to exert considerable power in Asia. China's revolution can still serve as an example and encouragement to others. She can, as she has in the past, actively and dangerously assist others in so-called wars of national liberation. Nor can we ignore the possibility that Chinese efforts to assist and even dominate Communist movements in other countries may ultimately meet with occasional triumphs—though our expectations should be tempered by the knowledge that in North Korea, where China left almost a million dead, her troops were withdrawn and the North Koreans have strongly declared their independence if not their hostility.

We will ignore China, or think of her as weak, only at great danger to ourselves. But we will never have a sound policy if we assess Chinese power in anything but realistic terms. And we should not, in order to arouse others to a real threat, exaggerate that threat to a point where our statements are simply not credible to those whom we wish to influence. Yet mutual misunderstanding and ignorance have often led us to wrongly estimate the danger of China, and have often distorted the Chinese view of our attitude and intentions. Because we did not understand the deep Chinese roots of Chinese Communism and China's great xenophobia, we underestimated and ignored, for several years, the fact and significance of the Sino-Soviet split; our policy has not fully recognized it to this day. Because we forget so easily the last century of history, some of us underestimate Chinese hostility to the West, or fail to understand that in their eyes we stand as the inheritors of the Japanese—even as the physical inheritors of their bases: Korea, Formosa, Okinawa, Japan itself.*

---

* Another example of our lack of understanding about China has less immediate implications for policy, but is nevertheless worth noting. Seeing the chaos and disorganization of the Great Proletarian Cultural Revolution and the fantastic doings of the Red Guards,

But even this misunderstanding, the miscalculations and ignorance, are not the most serious consequence of these past years. What is most troublesome is not what we do not know about China; it is what we do not know about ourselves—about our own goals, our own policies, our own conception of the national interest in Asia. For more than twenty years we have been the strongest power on that continent. Our aid and our armed forces, bases, and the flow of commerce give us greater influence in Asia than any other nation. Across the vast sweep of that continent in which we are so deeply involved, China looms more importantly and dangerously than any other nation. Indeed, it was the fact of Chinese Communist power that led us, through treaty and the movement of forces, to assume, over the last decade, the position we hold today. Yet, for many years we have disposed our forces, made commitments, conducted our enterprises, and fought wars, virtually without conscious policy and direction, unaware of what we seek and the price we are prepared to pay. We have striven to isolate China from the world and treated it with unremitting hostility. That, however, is not a policy. It is an attitude founded upon fear and passion and wishful hopes. In Korea, the Formosa Straits, and India, we responded to immediate situations of danger; those actions were necessary, but they were designed to protect the present rather than to

---

some tend to write off Mao Tse-tung and his followers as madmen, and abandon further efforts at analysis. Some scholars, however, contend that there is a rational explanation. They say that the peasantry would not continue its terrible sacrifices while a New Class of bureaucrats and technicians lives in comparative luxury, but would rebel, as many did in the wake of the Great Leap Forward. They note that while the Soviet Union, needing to squeeze capital from the Russian peasant in the 1930s, killed over fifteen million of its own people, the equally hard-pressed Chinese regime pays hard cash for seven million tons of Canadian and Australian wheat each year. In this view, the upheaval is intended to discipline or even destroy the new privileged classes—especially in the party hierarchy.

This explanation, of course, may be entirely wrong; its proponents seem to have no special evidence to support it, and I, of course, cannot judge between the competing views. My point is only that the evidence in their support seems as good (or bad) as the evidence that Mao is demented—and that underestimation of one's enemy is always dangerous.

prepare for the future. It should be clear that these responses and actions, this lack of knowledge and consistent direction, are not the failure of any one Administration or any one political party. Indeed, there has been more growth in our awareness and knowledge of the problem in the past year than in the past decade.

But we still lack, and still need, a policy; and the time to at least begin to develop one is now. Political passions have dimmed. Understanding and concern are rising. The Cold War in the West is calmed, allowing us to divert some energy and thought to Asia. Most importantly, as the war in Vietnam unveils the possibility of recurring and draining conflict, necessity—the midwife of foreign policy—crowds in upon us. We shall grope on our way toward a new China policy; limited knowledge, present uncertainty, and the random obscurity of the future require us to be at least that realistic. Such a policy will emerge, not as a sudden revelation, but slowly out of discussion and danger, from shifting events and painful battles. It will not, however, come of itself. We must make active efforts to think and plan, learn, decide, and act. We can discuss what a policy is and begin to glimpse some general direction for the policy that must come. But let us be sure we know what policy is not.

First, a position that pleases us without a reasonable chance of acceptance or accomplishment is not a policy. Thus the liberation of the Mainland by the Nationalist Chinese was at best empty rhetoric, and at worst a dangerous illusion. Similarly it is not a policy to say that we would now work for the admission of both China and Formosa to the United Nations. China does not and will not admit Formosa's independence, which in their eyes would legitimize our intervention in their unfinished civil war; neither is "two-Chinas" acceptable to the Nationalists on Formosa, for whom it would destroy any pretense to legitimate ruling authority on that island.

Second, faith in the ultimate goodness of human nature or the ameliorating impact of progress is not a policy. We cannot await with confidence the day when material wealth and a better understanding of economic reality will "bring China (or a new generation of Chinese leaders) to its senses." The history of our time gives ample proof that advanced, cultured, and self-confident nations are fully capable of dark disorder, violence, and aggression. It was not Stalin but Khrushchev who, in the fortieth year of the Russian revolution, crushed Hungary, and seven years later came to the brink of nuclear war in his Cuban adventure. It was a Germany "advanced" far beyond the distant goals of China that half destroyed a continent and slaughtered millions. Moreover, nuclear weapons today can give a country a capacity to destroy far greater than its real power or wealth. That fact, by itself, will undoubtedly influence Chinese leaders in a dangerous although still unpredictable way; thus the conflict in Vietnam would certainly be quite different if China had the capacity to destroy Chicago or New York with nuclear missiles. As Homer said long ago, "the sword itself often provokes a man to fight." China may or may not become less aggressive and dangerous as it progresses—as the Soviet Union may, as Germany or Japan may, as we ourselves may. It is praiseworthy to hope and work for Chinese moderation; but to look upon moderation as the certain fruit of time, and act accordingly, is to tempt fatal danger.

Third, the desire for reconciliation or the hope of friendship is not a policy. Hostility springs from the clash of interests and ambitions, and their resolution or compromise—the mutual acceptance of legitimate claims and interests—is at the heart of accommodation. That resolution, that compromise, must precede, not follow, reconciliation. Policy is the determination of terms on which reconciliation can and will be carried out.

Fourth, faith in the certainty of our historical judgment is not a policy. We cannot act as if we know China will certainly try to expand by force or that it will never try. We cannot assume that Communist expansion in Asia will inevitably be swallowed up by the nationalisms of Asian states; nor should we assume that all revolutions will be captured by Communists, or that all who call themselves Communists will come under the dominion and control of Peking. Rather, we must prepare for all contingencies that threaten the clear national interests of the United States.

A policy is none of these; just as it is not fear or hostility or wish. Policy is the establishment of goals and of a course of action rationally calculated to achieve those goals. It must be ready to yield to the overriding logic of events, yet strive to shape circumstances rather than belatedly react to them. We do not have such a policy toward China. We have acted often, and these actions are supported by reasons of varying wisdom and persuasion. Yet rarely have our stated reasons and goals been pursued with the consistency and sustained application that would raise them to the dignity of policy. Thus they have often become justifications for particular acts rather than expressions of consistent national purpose.

It has been suggested, for example, that we are pursuing strategic interests in Asia, denying the control of other land and resources to Asian Communism. Yet less than two years ago we were quite prepared to accept the spread of Communism to Indonesia: a nation of one hundred million people, incomparably rich in resources, standing over the critical Straits of Malacca and flanking the Philippines. Of course, we want to prevent the expansion, the acquisition of vast new resources, by powers deeply hostile to the United States. That statement, however, is only the beginning of thought. How do we discriminate between Chinese expansion and autonomous revolt? Where and under what circumstances can we bring our power effectively to bear? Where and under what circumstances should we limit ourselves to helping others, without hazarding large-scale combat or major war? These are not easy questions to answer. But until we at least begin to discuss and debate them we will be unable to develop any kind of long-range planning, let alone policy. Even then, the application of that policy in any given situation may be painfully difficult.

More corrupting, if less dangerous, is the self-righteous assertion of sweeping moral principles as a substitute for policy, though we are willing to ignore those principles when our conception of national interest demands it. We proclaim our intention to assure self-determination, with American lives if necessary. Yet we support and defend a Formosa whose indigenous people have no voice in Government, and we do not even raise our voice in protest. We are told that "nations must learn to leave their neighbors alone." Yet we do not always leave our neighbors in this hemisphere alone. Nor can we righteously announce that "we seek only freedom and human decency throughout the world," when we have supported, for what we felt was good cause, repressive and corrupt governments in every continent of the globe.

I do not quarrel with the necessity of some of the actions that were inconsistent with these principles. But those actions do teach us that blanket moral statements cannot determine all strategic judgments, and that their enunciation does not constitute a policy. It may well be that greater consistency with the moral principles upon which this nation rests might, in the long run, lead to a sounder policy and greater protection for the interests of the United States. I believe this to be so. Yet if we solemnly pronounce principles that will not or cannot be consistently applied, we delude ourselves and invite serious charges of hypocrisy from others.

In Africa, I tried to answer those who asked, "If the United States is fighting for self-determination in Vietnam, then how can it not support the independence struggle of Angola and Mozambique?" I answered unsatisfactorily, for there is no real answer. Yet to the questioners, it is less our intention than our pretension that is objectionable. Thus does false principle destroy the credibility in our wisdom and purpose that is the true foundation of influence as a world power.

The same is true of another kind of blanket formulation—that we must keep our commitments or meet our obligations. Of course, we must keep our commitments and obligations. But by what standards, and toward what ends, are those commitments made? How deeply do they extend, and what means will be used to fulfill them? Thus it is one thing to defend a commitment in Vietnam; yet it is something else indeed to fulfill that commitment by extending military operations to Thailand, in return making a new commitment to that nation as well. What is to govern the form of the commitment—whether it is to be a commitment to help others help themselves, or a commitment to ensure victory whether they help themselves or not? When we make the first, do we slowly and inexorably and almost automatically accept the latter?

None of these—sweeping statements, pious hopes, grandiose commitments—constitute a China policy for the future. That policy must be based on the reality and diversity of today's Asia and on a discriminating evaluation of our own interests, capacities, and limitations. It will be formed out of an evaluation of the dangers and capacities, the capabilities and desires, of other nations. We are not alone with China in Asia. There is also India, the second most populous nation in the world, in itself a great civilization; Japan, soon to become the third leading industrial power on the globe, a nation whose certain future importance is matched only by our ignorance about her; Indonesia, with its resources and commanding strategic position. In the long run, the vision and commitment of these great Asian nations will determine in large part the course of affairs on the continent—just as it is Great Britain, West Germany, France, and Italy that now set the primary thrust of development in Western Europe. Our policy must be shaped, our actions undertaken, in full understanding of the interests and actions of these nations—and with a consciousness that we do not act as a substitute for, but rather as a supplement to, their policy.

Further, we must understand that our policy toward China must be a major factor in determining our policy toward those countries that border on China, indeed all of Asia. If a strong India is considered vital to the containment of China, and to our national security, the level of our economic and military assistance must reflect that priority. We now work as if in a vacuum: for example, by spending thousands of American lives and billions of dollars in part on the theory that Vietnam is essential to us, while refusing to assist others on the border of China whose demands may be less, but whose strategic importance and vulnerability to Chinese dominion or penetration may be greater. Yet surely we have learned that a failure to act can have the greatest consequences. If we choose to remain an Asian power, we must be prepared to pay the cost: for example, in economic assistance, increased greatly as it must be if we are to avoid again paying the price in blood and treasure we pay today.

Our China policy will be formed out of paradox and complexity. It will recognize that Asia in 1967 is not the Europe of 1949, where a grand alliance, constructed against one great threat, served as the framework of all policy. Thus the Soviet Union—our principal adversary and competitor in the post-War world—is, at least for the time being, China's violent ideological opponent, with what often seems a very different vision of the Asian future. Her mediation in the India-Pakistan war was only one dramatic illustration of this difference. Thus also Japan, our former enemy and present ally, China's historical rival and imitator, invader and economic partner, today at once contracts with the Soviet Union to develop the resources of Siberia; conducts a large investment campaign in China, among other things proposing to develop China's petro-chemical industry; serves as a major U.S. base; and contributes the first $200 million to the Asian development bank.

China policy must be formed against the probability that when present convulsions subside, we will still face a hostile China. We still have to refuse the temptation of assuming that any acts or gestures on our part will significantly improve relations. Yet hostile words and proclamations are not wars. They do not prevent us from reaching agreements on matters of mutual interest—as after the Quemoy crisis of 1958, when we agreed to restrain Chiang's aggressive activity, and China agreed not to attack Quemoy and Matsu. They do not prevent us from having contacts that could lead us to know more about China, and they about us, and thus prevent the miscalculation of intentions that could lead to nuclear holocaust. We should not discourage contact of any kind, by ourselves or other nations, whether economic or diplomatic, even tourism: For a rational or informed China may be easier to deal with, and will certainly not be harder to deal with, than an irrational and ignorant one. Still our expectations must be tempered by the realization that European nations, in "contact" with each other for centuries, have filled those same centuries with hatred, conflict, and mutual destruction.

Our policy must also rest on the knowledge that we cannot predict the possibility of Chinese military expansion. Therefore, we must be prepared to help others defend themselves, while refusing to base our actions and policies on the assumption that armed clash is inevitable. We must realize that every extension of Chinese influence does not menace us. We must be able to discriminate between armed attack and internal revolution, between Chinese direction of revolutionary forces and Chinese exhortation. Where Chinese force is not directly involved or borders crossed, we must ask whether we should be willing to rely above all on the strength and vitality of the desire for national independence. After all, it is that powerful desire, and not our military force, which ousted the Chinese from central Africa, Algeria, and Indonesia, and which is steadily eroding the Soviet empire.

Policy demands finally a conscious and open recognition that we live in the same world and move in the same continent with China—with its dangers and possibilities, strengths and terrible frustrations. Only when we accept this reality can we work toward our central task: to bring about Chinese acceptance of the fact that it too must live with us and the other nations of the world. These are, admittedly, general considerations rather than guides to specific action. Yet it will make a great difference to our acts and policies if we treat China as a potential danger and a possible opportunity rather than as a certain enemy and a lost cause.

Of course, the shadow of the Vietnam war hovers over all these deliberations. That is itself an immense and complex subject to which we will shortly pass. Still the resolution of that war will not resolve the problems of Asia, although the resolution must depend in large part on our attitude and policy toward China. Nor, despite Vietnam's intimate relationship with our China policy, will the war's solution remove the urgent necessity of the larger problem.

We cannot know the future course of our relations with China. All our intentions and labor may ultimately dissolve in violence and bloodshed. But there is another possibility. Perhaps some day an American diplomat may go to China, carrying with him the same instructions Daniel Webster gave to Caleb Cushing in 1843; to tell the people of China "that your mission is entirely pacific . . . that you are a messenger of peace, sent from the greatest power in America to the greatest in Asia, to offer respect and good will and to establish the means of friendly intercourse."

Vietnam

Author's Note

SINCE THE TEXT of the following chapter was written in the fall of 1967, the Tet Offensive of January, 1968 has taken place. I see no need to change the views originally expressed in the chapter. I have, however, brought certain of the factual material up-to-date and I have added the complete text of an address delivered in Chicago, Illinois, on February 8, 1968 following that offensive. New footnotes in this edition are set in italics.

It is appropriate to inject here a note both personal and public. I was involved in many of the early decisions on Vietnam, decisions which helped set us on our present path. It may be that the effort was doomed from the start, that it was never really possible to bring all the people of South Vietnam under the rule of the successive governments we supported—governments, one after another, riddled with corruption, inefficiency, and greed; governments which did not and could not successfully capture and energize the national feeling of their people. If that is the case, as it well may be, then I am willing to bear my share of the responsibility, before history and before my fellow-citizens. But past error is no excuse for its own perpetuation. Tragedy is a tool for the living to gain wisdom, not as a guide by which to live. Now as ever, we do ourselves best justice when we measure ourselves against ancient tests, as in the *Antigone* of Sophocles: "All men make mistakes, but a good man yields when he knows his course is wrong, and repairs the evil. The only sin is pride."

THE ASTOUNDING MIGHT of American power now falls upon a remote and alien people in a small and unknown land. It is difficult to feel in our hearts what this war means to Vietnam; it is on the other side of the world, and its people are strangers. Few of us are directly involved, while the rest of us continue our lives and pursue our ambitions undisturbed by the sounds and fears of battle. To the Vietnamese, however, it must often seem the fulfillment of the prophecy of Saint John the Divine: "And I looked, and beheld a pale horse: and his name that sat on him was Death, and Hell followed with him. And power was given unto them over the fourth part of the earth, to kill with sword, with hunger, and with death. . . ."

Although the world's imperfections may call forth the acts of war, righteousness cannot obscure the agony and pain those acts bring to a single child. The Vietnamese war is an event of historic moment, summoning the power and concern of many nations. But it is also the vacant moment of amazed fear as a mother and child watch death by fire fall from the improbable machine sent by a country they barely comprehend. It is the sudden terror of the official or the hamlet militiaman absorbed in the work of his village as he realizes the assassin is taking his life. It is the refugees wandering homeless from villages now obliterated, leaving behind only those who did not live to flee. It is the young men, Vietnamese and American, who in an instant sense the night of death destroying yesterday's promise of family and land and home.

It is a country where young men have never lived a day in peace and where families have never known a time when it was not necessary to be afraid. It is a land deafened by the unending crescendo of violence, hatred, and savage fury, where the absorbing goal for millions is not to live well or to improve their lives, but simply to survive. It is a country where hundreds of thousands fight, but millions more are the innocent, bewildered victims of brutal passions and beliefs they barely understand. To them peace is not an abstract term describing one of those infrequent intervals when men are not killing each other. It is a day without terror and the fall

of bombs. It is a family and the familiar life of their
village. It is food and a school and life itself.

All we say and all we do must be informed by our
awareness that this horror is partly our responsibility;
not just a nation's responsibility but yours and mine. It
is we who live in abundance and send our young men
out to die. It is our chemicals that scorch the children
and our bombs that level the villages. We are all partici-
pants. To know this, to feel the burden of this responsi-
bility, is not to ignore important interests, nor to forget
that freedom and security must sometimes be paid for
in blood. Still even though we must know as a nation
what it is necessary to do, we must also feel as men the
anguish of what it is we are doing.

ANOTHER KIND OF WAR

President Kennedy said in 1961 that technology had
made all-out war highly unlikely, because if it came, it
would mean the end of civilization as we know it. We
face instead, he said, "another kind of war—new in its
intensity, ancient in its origin—war by guerrillas, sub-
versives, insurgents, assassins, war by ambush instead
of by combat; by infiltration instead of aggression, seeking victory by eroding and exhausting the enemy instead
of engaging him." In the last twenty years, most of the
world's struggles have been this kind of war; though the
struggles have sprung from many causes and have sought
different ends. In Algeria and Cyprus, the goal was
national independence from foreign domination. In
Burma, Iraq, and the Naga Hills of India, it was to
establish regional or tribal identity against the central
national authority. In Malaya and Greece, Communist
minorities sought to dominate a nation.

This is the war that we face in South Vietnam today.
Its character has been obscured by the smoke of conventional combat. Thousands of Americans have gone
into battle, confronting North Vietnamese regulars and
"main force" Viet Cong units. Our Navy and Air Force
planes have dropped a greater tonnage of explosives than
we dropped in all the European Theater in World

War II: in 1966 alone, five tons of bombs for every square mile and one ton for every forty people in all of North and South Vietnam. Yet these conventional efforts, the divisional operations and massive raids, are taking place because an earlier struggle failed. That was the attempt of the Government of South Vietnam, with our aid and assistance, to build a viable government and society and to stem an insurgency that as late as 1959 (according to the late Bernard Fall) had an active strength of only three thousand men. The struggle of "revolutionary war" continues unabated today, carried on in the 15,000 hamlets of South Vietnam and in secret quarters of the cities. This war continues, defying our massive sweeps. It still saps and enervates the society of South Vietnam and our war effort. It still energizes the enemy, still provides the base of his strength, supply, and survival.

The regular North Vietnamese units are only one of three forces arrayed against us in the Southern combat, and are by no means the most important. According to General Westmoreland, there are about 50,000 regulars* of the North Vietnamese People's Army facing us in the South. In most of the country, however, the forces opposing us are Viet Cong: South Vietnamese in rebellion against the Government of South Vietnam, though often Northern-trained or Northern-led, and to a degree dependent on Northern supply and direction. One hundred thousand of the Viet Cong are organized in the "main force" military units. Underlying these units are what former Ambassador Henry Cabot Lodge called "the real cancer": 150,000 Viet Cong guerrillas working throughout Vietnam, from tiny villages our forces have never seen to the gates of our great bases and to the very doors of our Embassy in Saigon. These South Vietnamese guerrillas have struggled almost continuously for over twenty years—against the French, against other nationalist groups, against the South Vietnamese government, against us. Throughout, they have worked and fought "in place," organizing and fighting in and around their own villages and districts. They have supplied rice and

---

* *Now estimated at 110,000.*

recruited soldiers, assassinated government officials and planted booby traps, and above all organized a substantial part of South Vietnam's people into a disciplined and effective opposition to the official government. Ambassador Lodge stated that not even the defeat of his main force units, but only the destruction of the Viet Cong infrastructure, would be regarded as decisive by the adversary himself. Behind the clamor of combat, Vietnam is still a revolutionary war—at least on the other side.

This must be remembered and stressed because our escalation of the war has concentrated on North Vietnam. It is dangerously easy, even seductive, to concentrate on what we know best: conventional warfare, bombing from the air, technology, and armies that do not meddle with politics. But to do this is to ignore every past lesson of this war, and of all the "new wars" of the last twenty years. For if these conflicts are called wars, and have deep international consequences, they are at the same time not wars, and their outcome is determined by internal factors. Their essence is political. They are struggles for the control of government, contests for the allegiance of men. Allegiance is won as in any political contest, by an idea and a faith, by promise and performance. Governments resist such challenges only by being effective and responsive to the needs of their people.

Men's allegiance and this kind of war are not won by superior force, by the might of numbers, or by the sophistication of technology. On the tiny island of Cyprus, the British Army had 110 soldiers and policemen for every member of EOKA, which never numbered more than a few hundred terrorists. Yet Britain had to surrender control of the island within five years after the rebellion began. In Algeria, the French army had, throughout the conflict, overwhelming superiority in men, firepower, and communications, as well as complete control of the air, and the technological and support capability to physically seal off the country from neighboring states. But again within five years, France had to sever its ties to Algeria and leave it in control of the rebels. In Vietnam itself from 1955 to 1959, the government and army of Ngo Dinh Diem had overwhelming numerical superiority over the Viet Cong, including all those infiltrated from the North. Expert observers seem agreed that the guerrillas were all but crushed. Yet the government did not grow correspondingly stronger. Within five years, the threat of the Viet Cong had grown to such proportions that, according to Senator Mansfield's report,* "A total collapse of the Saigon government's authority appeared imminent in the early months of 1965." Even today the Army of the Republic of South Vietnam outnumbers its opponents by at least three to one, but no one thinks it would last a month if the United States were to suddenly withdraw.

Mere numbers or the possession of advanced weapons are not conclusive for several reasons. One is the character of military force itself. Conventional military force and advanced weapons technology are useful only to destroy. But a government cannot make war on its own people, or destroy its own country. Suppose, for example, that a government force is fired upon from a village. A government that attacks that village from the air, or with heavy artillery, abandons all pretense of protecting the people of the village. But such protection is the first duty of any government worthy of the name, and its absence is not ignored by the village. Rather, as General Edward Lansdale has told us, "civilian hatred of the military resulting from such actions is a powerful motive for joining [the insurgents]."

There is another side to this coin. When an insurgent uprising threatened to unseat Jerome Bonaparte, his brother Napoleon told him "use your bayonets." Jerome replied, "Brother, you can do anything with bayonets—except sit on them." That is also true of more advanced weapons. Guns and bombs cannot fill empty stomachs or educate children, cannot build homes or heal the sick. But these are the ends for which men establish and obey governments; they will give their allegiance only to governments that meet these needs.

The most convincing government victory in any modern insurgency was in the Philippines. When Ramón

---

* "The Vietnam Conflict: The Substance and the Shadow."

Magsaysay became Defense Minister there, the Huk-balahap insurgents were on the outskirts of Manila. He had an army of only 50,000 to fight 15,000 insurgents, far below the ten-to-one superiority usually considered necessary to defeat guerrillas convincingly. The government forces had no special modern armament, and their air and communications superiority was limited. But Magsaysay placed only limited reliance, and secondary priority, on military actions. His first concern was to secure an honest election throughout the country. Next he began a thorough land reform, enforced by such innovations as mobile landlord-tenant courts held from jeeps to ensure that fair-minded judges would protect peasants from powerful local interests. Other reforms followed, all directed at the welfare of the people, including amnesty and land for rebels who ended fighting. Aided by his own charismatic qualities as a leader, Magsaysay's reforms attracted the allegiance of the people. Within four years, the rebellion was crushed and its leaders surrendered.*

While nearly everyone seems to acknowledge this political dimension to our actions, it is too often refused the priority it demands: The military dimension seems more urgent and insistent. But reform, and the hope it brings, cannot be postponed. The essence of insurgency, as Bernard Fall and Douglas Pike have authoritatively shown, is intense and extensive political organization of an ever-increasing proportion of the nation. That organization is based on the immediate and pressing needs of the people, on their grievances and injustices. Often this will be the first time these people have ever participated in organized political activity, or in a major effort to improve their lives. Moreover, the insurgents are likely to institute at least a facsimile of actual reform in areas they control, even in the midst of the struggle. In Vietnam as in the China of the 1940s, they have distributed land, organized schools and adult-education classes, and established courts, thus entering into direct competition with the established government. If the government ignores or postpones reform while attempting

* Its later resurgence has been in direct proportion to the relaxation of reforms which followed Magsaysay's death.

to repress the insurgency with military force, it only confirms the insurgents' claim to represent the forces of justice and progress. If the government goes further and actively tries to dismantle the rebel reforms—as by helping landlords collect back taxes from peasants who have been "given" their land by the insurgents—it can recruit rebels more effectively than any Communist. It does little good to warn that the end result of Communism will be dictatorship and exploitation; the deeds of today speak most loudly, if not most truly, on whose promises will be kept tomorrow.

The final reason for the inadequacy of military power is that it can give no hope. Force is neutral; it has no program. Every insurgent movement lives not primarily on force, but on a dream—of independence, of justice, of progress, of a better life for one's children. For such dreams, men will undergo great hardship and sacrifice, as we have done and will do again for our own. Without a vision of the future to offer, a government can demand no sacrifice, no resistance to insurgent terror or blandishments. Only a spirit of sacrifice and determination, greater than that of the insurgents, will win such a war.

What is true of military force in general is true in far greater degree of military force applied by a foreign power. Whatever appeal an insurgent movement can gain through a program of reform, its appeal will be enormously enhanced if it can seize the banner of nationalism, the strongest political force in modern life. The underdeveloped nations of Asia and Africa, with rare exceptions, are former colonies and dependencies of the Western powers. Only recently have they emerged into political independence; they are still struggling to establish economic, cultural, and intellectual independence and power. For a government to rely excessively on a foreign power, to invite Western armies to take the field against native insurgents, is at once a terrible confession of national weakness and a direct threat to the independence so recently achieved. It allows the insurgents to picture the government as colonialist puppets. Perhaps most seriously of all, every insurgent blow against the foreigner may raise a thrill of national pride even in supporters of the government; and at the bottom of his heart, no man who loves his country can rejoice when his fellow-countrymen are defeated in battle, even if he himself is strongly opposed to their politics. A basically sound and independent government, commanding the allegiance of its people, can survive and profit from foreign assistance, as in Venezuela, the Philippines, or post-war Greece from 1947-1949. But a weak government, without support from its own people, may only be further weakened, perhaps fatally, by foreign assistance or intervention. Foreign assistance can reinforce a national will, but foreign intervention cannot provide a substitute where a national will is lacking.

This does not mean that military force is ineffective or unnecessary. The most loyal citizens may deny allegiance to his government if insurgent terror is not prevented and overcome by government force. The most developed and unified societies often find force necessary to defend themselves against those who reject peaceful political processes. Force is the last resort of all states and societies, and we ourselves have used it to repress internal disorder several times in this decade. Military force can and must be a part of any effort to combat insurgency. Citizens and governments need protection, a shield behind which reforms can be carried out.

But no primarily military effort can be successful against a deeply rooted insurgency with any degree of popular support. Still less can any amount of force redeem political failures, or win the allegiance of the people to a government that does not earn that loyalty. Rather I think that the history of the last twenty years demonstrates beyond doubt that the only sound approach to revolutionary war is above all political. Where the needs and grievances of the people, whether for social change or national independence, begin to be met by the political process, then insurgency loses its popular character and becomes a police problem—as it did in Venezuela and the Philippines and Malaya. George Marshall once said, "Let's not talk about this matter too much in military terms; to do so might make it a military problem." But that is a fair account of what has happened in Vietnam.

THE "OTHER WAR" IN VIETNAM

The political war in Vietnam has been called by many names: pacification, civic action, New Life Hamlets, "winning the hearts and minds" of the people, and Revolutionary Development. Since 1966, it has often been referred to as the "other war," to distinguish it from the active large-unit combat operations, fought principally by American troops. By itself, the name "other war" tells us that the "real war," in the minds of those who use the phrase, is the large-scale military combat.

Yet it is the "other war," the political contest for the allegiance of the people of Vietnam, that is in fact *the* war. And this "other war" has been lost repeatedly in the last two decades: first by the French, then by Diem, more lately by the governments that followed him. Each time it was lost not only from Communist strength, but more importantly from the weakness, ignorance, and greed of the successive governments. The French refused self-government to Indochina, and the Viet Minh became representative, leader, and organizer of those who wished independence for their nation; their elimination of other nationalist groups, often by bloody force, is itself evidence of how eager they were to seize the advantage and control of the independence cause. By its end, Diem's regime was so repressive that it alienated its people and drove many to join the insurgents, yet was too corrupt and inept to suppress them. When Diem was overthrown by his own generals, the fifteen months of governmental chaos and internal power struggles that ensued led directly to that "total collapse of the Saigon government's authority" which Senator Mansfield found imminent in 1965.

It is these political failures that have led to ever-greater war, and at the same time have recklessly thrown away the time and opportunity bought by the blood and sacrifice they called forth.

Above all, Vietnam teaches us that a government must command the willing allegiance of its people, and make itself a vehicle for the satisfaction of their national and personal aspirations. Yet there is no sign, in the early fall of 1967, that the lesson has been absorbed.

LAND AND OTHER REFORM:
THE SOCIAL QUESTION

Look first at the issue of land. Vietnam is an agricultural country; to talk of land is therefore to go to the heart of the social and political structure. In the greatest part of South Vietnam, 6300 (mostly absentee) landlords—two percent of landowners—own forty-five percent of the land. 183,000 small-holders, seventy-two percent of all landowners, own fifteen percent of the land. Another four million potential workers are unemployed essentially landless peasants without support; many more are tenant farmers. Virtually every observer of Vietnam since 1945 has declared land reform, comprising both redistribution of ownership and restriction of the landlords' power over their tenants, to be a central element in the struggle. Anti-Americanism has now largely replaced land reform as a propaganda vehicle for the Viet Cong. But for many years it was one of the most important insurgent issues; and even today, especially in the Mekong Delta where half of South Vietnam's people live, it retains much force. And the adherents it once gained are, in a real sense, in large part responsible for our difficulties today.

But despite the promises of a dozen regimes, despite laws and ordinances and decrees, no non-Communist Vietnamese government has ever carried out a serious land reform. Two ordinances, promulgated by Diem in 1955 and 1956, did limit riceland holdings of any individual to 100 hectares (about 247 acres), and rents for tenant farmers to twenty-five percent of the crop. (By comparison, the thoroughgoing land reforms in Taiwan and Japan limited holdings to any family to seven and ten hectares respectively.) Yet even the limited Diem ordinances are not enforced: In government-controlled areas, tenant farmers (who are seventy percent of all farmers in the Mekong Delta) must still pay fifty percent or more of their rice crops to absentee landlords. When government forces move into Viet Cong areas, they are still sometimes accompanied by absentee landlords, who rely on the troops not merely to recapture their lands, but also to collect back rents for the years they have lived in Saigon, safe from the Viet Cong.

There are simple and practical land reforms that could be undertaken and enforced in the areas securely under government control, and thus automatically extended to other areas as an inducement for coming under government control. Land could be redistributed to the peasants who till it, with all land holdings limited to a number of hectares (allowing for varying local conditions) comparable to those in Japan and Taiwan; land rents, both back rent and future payments, could be abolished. Compensation for landlords would be relatively inexpensive. We could always have said, as we still could say: Let it be the Viet Cong, and not the South Vietnamese government, who tax and exploit the peasants. No doubt land redistribution would be difficult in the midst of this savage war. But the entire war is difficult for us all, particularly for the young Americans who are fighting and dying, and for their families; there must be a better reason for the lack of reforms than that they would be "difficult" to carry out.

The declaration of the United States at the Honolulu Conference of February 1966 pledges our "full support to measures of social revolution, including land reform." The Vietnamese declaration at that same conference, and the joint declaration of the two governments, however, omitted any reference to land reform. This was not an accident. For years, the rulers of South Vietnam have refused to undertake the real land reforms we have urged them to make. At best they have made token efforts, ordinances and laws not enforced in the countryside, because land reform has not been in their narrow self-interest. The government of South Vietnam—not only the cabinet officials, but also the civil servants, the military officers, the province chiefs—was and is largely made up of, or allied with, a privileged class, for whom land is the basis of wealth and power. Faced with a choice between the welfare of their nation and the preservation of their privileges, they have chosen the latter. For them, with some individual exceptions, it seems that the war is not worth winning if the price is the sacrifice of their land, wealth, and power. It is this continued dominance of the wealthy and privileged, and not the war or Communist terrorism, that has prevented land reform in the past, and prevents it today.

The problem of corruption is a second example. We have known for years that corruption is pervasive; though chagrined at its extent while Americans are dying, we have tended to regard it as an issue peripheral to the main war effort. But corruption is not a matter just of spectacular individual cases, such as the cabinet minister who took almost $1 million in payments from American firms selling medicines to the government. It is a whole system, under which the army and social elite further exploit the mass of the people: selling government posts, siphoning off American aid at a dozen levels before it reaches the peasant, keeping incompenent officials in office. When generals and officials live in luxury far beyond their official means, the effect on our efforts is much more than wasted money. It results also in pervasive cynicism and political defeats. Lieutenant Colonel William Carson, head of the Marine Combined Action Program in Danang, has succinctly described this process: "The peasant sees that we are supporting a local government structure he knows to be corrupt. So he assumes that we are either stupid or implicated. And he decides that we are not stupid."

The social question also reaches deeply into the army, still enmeshed in the system of corruption and misgovernment, despite all our efforts, too often indifferently led by members of the elite. Its common soldier, who sometimes fulfills his potential as a brave and tenacious fighter, still labors under awful burdens: poorly paid, badly fed, little or no attention devoted to the welfare of his family, fighting for years on end against the Viet Cong, but also to preserve the same system that exploits him and his family. The consequence is apparent in the staggering desertion rate. The United States command in Vietnam reported over 18,000 desertions from the Army of the Republic of Vietnam (ARVN) forces in the first three months of 1967. Now it is estimated that 1967 desertions may be at a lower rate—perhaps 50,-

000, nearly ten percent of South Vietnam's army; still more men than the United States will add to its forces this year. Even so, achieving this rate would be an improvement over the 116,000 desertions of 1966, or the 113,000 of 1965. A knowledgeable observer has said that "in Vietnam all statistics are poetry," and these like others may overstate or understate their case.* But however inaccurate they may be in detail, there is no avoiding their general implications about the depth of the ARVN commitment.

Evidence of the ARVN's weakness is the increasing combat burden on the American forces, who, it was announced in late 1966, would thenceforth take over all offensive and major combat operations, leaving to the South Vietnamese army only rear-guard protection and pacification activities. Even in those areas where the ARVN has retained combat responsibility, it has engaged in progressively less fighting: declining from an average of one contact in every 200 small-unit operations in 1965, to one in every 400 operations in 1967. (American forces make contact in one of every thirty-eight such operations.) Now, as the pacification program flounders, there are suggestions that there must be more Americans to do that job as well; some American commanders, notably among the Marines, have already felt it necessary to put their troops to the work of pacification.

That we have done as well as we have in Vietnam is therefore a great tribute to the valor and effectiveness of our own young men, who have equaled the performance of any American army in our history. It is a tribute also to those isolated hamlets or villages where the will to resist the Viet Cong has survived despite the failures of the Saigon government. It is a tribute finally to those South Vietnamese, principally in the elite combat units, who have continued the struggle notwithstanding the apathy or ineffectiveness of so much of the ARVN. These, however, are not representative of the South Vietnamese Army.

---

* They do not, for example, expressly make clear that most deserters do not go over to the Viet Cong but simply go back to their homes.

WHOSE SIDE ARE WE ON?

The absence of reform, the corruption and weakness, an army relegated to the work of pacification while American troops assume the burden of combat—these are measures of the extent to which this has become an American war. And this is the crux of our difficulties in Vietnam. As part of a world-wide struggle against the extension of Communist power, and to protect the self-determination of the people of South Vietnam, we committed ourselves to the support of its government. To this day, the primary reason for our continued support of South Vietnam is in the interest of the people of the country, and not its government. But in our effort, we became allied with a regime and a class that, given repeated chances to change its ways, has shown neither the will nor the capacity to meet the needs of its own people. Our constant hope and purpose was to induce that government to make the needed reforms and to assist them in doing so. Our efforts were grounded not only in a realistic knowledge that the struggle must otherwise be unsuccessful, but also in the nature of our commitment: to the South Vietnamese people as a whole, rather than any narrow element. But the obstinacy of the government has worked to the detriment of their own people, to the advantage of the Communists, and at the cost of American lives.

Nevertheless, it is important that we preserve a sense of proportion. Some Americans, repelled by American support for a selfish and repressive government, have swung so far in the other direction as to romanticize our adversaries: to see in kindly "Uncle Ho," and the Vietnamese Communists he leads, nothing more than a relatively benign nationalist force. Only a frightening insensitivity to the human cost of North Vietnamese nationalism could regard its extension as a desirable end. The North Vietnamese regime is far more repressive, and more ruthlessly efficient, than any of the various Southern governments. Its "land reform" program of 1954-55 was a forced collectivization on the Chinese model, so brutally carried out that the peasant rebellion that it caused could be suppressed by Ho's army only at the cost of over 100,000 lives. There is nothing we would recognize as freedom in North Vietnam today. In the South, the Viet Cong program has been advanced by terrorism in its most cruel and literal sense: beheadings, disembowelments, the killing of women and children. It has been more effective, in large part because more selective, than our bombing and shelling, as I will discuss later. That, however, is not a matter for moral approval, much less for welcoming Viet Cong victories.

Therefore, the point of examining the shortcomings of the Saigon regime is not to decide whether it "should" fall, or its enemies "deserve" to win. The losers, in either case, are the people of South Vietnam, the majority of whom by all evidence have little desire to be ruled either by the generals in Saigon or by the Viet Cong in the countryside. The point of such examination is to decide where the American national interest lies, and how it may best be served. It is not always possible to pick our allies, nor to ally ourselves only with governments whose conduct we approve. For all the courage of its armies and people in World War II, our wartime Soviet ally had murdered several million of its own citizens, party leaders, and military officers in the Great Purge just three years before, and maintained throughout the war its Arctic and Asian death camps, which claimed many millions of victims from 1925 to 1950. The obvious necessity of the alliance against Nazism warns us that distaste for a government should not and cannot be our sole standard for alliance. But our own self-respect, as well as the national interest, does demand that such alliances be weighed with a careful eye to their necessity and effectiveness.

These are general considerations. What they mean in more concrete terms can be found in the vexing question of the war's damage to the civilian population. Since the beginning of the direct American involvement, we have been warned, often by our own experts, that the indiscriminate use of heavy artillery and air strikes against peasant villages would kill thousands of innocent civilians, and create more Viet Cong than it could destroy. Despite these warnings, unobserved artillery fire is still a prominent feature of the war; air strikes are still too often called in on the basis of insufficient information; and large areas of the country are designated as "free bomb zones," in which any person or hut is assumed to be Viet Cong, and subject to air attack. No one can say how many have joined the Viet Cong as a result of such random destruction. We do know that one out of every eight South Vietnamese is a refugee, principally fleeing from bombing and shelling. We know there have been hundreds of thousands of civilian casualties—a heavy percentage of which are our responsibility. And we also know that despite a claimed 227,000 Viet Cong deaths—115,000 just from January 1966 to August of 1967—estimated Viet Cong forces have risen from a maximum of 115,000 in 1965, to a minimum of over 250,000 in 1967, all by the count of our own command in Vietnam.* Clearly the Viet Cong have substantially increased their recruitment in South Vietnam.

Many critics of the war have decried the damage to civilians, and our lack of sufficient effort to assist the victims. No one can fail to be shocked by the photographs we see every day, of the children burned or drowned or bombed. The war's supporters counter with a demand that the critics also condemn the Viet Cong. Certainly their terrorism is as personally and inhumanly brutal as anything in the war: attacking, torturing, and killing not only village officials and civil guards, but teachers and nurses and ordinary citizens, and the wives and children of those in whom they wished to strike fear. In condemning that moral blindness that reproaches only the United States, while refusing to recognize the terrorism of the Viet Cong, the war's supporters are unimpeachably right. There are no moral excuses to be made for the brutal terror of the Viet Cong.

But the morality of our actions will not be elevated by the sins of others. Moreover, their terrorism has not prevented the Viet Cong from convincing large numbers of South Vietnamese to work and fight and sacrifice for their cause; while there is every evidence that the

* According to The New York Times Report March 18, however, the CIA reported substantially greater forces available to the enemy when the Tet Offensive was launched on January 30, 1968. The figure reported was 515,000 to 600,000 as compared to the 448,000 to 483,000 figures reported by the "national intelligence estimate."

destruction our modern weapons have brought to the countryside has pushed large parts of the population into apathy, into becoming embittered refugees, and others into the camp of the enemy. It is not Americans, but Vietnamese, who seem to weigh our nations on a different scale from those of the Viet Cong. Nor is this surprising. Whatever else they may be, the Viet Cong are Vietnamese; and we are fighting a white man's war in an Asian land. John Fairbank said of the United States in Vietnam that "we are sleeping in the same bed the French slept in even though we dream different dreams." We want no colonies, no territory, no permanent bases. But it seems to be the bed that counts. For our presence in Vietnam has led us to identify with and rely on the same groups, even the same individuals, as the French. President Thieu, Vice President Ky, and most of their senior colleagues fought with the French.* Of all the officers in the Vietnamese army, only two now holding the rank of lieutenant colonel or above fought against the French (although there are lieutenants and captains who commanded battalions for the Viet Minh while the present group of generals were corporals and sergeants under the French).

These are facts we often ignore, perhaps because we think of Communists always as Communists first and Vietnamese a distant second. Over many years, our experience with the Communist parties of the West, including the United States, was that of slavish obedience to the Kremlin, even to the profound detriment of their own interest. Few will forget the ugly and degrading spectacle of Communists defending Hitler and damning the democracies as soon as the Nazi-Soviet Pact was signed in 1939, and then rushing to form anti-Fascist popular fronts when the Soviet Union was invaded. The Vietnamese Communists are Communists, and they have in the past subordinated their national interest to that of

---

* In addition they are overwhelmingly Catholic, in a country predominantly Buddhist; Northerners (though Thieu himself is Southern) in a country where regional loyalties may be as strong as national ones; military men, in a society that does not hold the military in high regard; young, in a culture that venerates age. This reflects not on them—they after all cannot change their origins or age—but on the weakness of our position in identifying so strongly with them.

the Soviet Union: At Geneva in 1954, on the verge of complete victory over the French, Ho Chi Minh was persuaded to postpone half the fruits of that victory, apparently for reasons relating only to the interests of the Soviet Union and China.

But the Viet Cong are also Vietnamese nationalists, heirs of the Viet Minh who defeated France and gained independence. Ho Chi Minh is the leader and symbol of their independence struggle. The proudest achievement in modern Vietnamese history, the defeat of the French, was accomplished by the Viet Minh. It is perhaps because of this, says Neil Sheehan, an experienced and knowledgeable reporter of the war since 1962, that "the Communists, despite their brutality and deceit, remain the only Vietnamese capable of rallying millions of their countrymen to sacrifice and hardship in the name of the nation and the only group not dependent on foreign bayonets for survival." Sheehan concludes that "Vietnamese will die more willingly for a regime which, though Communist, is at least genuinely Vietnamese and offers them some hope of improving their lives, than for one which is committed to the status quo and is the creation of Washington." This view may be overstated. Still it should alert us to the futility of any program that asks the people of South Vietnam to fight just in the name of anti-Communism. The majority of the people undoubtedly do not want a Communist government, but neither do they want their present rulers in Saigon; no political force effectively represents their interests. Certainly there are dedicated Vietnamese nationalists who are firmly opposed to the Communists, some of whom are veterans of the independence struggle. But they are not the South Vietnamese government.

THE ELECTIONS.

In the spring of 1966, Buddhists in the northern part of South Vietnam engaged in demonstrations against the government of Premier Ky. After a period of confusion and indecision, Ky repressed the demonstrations, although he was forced to pledge free elections within a year. During 1966 and 1967, Americans increasingly looked toward these elections as a possible turning point in the "other war": an opportunity to engage the energies and loyalties of the people for the Saigon government, to weld a national force able to compete with the Viet Cong, possibly even to open the way to peace among the South Vietnamese. The Marines' Colonel Carson put it most sharply: "As for the elections, if they provide the leadership . . . then we have a chance. If not, we've had it. The ball game is over."

Why were these elections so important? It was not just for their own sake; South Vietnam had presidential elections in 1955 and 1961, and assembly elections in 1956, 1959, 1963, and 1966. They were not important because they might return the country to civilian rule; Diem was a civilian president ruling under a constitution. Nor were the elections important as an abstract test of democracy or a demonstration of fair procedure. The elections of September 3, 1967, were relevant only by one test: whether they would result in real effort and progress in the "other war," in attracting the willing allegiance and forthcoming support of the South Vietnamese people. They were, quite possibly, the last effective chance for the governing group to demonstrate its willingness to make sacrifices comparable to those of our own young men.

Unhappily, that question was answered long before a ballot was cast. The Constituent Assembly that drafted the present constitution, while more representative of Vietnamese opinion than the military junta, was still far from representing the aspirations of the peasants. Dr. Phan Quang Dan, a stout anti-Communist and a supporter of American involvement, proposed in the Constituent Assembly an article that would have guaranteed peasants the right to own the land they work. The proposal got three votes out of 117. (There was no difficulty, on the other hand, in making certain that the constitution guarantee the property of landlords.)

Still the Assembly might have provided an opening for other elements to enter the government—especially if it had received the strong support of the United States. But its attempts to assert its independence of the military

Directory were ignored or defeated, under the constant surveillance and often the intimidation of the military police. Under the electoral law, not only Communists but also "neutralists" were barred from participation. The supporters of any candidate so labeled would be subject, under South Vietnamese law, to a five-year jail term for advocating "neutralism." Other candidates were excluded because their views were "unacceptable." One of these, General Duong Van Minh, was perhaps the South Vietnamese with the broadest popularity and support in the country. Although his leadership of the 1963 coup against Diem had given him the potential ability to compete effectively against the Viet Cong, he was not allowed to return from exile in Thailand—perhaps because, in the view of many observers, he was a likely winner. Another candidate, Au Truong Thanh, was barred because his advocacy of peace was considered to be evidence of Communist sympathies; he had served as the Government's Finance Minister until 1966, appointed by the very government that now ruled him off the ballot, and had received high praise for his performance from Vietnamese and American officials.

No candidate representing the views and interests of the militant Buddhists was allowed. No run-off between the two leading candidates—in the event no candidate won a majority—was permitted, since this would certainly have resulted in a civilian victory. Not only many Buddhists, but also the non-Communist trade-union movement, were barred from the senatorial campaign; although the same former government official, a close friend of Marshal Ky, who took $1 million in "commissions" on imported American medicines, remained at the head of a major senatorial slate. The military ticket used the full resources of the government to promote its own cause.* Any voters inclined to doubt their power were reminded of it on the eve of the election, when two Saigon newspapers were closed down and a former National Police Chief who supported another candidate was arrested. It was in these and many similar ways, and not in

---

*The Electoral Law, however, provided that "government officials and military men, to run for elections, must file and take a leave of absence for the duration of the campaign."

the crude stuffing of ballot boxes, that the election that had so much promise and that might have captured the imagination and support of the Vietnamese people, was such a disappointment.*

The September election brought 4.9 million voters to the polls, eighty-three percent of the eligible electorate, which may comprise (statistics again are uncertain) as much as three-fifths of South Vietnam's adult population, the rest living in Viet Cong or insecure areas. This was an impressive number, though we cannot know how much it was affected by the fact that registration cards were stamped by policemen at the time of voting, and those without stamped cards are liable to arrest as Viet Cong sympathizers. In Algeria, as former French Prime Minister Pierre Mendès-France pointed out to me, a much higher proportion of the population voted in each of a series of French-sponsored elections throughout the year and a half before the French were forced to leave.

Most significant, however, is the result: for with all the advantages of incumbency, with the support and votes of the armed forces, with their strongest rivals excluded from the contest, running against candidates who themselves did not represent social change or identification with the peasantry—with all this, the military ticket could still win only thirty-four percent of the vote of three-fifths of the nation. The direct result of not providing for a run-off is a government clearly rejected by two-thirds of those who voted—not to mention the insurgents. General Thieu warned before the election that a majority or more would be required for a truly effective government. There is little reason to doubt that judgment.

Thus the 1967 elections resulted, as they had to result, in the victory of the same class, the same ruling order, that has presided over the disastrous decay of South Vietnam in the last thirteen years. The elections have given a paper veneer of respectability to a ruling group that survives by the strength of American arms. They have not affected the allegiance of the South Viet-

---

* Other devices, such as the harassment of candidates, and the issuing of two voting cards to soldiers, seem to have been abandoned or modified under criticism in the United States.

namese people; though they may, if we so desire, allow us to delude ourselves. The elections of 1967 thus appear as another event in the long history of missed opportunities, failures of essential political action, which at each turn of the road have had to be rescued by the application of greater military force.

Unhappy as this result is for the people of South Vietnam, it has serious consequences for the United States. For as we have sent more troops, and extended our bombing, the South Vietnamese have done less; and thus fueled the demand for more bombing, more American troops, to support the men already committed. Already, in the first months of 1967, American casualties were at a higher rate than South Vietnam's draft calls. Their draft age is maintained at a year higher than our own, while their Chief of State has called for 100,000 more American troops.* He refuses to order general mobilization of South Vietnam because, as he said, it would disrupt the nation. President Kennedy said in 1963, "It is their war. They are the ones who have to win it or lose it. We can help them, we can give them equipment, we can send our men out there as advisers, but they have to win it, the people of Vietnam, against the Communists." Similarly, when President Eisenhower sent American troops to Lebanon in 1958, he ordered that they occupy only the capital and the main airport: "If the Lebanese Army were unable to subdue the rebels when we had secured their capital and protected their government," he has written, "we were backing up a government with so little popular support that we probably should not be there."

We cannot remake South Vietnamese society, or ask the South Vietnamese people to give their national allegiance to the United States. Nor can American troops, for all their genuine concern, run the "other war." American troops can, as they have done with commitment and great skill, hold clinics, build schools, dig wells, and otherwise improve their relationships with the people. But if the South Vietnamese government does not itself engage in even more extensive efforts, then American actions may

---

* In March, after strong protests in the United States, the Saigon government proclaimed its intention of drafting 18 year-olds. No time-table has been set on implementation of this plan.

not strengthen, and may even further weaken, the government in the eyes of its people. Only South Vietnamese political efforts, in the villages, in the countryside, in Saigon, can bring cohesion and effectiveness to the fight against the Viet Cong. More fundamentally, basic and lasting social change can only be carried out by Vietnamese. Without that change, our efforts, whether military or political, will be expended in vain. But the change has not come. Nor does it seem likely in the future.

This is a war for the allegiance of the people. If after thirteen years of American involvement, and over two years of major combat participation, the "other war" has failed to attract the allegiance of the people of Vietnam, we must ask ourselves whether all the sacrifice—the scars of which will still be borne twenty and more years from now by today's Vietnamese children and American young men—will have been for the benefit of forgotten generals and a selfish elite.

The Road To A Settlement

There are three possible routes before us: the pursuit of military victory, a negotiated settlement, or withdrawal.

Withdrawal is now impossible. The overwhelming fact of American intervention has created its own reality. All the years of war have profoundly affected our friends and our adversaries alike, in ways we cannot measure and perhaps cannot know. Moreover, tens of thousands of individual Vietnamese have staked their lives and fortunes on our presence and protection: civil guards, teachers, and doctors in the villages; mountain tribesmen in the high country; many who work for the present benefit of their people, who have not acceded to the Viet Cong even though they may not support the Saigon government. Many have once already fled the dictatorship of the North. These people, their old ways and strengths submerged by the American presence, cannot suddenly be abandoned to the forcible conquest of a minority.

Beyond this is the more general question of the American commitment, and the effect of withdrawal on our position around the world. Without doubt, the so-called "domino theory" is a vast oversimplification of international politics. In Asia itself, China is the biggest of all possible dominoes; yet its fall to the Communists in 1950 did not cause Communist takeovers in its neighbors (though it participated in the Korean war and aided the cause of the Viet Minh rebellion already underway). Burma, which refused military and economic assistance from the United States, repressed two Communist insurgencies without interference or disturbance by the Chinese. The Cuban domino did not lead, for all Castro's efforts, to Communist takeovers elsewhere in Latin America. Nor did the collapse of Communism in Indonesia in 1965 seem to weaken the Communist regime in North Vietnam. Moreover, North Vietnam and the Viet Cong draw their strength, not from Communist theory, but from their own dynamic of nationalist revolution, and from the unique weakness of the Saigon government. Vietnam's neighbors do not share this combination of government weakness and revolutionary strength; if they did, surely we could expect that they would long ago have erupted in insurgency, while the United States is so heavily engaged in Vietnam.

If the domino theory is an unsatisfactory metaphor, still it contains a grain of truth. World politics is composed of power and interest; it is also spirit and momentum. A great power does not cease to be that because it suffers a defeat peripheral to its central interests. The Soviet Union is still a great power notwithstanding the collapse of its Cuban adventure in 1962. But in some degree, the aftermath of Cuba was a perceptible lessening of Soviet prestige and ability to influence events in many parts of the world. I saw this to be especially true in Latin America when I visited there two years later. So, I believe, would defeat or precipitous withdrawal in Vietnam damage our position in the world. We would not suddenly collapse; Communist fleets would not appear in the harbors of Honolulu and San Francisco Bay. But there would be serious effects, especially in Southeast Asia itself. There, as Prince Norodom Sihanouk of Cambodia said in 1965, the result of intervention (which he opposed) and retreat would be that "all the other

Asian nations, one after another (beginning with the allies of the United States), will come to know, if not domination, at least a very strong Communist influence."* Prime Minister Lee Kuan Yew of Singapore, an independent leader often at odds with the United States, has stated similar views.

Beyond Asia, in other nations that have ordered their security in relation to American commitments, a sudden unilateral withdrawal would raise doubts about the reliability of the United States. Our investment in Vietnam, not only in lives and resources, but also in the public pledges of presidents and leaders, is immense. It may be, as some say, that the investment is grossly disproportionate to the area's strategic value, or to any ends it may conceivably accomplish. But it has been made. Simply to surrender it, to cancel the pledges and write off the lives, must raise serious questions about what other investments, pledges, and interests might be similarly written off in the face of danger or inconvenience. Of course, other nations will not cease to defend themselves, or surrender themselves to our adversaries, simply because they do not regard us as reliable protectors. But the relationships that they might develop with other countries might not be completely to our liking. We cannot discount the likely effects on the morale of other nations, especially those now narrowly balanced between stable progress and revolutionary upheaval. Forces antagonistic to us within those countries would be strengthened—such as the Indian Communist Party—and these nations' ties to us weakened or strained.†

* It should be added, however, that while Prince Sihanouk has now expelled the pro-Chinese elements from his cabinet, and has taken other action against Chinese influence in his country, he still insists that the security of Cambodia would be strengthened by American withdrawal from Vietnam.

† Two other arguments often advanced seem to me of questionable merit. One is that withdrawal would strengthen Chinese expansion. The most constant thread of Vietnamese history, however, seems to be hatred and fear of China. North Vietnam seems to have maintained its independence of China despite its need of Chinese supplies. At any rate, the war in all probability increases, rather than lessens, Vietnamese dependence on China. Any extension of Chinese power would also probably be resisted, as it was in Laos, by the Soviet Union. Further, despite the hundreds of thousands of battle dead

These are the arguments against withdrawal. But these arguments do not in any way support a policy of continuing the present course of conflict, or continuing it at its present level, or in the same way. Still less do they support a search for nonexistent ways to military victory.

We are now steadily widening the war in order, we are told, to increase the costs to Hanoi. Yet, in our concern with the price our adversary must pay, let us not omit our own costs from the war's account. The mounting devastation of South Vietnam is more and more eroding the fabric of that society, making its ultimate reconstruction more remote and difficult. Yet lasting peace depends upon the strength of the nation we leave behind. The war has also made far more difficult the hopeful pursuit of fresh understanding and diminishing tension between the two great nuclear powers: the United States and the Soviet Union. One concrete consequence, in all probability, is our inability to reach agreement on the antiballistic missile question—leading us to the expenditure of billions of dollars in a new and profoundly dangerous spiral in the arms race. The war has estranged and alienated us from our closest friends in the Western Alliance. Not one has seen fit to aid us in Vietnam; they continue to trade, both with North Vietnam and China; and some European church organizations are extending assistance to North as well as South Vietnam—an action that would have been unthinkable in Korea or World War II. I found in Europe, among men and nations who

China left there, North Korea has strongly asserted its independence of China.

A second related argument is that the seventeenth parallel marks, roughly, one of those truce lines established after the Second World War across which movement is simply not to be allowed: just as we could not allow movement across the thirty-eighth parallel in Korea, or across divided Germany. One difficulty with this argument is that the bipolar world is gone; in any case, to the extent there is a line, countries like Indonesia, Ghana, Yugoslavia, Egypt, and Algeria have either moved across or astride it in recent years. The "line" is no longer fixed, and will become less so with time. The second difficulty with the Korean analogy is that there were almost no South Korean insurgents, but only two nations where once there had been one. Our troops were not asked to occupy South Korea but to repel a physical invasion. Syngman Rhee, moreover, was for all his faults the outstanding Korean nationalist leader; his closest counterpart in Vietnam is Ho Chi Minh.

wish only good for the United States, deep anxiety and fundamental disagreement with our policy; we were, they felt, becoming dangerously irrelevant. Beyond Europe, in the Near East, Latin America, and Africa, the diversion of our attention, resources, and energies has seriously limited our capacity to affect the course of events, and protect far more important national interests. Thus while we spend our thirty billion dollars annually in a country of small strategic importance, India—one of the truly important areas of the world—slides into starvation and possible chaos, in large part for want of development capital. The war is also diverting resources that might have been used to help eliminate American poverty, improve the education of our children, enhance the quality of our national life—perhaps even to save the nation from internal violence and chaos. Less measurable but equally serious, the war has divided Americans from each other, and some from their government, in ways whose effects we may feel for years to come.

Thus there is another domino theory, another kind of momentum to this war. The mounting cost is an increasing deterrent to action elsewhere. Though portrayed as a necessary proof of our will and ability to "keep our commitments," the war in Vietnam is very likely to have the opposite effect. We are not only less likely to assume other commitments, but also less likely to fulfill those we have with great support or enthusiasm. During the days leading up to the Arab-Israeli confrontation of 1967, it was clear that our involvement in Vietnam had seriously weakened our firm and long-standing commitment to Israel. In the Congress, liberals and conservatives alike have firmly stated their conviction that the United States should never again engage in an effort like Vietnam. Some would have us prove in Vietnam that "wars of national liberation cannot succeed." But the longer the conflict goes on, the more likely we are to "prove" that the United States will not oppose them in the future. Certainly the sight of the world's largest and most powerful nation, so frustrated by one of the smallest and weakest of nations, must hearten believers in revolutionary war and the efficacy of Communist tactics of organization.

Growing awareness of these realities has led some to call for a quicker end to the war through application of greater military power: the pursuit of total military victory. But this is a phantom. Military victory would require that we crush both our adversary's strength and his will to continue the battle; that the forces from the North be compelled to withdraw beyond the border; that much of Vietnam be destroyed and its people killed; that we continue to occupy South Vietnam as long as our presence is required to ensure that hostilities, including insurgency, will not be resumed. This will be a very long time indeed; and its coming is beyond our present vision. Most disinterested observers agree that victory—in any sense other than obliteration of both North and South Vietnam—is not near. American officers have, only half in jest, suggested that their sons may grow up to fight the same war in Vietnam.

These somber estimates are grounded on undeniable reality. Despite the brave and dedicated efforts of American forces, the enemy forces continue to grow, both by recruitment in the South and infiltration from the North. Increasing support from the Soviet Union and China has given the Communist forces a range of sophisticated and destructive weapons: not only submachine guns to replace the homemade rifles that the Viet Cong once used, but also long-range rockets and mortars with which to strike at our air bases.* Security in the countryside depends, perhaps more than ever, on the physical presence of American troops. The South Vietnamese army assumes less and less of the burden, requiring the United States to run harder just to prevent further deterioration of the overall effort. Yet already, as the Senate Preparedness Subcommittee has found, our resources of planes, pilots, and trained combat leaders are under serious strain everywhere in the world.

Here is sober medicine indeed. For if there is virtually no limit to the power we possess, still the exercise

---

* These attacks also demonstrate that despite our best efforts, we are still without enough local support in areas near our bases such as Danang to prevent their use against us.

of power must be matched to the ends we seek. And these facts tell us that the pursuit of victory would require an expansion of the war, far beyond even the massive efforts we now are making. It would mean rapidly increasing commitments of American forces—to a million or more, who can really say—the call-up of reserves, and something close to general mobilization. It would mean a growing risk of widening war with China, even with the Soviet Union. It would lead, indeed already has led, thoughtless people to advocate the use of nuclear weapons. And it would involve all these things—commitment, risk, and spreading destruction— in pursuit of a goal that is at best uncertain and at worst unattainable. It was for these reasons that General Douglas MacArthur advised us in 1962 that we should under no circumstances go beyond the sending of advisers to become involved in another land war in Asia.

There is a tendency, born of impatience and frustration, to assume that a freer exercise of our great power, especially the destructive power of our Air Force, could quickly end the war. But the claims of airmen to omnipotent destruction have (fortunately for the human race) not proven sound in the past. Goering promised to obliterate Britain, but succeeded only in hardening British resistance. The Allies in their turn undertook to destroy Germany's warmaking potential from the skies; the result, as the Strategic Bombing Survey later showed, was that German war production steadily increased through the heaviest raids. By 1944, though Berlin had lost two-thirds of its homes and over a million Germans had been killed or wounded in the bombing, production was three times as great as in 1941. North Vietnam, moreover, is not an industrial but a peasant society, not seriously vulnerable to air attack. For over a year, Air Force partisans have protested that the bombing targets assigned—crude bridges, fords, dirt roads, small "structures"—were not worth the losses incurred in planes and pilots, perhaps not even equal to the costs of the bombs dropped. The port of Haiphong, says the Secretary of Defense, is a "convenience rather than a necessity" for imports and could easily be replaced by overland supply routes. Destroying the capital of Hanoi would mean little to an enemy who defeated the French without holding a single major city anywhere in Vietnam, North or South.* Bombing the cities, or the dikes that keep the Red River Delta from flooding. would amount to the deliberate destruction of the North Vietnamese people: an action out of all proportion to the threat they pose to us, and certain to provoke the justified condemnation of the world.

If the bombing cannot destroy North Vietnam's *capacity* to fight, can it destroy its *will* to continue? Can the bombing exact such a price from the leaders and people of North Vietnam that they must come to our terms? Bombing did not have that effect on Great Britain or on Germany. Mussolini could not force Haile Selassie to surrender with bombing, nor did Japanese bombing succeed in forcing Chiang Kai-shek to negotiate. On the other hand, bombing seems to have played a part in inducing Italy to surrender in World War II. The Tokyo fire raids and the use of the atomic bomb certainly were a major factor in the Japanese surrender. Of course, none of these are precise analogies to the Vietnam war: The leaders, nations, and strategic situations involved are all different in ways that cannot be reduced to numbers. It is impossible to say that bombing will or will not, as a general principle, bring a country to terms. Apart from total destruction, it has been well said, "War is all in the mind. If you believe you have not been defeated then you are not defeated." Secretary of Defense McNamara, as late as August 1967, told the Senate that "I have seen no evidence in any of the many intelligence reports that would lead me to believe that a less selective [that is, intensified] bombing campaign would change the resolve of North Vietnam's leaders or deprive them of the support of the North Vietnamese people. . . . There is also nothing in the past reaction of the North Vietnamese leaders that would provide any confidence that they can be

---

* I visited Hanoi when the French held it. It was clear that holding the city meant nothing while the Viet Minh were slowly winning the countryside; Ho Chi Minh controlled North Vietnam and waged a war without Hanoi or Haiphong before, and can probably do it again.

bombed to the negotiating table." We cannot even predict with certainty the response of Western leaders, or of our own government, to uncertain future events. Still less should we risk great national interests in predictions about the minds of men far away from our experience and knowledge.

What we do know, perhaps all that we are capable of knowing, is that escalation of the bombing of North Vietnam, as an answer to this war, has been at every point thus far a terrible and dangerous illusion. Escalation is not our sole prerogative, but a mutual activity. North Vietnam cannot precisely duplicate our escalations, by bombing the sources of our strength in Guam or Pearl Harbor, not to mention Detroit or Washington. But with the assistance of the Soviet Union and other Communist nations, they can match our escalation where they are relatively strong: on the ground in South Vietnam. When we began bombing the North, in February of 1965, there was one battalion of North Vietnamese regulars confirmed as fighting in South Vietnam, and our combat deaths numbered in the hundreds. As we introduced ground combat forces (over 300,000 by the end of 1966), the North Vietnamese also increased their commitment (to over 40,000 men), the Viet Cong stepped up their recruitment—and by the end of 1966, over 6000 Americans had died. In 1967, we have escalated the war both on the ground (200,000 more troops), in the air (destroying North Vietnam's infant industry, bombing within the city limits of Hanoi, Haiphong, and other centers), and in other ways (firing artillery across the Demilitarized Zone directly into Vietnam, naval bombardment of the North Vietnamese coast). This escalation has been matched by the introduction into Vietnam of whole families of sophisticated new weapons that have worked great damage on our forces. Our combat deaths were greater, in the first six months of 1967, than in all the six previous years combined.

This may be only a foretaste of what is to come. Clearly, the Soviet Union feels that it must maintain its support of the North Vietnamese effort so long as the fighting continues. Neither China nor the Soviet Union can accept the defeat or destruction of North Vietnam; just as our government feels it cannot abandon the South Vietnamese. Moreover, the Soviet Union can maintain this support at little cost to itself, meanwhile helping to seriously sap the strength of the United States: perhaps $1 billion next year, with no casualties, for the Soviet Union, compared to over $30 billion, and thousands of casualties, likely for the United States. We can extend our bombing—and as Secretary McNamara has told the Congress, the Soviets can give North Vietnam weapons capable of striking at our aircraft carriers and air bases, such as rocket-firing patrol boats or ground-to-ground missiles. We can introduce more troops into the South—and the North Vietnamese can match them with another segment of their regular army, only one-fifth of which has thus far been committed to combat.

We can invade the North—and thereby assure ourselves of the opportunity to engage another quarter of a million of the enemy in combat; somewhat as if a man afflicted with one migraine were to request another head in which to have a second. We can, as some generals tell us we are doing, engage in a "war of attrition" on the Asian mainland, where our adversary has a strategic reserve of 700 million Chinese. In 1964, a former chief of the Strategic Air Command told us that an ultimatum, coupled with the bombing of selected military depots, would bring Vietnam to its knees "within a few days": another of the promises of easy and imminent victory that have not ceased since the French began them in 1946. It is perhaps too much to expect that these promises will no longer be made. It would be incredible if they would any longer be believed.*

The third alternative is a negotiated settlement—as we have known for more than two years, the only satisfactory solution to the war. This course is our stated government policy. This is the course that I favor, and that I believe is in the best interests of this country. Only negotiations could allow us to end the fighting without

---

* The advice, "bomb them back to the Stone Age," may show that the speaker is already there himself, but it could, if followed, force all of us to join him.

precipitate withdrawal: to avoid the progressive destruction and weakening of South Vietnam, and end the drain on our own energies and resources, without great damage to our position in Asia and the world. An honorable negotiated settlement, moreover, has been the overwhelming preference of most Americans, a course on which the nation could again unite.

Throughout 1966 the chances for such negotiations were present. They reached their height in the winter of 1967. At that point, with a false scent of victory leading us on, the United States cast away what may well have been the last best chance to go to the negotiating table, on terms we clearly would have accepted before. The months of war that have followed have been as destructive, to our own forces and to North Vietnam, as all the years of war before 1967. The damage, and hardening attitudes, may make a negotiated peace impossible for some time to come.

The alternatives to negotiation are so unacceptable that I continue to believe the effort should be made. Ultimately no other solution is possible. Despite the killing and the destruction, we are in no better position now than we were a year ago—and we will not be in any better position a year from now. I think now, as I have always believed, that we should go to negotiations in an effort to reach a peaceful and honorable settlement. Perhaps we cannot; but we should try, and we shall never know until we do try. But we must clearly understand that intervening events in this period, on all sides, have made the prospects far less hopeful. An effort for negotiation now may well be rejected. The pages that follow set out the framework of negotiations, a discussion of the events of the winter of 1967, a program for negotiations that I then believed possible—and a brief assessment of the prospects as I write in September of 1967.

First, however, let us understand what negotiations are. A negotiated settlement must be less than a victory for either side. Both sides must come to any discussion with at least one basic condition, one irreducible demand, one point they will not yield. For the United States it must be that we will not abandon South Vietnam to forcible takeover by a minority. For our adversaries it must be that they will not accept a settlement that leaves in the South a hostile government, dedicated to the final physical destruction of all Communist elements, refusing any economic cooperation with the North, dependent upon the continued presence of American military power. These conditions, these minimum terms, can be breached only at sword's point; only by driving the adversary's forces from the field. For either side to yield its minimum conditions would be in fact to surrender. If we intend to deny these minimum conditions to our adversaries, then we must defeat them completely. If this is what we intend, we should understand it clearly— and understand as well the full costs of this course, costs out of all proportion to any benefits we might attain. For to say, which is true, that we will do whatever is necessary to preserve our vital interests, does not define what those interests are. In the world as in our own lives, wishing does not make it so; every achievement or gain must be paid for. It is not wise policy; it is in the real sense not policy at all, to commit a nation to the achievement of all goals that might be desirable or even important. Wise policy is a setting of priorities—differentiating between that which is merely important and that which is truly essential. And it would be both callous and self-indulgent for those of us who sit comfortably at home to form policy without full knowledge and consciousness of the cost to others, the young men and women and children, whose lives turn on the abstractions of our discussion.

NEGOTIATIONS: GETTING TO THE TABLE

First, we must get to the negotiating table. For more than two years we proclaimed and published our unwavering desire to begin negotiations with our Communist enemy: "Anywhere and anytime," the President said. Since the first mention of negotiations in 1965, North Vietnam and the National Liberation Front (NLF) had established their conditions for such talks. Hanoi's position, known as the Four Points, had been regarded as unacceptable by the United States. Our interpretation was that it required the withdrawal of American forces from South Vietnam, and the recognition of the NLF as the "sole genuine representative" of the Vietnamese people, even prior to discussions.

In January of 1967, however, Premier Pham Van Dong told Harrison Salisbury of *The New York Times* that the Four Points should be considered as an agenda for discussion at negotiations rather than conditions that must be met prior to negotiations. It was an indication that Hanoi had altered its position: From minimum demands, these had become only bargaining points. Then Secretary General U Thant, after confidential investigations, said that cessation of the bombing was all that was required for negotiations to begin. United States spokesmen, through January, made clear that we were awaiting a "signal." Since previous Administration statements had focused on the lack of response by Hanoi to the bombing pause of 1966, this was widely interpreted as a demand for evidence that if the bombing were suspended, negotiations would actually begin. Then, on January 28, in an interview with Australian Communist reporter Wilfred Burchett (often an unofficial conduit for official Hanoi views), the Foreign Minister of North Vietnam, Nguyen Duy Trinh, said, "If the United States really wants talks, it must first halt unconditionally the bombing raids and all other acts of war" (this referred to such acts as coastal shelling then in progress) against North Vietnam. The interview continued, "If the bombings cease completely, good and favorable conditions will be created for the talks." The Foreign Minister concluded, "President Johnson said he was only awaiting a sign. Well, he's had the sign." The interview went on to make it unmistakably clear that Hanoi was dropping its Four Points as a precondition for negotiations to begin. It was a major change in policy; an important retreat from their previously held position.

Then, on a visit to London which coincided with the four-day Tet Truce, Soviet Premier Alexei Kosygin joined the Soviet Union, for the first time in the history of the conflict, in the public search for peace. In formal statements on two separate occasions Kosygin said that the first step toward peace "should be the unconditional cessation of the bombing of and all other aggressive acts against the Democratic Republic of Vietnam [North Vietnam]. As the Foreign Minister of the DRV declared recently, this step is necessary to enable talks between the DRV and the United States to take place. The Soviet government welcomes this statement and regards it as an important and constructive proposal for ending the war." Then, in a press conference, he went further, referring to "only one circumstance which must be considered": "I have in mind the statement made by the Foreign Minister of the Democratic Republic of Vietnam in an interview with an Australian journalist. In this interview he voiced a proposal which, essentially, boils down to the following: The United States of America must unconditionally stop bombings of the Democratic Republic of Vietnam and then it would be possible to open negotiations to explore avenues of a political solution of the Vietnamese problem."

"We fully add our voice to the statement by the Foreign Minister of the Democratic Republic of Vietnam," he continued, "and believe that the United States should take advantage of it. This is a very constructive proposal which makes it possible to get out of the impasse the United States landed in now. I think that public opinion in the United States should exert its efforts in this direction, compel the leaders of the United States to respond to the proposal set out by the Foreign Minister of the Democratic Republic of Vietnam. We fully support this proposal."

A reporter asked: "If all military actions against North Vietnam are stopped, do you think the DRV Government would be ready to start peaceful negotiations with the United States? Do you see any other preliminary conditions for such talks?"

Kosygin answered: "I have already answered this question. I would suggest that the author of this note just read the statement of the DRV Foreign Minister to which I already referred and the statement specifies on what conditions the DRV would agree to meet around the conference table and, I repeat again, we fully share these views." The statement of the DRV Foreign Minister had referred only to halting the bombing.

This declaration came from a man of enormous authority in the Communist world, whose country, then and now, sustains North Vietnam's effort, and supplies them with the mortars and artillery, the antiaircraft guns and ammunition with which they combat our forces. The statement did not demand that we withdraw our forces, slow down our military effort on the ground, or even halt bombing in South Vietnam or of the infiltration routes in Laos. It did not demand an indissoluble and binding guarantee that we would never use our planes again at any future time, no matter what our adversary did to enlarge his effort or change the nature of the war. There was no demand that we accept any terms or conditions, such as the Four Points, in advance of talks. We were simply informed that "to enable talks" we should stop bombing—something we had done before.

We were willing to do this in 1966, when we suspended the bombing of North Vietnam for thirty-seven days, without asking any prior act, signal, or statement in return, hoping that our restraint might bring negotiations.* In 1966, it was our adversaries who publicly laid down conditions for negotiations—acceptance of the Four Points or withdrawal of American troops. In 1967, however, Premier Kosygin and President Podgorny of the Soviet Union and more importantly, the government of North Vietnam itself, said negotiations could begin on terms we clearly would have accepted in 1966. Why then did we not try again in this far more hopeful moment?

The answer, in the winter of 1967, was that our negotiating position had changed. In his February letter to Ho Chi Minh (released to the press by North Vietnam in March, and subsequently confirmed by our govern-

* It was later suggested that the 1966 suspension was not only in hope of negotiations, but also of military steps by our adversaries. In 1966, however, the understanding was quite different. On March 13, 1966, Vice-President Humphrey said that we undertook a bombing suspension because we thought "Hanoi during those 37 days might . . . indicate that maybe they would like to negotiate—which obviously would have kept the bombing pause going." Secretary of State Rusk made the same point in February 1966.

ment), President Johnson wrote that "I am prepared
to order a cessation of the bombing against your country
and the stopping of further augmentation of U.S. forces
in South Vietnam as soon as I am assured that infiltration into South Vietnam by land and by sea has
stopped."

In 1966, we had halted the bombing without such a
demand. But without further support of any kind,
Hanoi's 50,000 regular troops in the South would be
hard-pressed and at a significant military disadvantage
before the 400,000 Americans already there, especially
since our great superiority of firepower could be indefinitely maintained by ship and plane. Thus our 1967
offer was in effect a demand for the North Vietnamese
to withdraw their forces, to abandon the Viet Cong in
the South. This was quite clearly understood in the
highest circles of our government at the time the letter
was dispatched. In the winter of 1967, important United
States officials felt we were on the brink of a military
victory, that our position was considerably stronger and
our adversaries considerably weaker than had been true
a year before. Therefore, they thought, we could afford
to stiffen our position. And we did.

Objective assessment of the prospects for a negotiated
settlement rests on clear analysis of the minimum goals
of both sides, our adversary's as well as our own. To say
that the Communists have a certain requirement—for
example that they cannot negotiate while bombing continues—is not to take up their cause or become their
partisan; it is only to state a fact. To say, therefore, that
North Vietnam "cannot" negotiate while bombs are falling on Hanoi is not an approbation of their refusal to
come to the conference table, but merely a prediction
that as long as the bombs fall the war will go on. And to
say that the bombing will not cease until we are "assured
that infiltration into South Vietnam by land and sea has
stopped" is only to ensure that bombing and infiltration
will continue, that there will be no negotiations, and the
war will go on. That, in fact, was the result of our position in the winter of 1967. Our public position at the
time was that we wanted "just almost any step" in return
for a bombing halt. If such a small step was at issue,

why should it be allowed to determine such a weighty matter? In fact, as was later revealed, our demands were much more serious than the public phrase indicated. The new demands of the February 2 letter bore little relation to the actual military situation. Therefore our offer could not be successful.

President Johnson's letter on the bombing was delivered to the North Vietnamese representative in Moscow in the midst of Premier Kosygin's discussions on the same subject with Prime Minister Wilson in London. It was delivered in Moscow on February 8, but did not reach Hanoi until February 10. On February 13, before any response had been received from the North Vietnamese, bombing of North Vietnam was resumed.* When Ho Chi Minh's answer came on February 15, two days later, it was harsh and bitterly critical in tone. Nevertheless, despite the bombing resumption, it reaffirmed the possibility of negotiation, if the bombing of the North would cease.† Negotiations, of course,

* The stated reason for our resumption was that North Vietnam had used the Tet Truce to resupply its forces in South Vietnam. Leaving aside the fact that these efforts, according to the Department of Defense, were restricted to the southern part of North Vietnam, resupply in any case was not a violation of the truce. We of course continued and intensified our resupply efforts during the same period, as we had every right to do. Not only did we continue to unload ships and planes, but also undertook major road shipments within South Vietnam. If not for the truce, these would have been subject to harassment and ambush by Viet Cong forces.

† Much debate in the United States at this time was preoccupied with an inordinately complex argument over whether any bombing cessation would have to be "unconditional" or "permanent."

In the terms of this debate, an "unconditional" cessation was one that did not explicitly demand some direct concession in return. A "permanent" cessation was interpreted as being one that promised that under no conditions would the bombing be resumed. Clearly, a "permanent" cessation of bombing would be unacceptable to any sovereign state; certainly we would not promise never to bomb North Vietnam, whatever it might do in future to change the course of the war. But an "unconditional" cessation—simply stopping and stating the fact, "we are not now engaged in the bombing of North Vietnam"—carried no such difficulty.

At the time, opponents of a bombing cessation said that simply stopping the bombing would not work, since what the North Vietnamese were really demanding was a "permanent" halt (sometimes described as a "definitive" halt). This apparently was the understanding of President Johnson as set out in his letter to Ho Chi Minh. Ho's reply seems clearly to have set this question at rest. His would be only a first step toward an acceptable peace, as I will discuss later. But they were an essential first step.

Throughout the spring and summer, the message was repeated, through friends and adversaries alike: only cease the bombing, and there will be negotiations. As late as May, Premier Pham Van Dong said the offer "still had full value," and the Foreign Minister referred to Hanoi's "expressed willingness to work out a political solution, including negotiations"; the sole requisite was that "the United States should indicate its good faith with actions."

Throughout this same period, however, the bombing continued. It was argued that the United States could not be absolutely certain that Hanoi and Moscow would negotiate if the bombing were stopped; some of the Hanoi statements, it was further argued, conflicted with one another. In my judgment, examination of the public statements of Hanoi and Moscow through those months

---

letter set out two separate sets of conditions. The first, described as "the basis of a correct political solution to the Vietnam problem"— that is, the settlement which would result from negotiations—included a demand that "the United States government must stop definitively and unconditionally its bombing raids and all other acts of war" against North Vietnam: in other words, if the war is settled, the U.S. would formally undertake not to bomb North Vietnam, a self-evident fact. In a separate, distinct paragraph dealing with "direct talks between the Democratic Republic of Vietnam and the United States"—that is, the negotiations themselves—the letter stated, "If the United States Government really wants these talks, it must first of all stop unconditionally its bombing raids and other acts of war" against North Vietnam—in other words, to arrive at negotiations, simply cease the bombing, without any promises not to resume at some future time. The first paragraph mentions the Four Points; the second does not. The first uses the word "definitively" to describe the bombing halt; the second does not. Thus the letter clearly recognizes the distinction between what North Vietnam might expect in advance of negotiations, and what they must come and bargain for, making concessions acceptable to us in return.

Much more to the point, words like "unconditional" and "permanent," in dialogue between nations, are obstacles only if one side or another is determined to make them so. Action—such as stopping the bombing—brushes all the metaphysical cobwebs away, creating a new reality and a new context for all old positions. There were enough statements made, by Kosygin in London and by North Vietnamese officials, where the word "permanent" was quite clearly not used. All we had to do was publicly accept their offer for negotiations on their publicly stated lines.

clearly indicates that a major shift in the North Vietnamese bargaining position had occurred since 1966, showing a firm intention to come to the negotiating table once the bombing of North Vietnam was suspended. In any case, the varying interpretations of the Communist statements were not serious questions. They meant everything if there was no will to compromise, and nothing if compromise was desired.

In the most serious and urgent crisis of the Cold War, we moved toward peace by accepting, as we wished to interpret it, that position of our adversaries which contained the greatest hope of swift settlement. This was, of course, the Cuban missile crisis of 1962. At the height of the crisis, President Kennedy received two conflicting messages from Premier Khrushchev. The first was received on Friday, October 26, offering under certain conditions to remove the missiles from Cuba. The next day, however, a second message demanded unacceptable concessions in return. President Kennedy simply ignored the second statement and announced his agreement to the first offer, as he wished to interpret it. The crisis thus was resolved without open conflict. Such a technique might have yielded fruitful results in the winter of 1967, when ambiguities in the statements of our adversaries were far less pronounced. Certainly it was worth trying.

During the February pause, I had made no comment on these developments. A trip to Europe, and information received on my return, indicated that negotiations might be possible, and I felt a public statement might hinder or prevent any progress. But when it became clear that these activities had been unproductive, I decided to speak; for the failure to reach the negotiating table was followed by new, "more far-reaching" escalation. The certainty of rising cost and danger, and the apparent determination to concentrate on military solutions, to have American forces assume the burden of the war, and to gloss over the importance of internal reform, led me to call for a cessation of bombing in a speech to the Senate. I urged "that we test the sincerity of the statements by Premier Kosygin and others asserting that if the bombardment of the North is halted, negotiations would begin—by halting the bombardment and saying we are ready to negotiate within the week;* making it clear that discussions cannot continue for a prolonged period without an agreement that neither side will substantially increase the size of the war in South Vietnam—by infiltration or reinforcement. An international group should be asked to inspect the borders and ports of the country to report any further escalation. And under the direction of the United Nations, and with an international presence gradually replacing American forces, we should move toward a final settlement that allows all the major political elements in South Vietnam to participate in the choice of leadership and shape their future direction as a people."

It is still my belief that that plan could have led to negotiations, and possibly to a settlement—and at a relatively small risk to us. Suspension of the bombing might have been more difficult if continued bombing of North Vietnam had been an indispensable, or even promising, way to secure our objectives in South Vietnam. For our policy was not to destroy North Vietnam, or overturn its government. But the bombing could have been stopped as a step toward peace without impairing the objectives for which it was begun in 1965. We had begun the bombing, as President Johnson told us at Johns Hopkins, for three purposes. The first was "to increase the confidence of the brave people of South Vietnam"; the second, "to convince the leaders of North Vietnam . . . [that] we will not be defeated. We will not grow tired. We will not withdraw." But these purposes had already been fulfilled by the huge resources and American lives that had been committed to South Vietnam since the bombing began. Our adversary, in the winter of 1967, had seen his hopes for victory destroyed, not by the bombing, but by the skill and bravery of our forces on the ground.

The third purpose, the President had said, was "to

* This figure of speech, intended only to demonstrate our own willingness to negotiate, was interpreted by some as a time limit on the bombing halt I proposed. Elsewhere in the speech I made clear that there could be no such limit, and that the distrust of the years of war might have to be alleviated by a halt of some duration, to be determined by the passage of time and events.

slow down aggression," to reduce the flow of men and supplies from North Vietnam to the Communist forces in the South. In 1965, General Matthew Ridgway, the commander of our last ground war in Asia, predicted that air attacks could not stop the infiltration of men and supplies through the scattered jungles, trails, and hills of Southeast Asia. It had not worked, he pointed out, even in the more open countryside of Korea. In hearings in early 1967, the Secretary of Defense had testified to the Congress that although the bombing of North Vietnam has other values which he supports, "I don't believe the bombing up to the present has significantly reduced, nor any bombing that I would contemplate in the future would significantly reduce, the actual flow of men and materials to the South." He was supported in this view by many greatly respected military observers, including General James M. Gavin, one of our most brilliant and seasoned combat commanders. Other military men have since stated their conviction that the bombing is an essential handicap to North Vietnamese infiltration, putting forward evidence that many infiltrators die of disease or bombing on the long trail through Laos and Cambodia to the South. In August of 1967, despite a considerable escalation of the air war since February, the Secretary of Defense, although still supporting the bombing, was to give to the Congress an estimate that "ten to twenty percent of the personnel dispatched to the South by the rulers of North Vietnam never reach the battle area—about two percent are casualties caused by air attacks." At any rate, bombing of the infiltration trails in Laos would not have been affected by a halt in the bombing of North Vietnam.

There is no question that the bombing makes infiltration much more difficult. But all of North Vietnam, so far as the war in the South is concerned, has been for some time a long supply trail; food, ammunition, and weapons are not manufactured in North Vietnam, but in China and the Soviet Union. It is these supply trails that, as in Korea, have not been severed from the air at any time during the war. Again according to the Secretary, the Viet Cong and North Vietnamese forces in the South require "significantly under 100 tons a day"

of military matériel (other than food) from the North—
"a quantity that could be transported by only a few
trucks." To move this small volume, the North Vietnamese have "a highly diversified transportation system" using "barges and waterways, trucks and foot
power, and even bicycles capable of carrying 500-pound
loads." Just 400 such bicycles could carry the 100 tons
of supplies needed. And the experience of the war thus
far is that the North Vietnamese and their allies have
made whatever effort is necessary to match our efforts
in the South.

When I offered my proposals on March 2, 1967, I
summed up my case for halting the bombing:

"It should be clear by now that the bombing of the
North cannot bring an end to the war in the South;
rather that it may well be prolonging the war. . . . Our
troops are being killed by the bullets and mines of forces
in the South. If by ending the bombing of the North
we bring peace in South Vietnam nearer, then we will
save the lives of thousands of our young men and of
thousands of Vietnamese. . . .

"It is not weakness for this great nation to take a
generous step toward ending the war. It is not bravery
to refuse an act which may save thousands of lives with
little risk to ourselves. Can anyone believe this nation,
with all its fantastic power and resources, will be en-
dangered by a wise and magnanimous action toward a
difficult but small adversary? Not escalation, but an
effort to achieve negotiation, now opens the most hopeful prospect to peace."

AFTER THE BOMBING

Stopping the bombing, then or at any possible future
time, would be not a program, but a device: only one
part of a coordinated plan for negotiations and settlement. As soon as the bombing was halted, international
teams under the United Nations, or perhaps a strengthened International Control Commission or even some
other international group established especially for this
purpose, should be asked to provide detached and ob-

jective information to the world about any large buildup of troops or supplies. They would patrol the borders, ports, and roads of Vietnam with equipment such as reconnaissance planes, and other intelligence facilities, placed at their disposal. Cooperation from the North Vietnamese would be helpful, but not essential; in any case, the offer to permit international inspection would help to indicate our sincerity.

Our next step should be to seek an understanding with our adversaries that neither side will substantially increase the rate of infiltration and reinforcements during negotiations. It is unrealistic to expect the North to cease its present support for its own troops and the Viet Cong, just as it would be for us to stop supplying our forces in the South; but it would be equally unrealistic to expect that peace can be discussed effectively or with confidence while casualties mount and the war gets bigger. Hostilities might well continue during negotiations, but it would be necessary for both sides to refrain from escalating the war on the ground and trying to change the military balance. With or without specific agreement from the North Vietnamese, the international inspection team would report any effort, by either side, to increase its strength during the peace talks. They would also monitor any agreement reached during the course of negotiations on suspension of military activity, hopefully including a cease-fire. Thus the detached and objective testimony of the international community would be witness to our sincerity, and to any attempt by North Vietnam to step up substantially its help to the National Liberation Front under cover of negotiations. And if the failure of negotiations, coupled with the actions of our adversary, made it necessary for us to reexamine our position, we would act with far clearer international understanding of our motives and necessities.*

---

* There is an important precedent for just such an action. During the Cuban missile crisis, the United States asked Secretary-General U Thant if the United Nations would be willing to inspect and verify the withdrawal of Soviet missiles from Cuba. He agreed that this would be an appropriate role for the United Nations. At the same time our military commanders determined that it would be both technically feasible, and consistent with our security, to turn over

Negotiations: The Settlement

Once at the conference table, our problem would in a sense be more difficult. Negotiations are not the end of the road, but only a bridge to the future of South Vietnam. That future must include the right of the people of South Vietnam to self-determination. How to accomplish this has always been at the heart of the problem of peaceful settlement. The negotiators must develop a program to dismantle the war: to establish procedures for a cease-fire, for the laying down of arms, and for the gradual withdrawal of foreign forces from the country —and all this accompanied by the political steps necessary to protect the safety of all sides while the war is being dismantled.

More difficult and intricate is the resolution of South Vietnam's tangled politics. This question is central, not only to a settlement, but to the preliminary question of arriving at serious negotiations. Stopping the bombing may bring Hanoi to negotiations. But the NLF seeks more than a halt to bombing of the North; it seeks a role in the South. Whether the NLF would come to negotiations, and the position they would take there, will almost certainly depend in large part on the terms of political settlement which are understood to be possible.

What should those terms be? We have not defeated the Viet Cong; they have not defeated us, nor can they. A military victory is not in sight for anyone. Any settlement must therefore be a compromise that, however imperfect, would protect the self-determination of the Vietnamese people. All the people of South Vietnam, Communist and non-Communist, Buddhist and Christian, should be able to choose their leaders and seek office through peaceful political processes, free from external coercion and internal violence. All should have the opportunity to seek peacefully a share of power and

---

many of our intelligence facilities—including high-flying aircraft— to a United Nations inspection team. Although that effort was blocked by Castro's resistance, in the case of Vietnam it should be possible, especially with recent advances in surveillance technology, to watch and report on most major routes of infiltration and supply even without North Vietnamese cooperation. This surveillance could be supplemented or replaced with United States intelligence activity.

responsibility, preferably through free elections. They should determine their future and the nature of their system and resolve the question of Vietnamese reunification.

The first step would be for the South Vietnamese government, as well as other political elements not represented in it, to begin their own discussions with the National Liberation Front. For many years, the people of South Vietnam have been divided in fierce and hostile combat. If they are to settle their own future, they must at least begin to talk to each other, try to eliminate unnecessary conflicts, and search out areas of possible agreement. Undoubtedly a cease-fire would allow this process to begin at the village and hamlet level, aiming toward village elections in which all sides, including the National Liberation Front, could freely participate.

I have always felt that the United States, as a major combatant, must also be ready to talk directly to all parties—North and South, military and civilian, Communist and non-Communist alike. Most directly we must negotiate not only with the North Vietnamese government in Hanoi but with the NLF in the South. The exact status of the NLF, whether puppet or partly independent, is a matter of some dispute among experts. Douglas Pike thinks them a complete creature of the North; while it was the conviction of Bernard Fall that the native fighters in the South, whatever their material dependence on Hanoi, have their own goals and their own plans for the future. Many of those who have talked with the NLF support this view, even to the point of asserting that the Viet Cong do not seek the reunification of Vietnam in the foreseeable future. Whatever the real relationship, which may well be seen differently by North Vietnam and the NLF themselves, the NLF has been, and is, our adversary in the field throughout most of South Vietnam; they are an indispensable part of any settlement; and this we will have to recognize through direct negotiations. If they are independent, we should talk to them. If they are not, it makes no difference that they are at the conference table with North Vietnam. The only objection to their participation is that it would confer status upon them. They have already achieved more status on the battlefield than we could give them at the conference table.

It was and is essential that non-Communist Vietnamese take a major role in discussions leading to a negotiated settlement, and exert effective force and influence in competition with the NLF for future leadership. The effectiveness of their participation in negotiations will largely depend on the extent to which they have the confidence of their own people and represent their aspirations. Therefore the failure of the 1967 elections is undoubtedly a handicap to fruitful peace talks. Had there been a free political process in South Vietnam during the spring and summer of 1967, it undoubtedly would have broadened the final government to include other elements of South Vietnamese society, thus making it clear to Hanoi and the NLF that they were faced with a formidable negotiating adversary, which represented the choice and objectives of the non-Communist majority in South Vietnam. As much as possible, however, that opportunity must be reopened: most particularly by broadening the base of the present Saigon government, and curbing the arbitrary use of police powers and censorship. The most distinctive legacy of the Diem period may have been the suppression of the new national leadership that might have arisen, but did not, over his decade of rule. If the present ruling group is all that is allowed to compete with the Communists, the Viet Cong would certainly dominate the peace.

Finally, a lasting settlement of the war would be extremely difficult unless all parties are secure in the knowledge that free elections open to all would ultimately be held, and that those who won them would take office. Confidence will depend on the structure of government between the end of hostilities and elections—perhap a prolonged period, certainly one in which the rights of all major political elements must be protected by any negotiated agreement. That, however, would not be enough; suspicion and fear are now too deeply ingrained. The Communists would fear a takeover by the military, just as we might fear a Communist coup. Thus, during the interim period between the end of hostilities and elections, it will be necessary to establish a ruling structure in which both sides have confidence. There are many possible ways of achieving this. It may be desirable to formulate a series of international guarantees, agreed upon by the major powers as well as by the combatants, perhaps by establishing an international force to supervise the political process and ensure against efforts to mount a coup. This might be accomplished through an expanded and strengthened International Control Commission, by the United Nations, or by agreement of the interested nations. To the extent the South Vietnamese share in this interim administration it will be necessary, as I have said before, for all important elements in the country to have a share of power and responsibility. The details of an exact formula must await actual negotiations. The important thing is that it provide enforceable and unbreakable guarantees against fraudulent elections and any attempt, by either side, to take power without or despite the elections.

The territory of South Vietnam is now divided. Each side controls certain areas, though each has partisans living in areas controlled by the other. Some are contested between the two. Over the long run, real peace in South Vietnam can come only when all elements and interests are able to move freely, and the government's writ extends throughout the country; and an effective government presence in all areas of the country would also be necessary to any free election.

Therefore, it is critical that those who are administering the interim period before elections—probably a mixture of international representatives and South Vietnamese—have the full confidence of all parties as well as the authority and power to guarantee an uncoerced choice by the people of the country. At such time as free elections are possible, the share of all elements would be determined by the people in South Vietnam. Until that time it must be determined by agreement.

In any case, it is clear that unless we accept the principle of Viet Cong participation in any interim government structure, albeit under international supervision or as part of an international framework, there is little hope for success in any negotiations. When I first made this proposal, in February of 1966, it was at first attacked by some officials of the Administration. The President's Press Secretary, however, later stated that the United States did not foreclose such participation. It did not, he said, guarantee the principle of NLF participation in an interim government, but felt that the issue should be left to the negotiators. This, in my view, was a step forward, though an insufficient recognition of the difficulties—especially in light of statements by Vice-President Ky that he would not accept an NLF role in the government even as a result of free and fair elections.

I did not offer this program as a fixed and frozen formula, but as a set of suggestions to be refined and revised by the critical examination of others; molded and reworked by shifting events, the responses of other nations, and the passions of people whose lives and homes are at stake. I did believe, however, that they pointed in a necessary direction.

It must be said that this plan involves risks. An adversary who lives may perhaps fight another day. A government that is not continuously sheltered by American military power may be again attacked or subverted or overthrown. But these are "risks" that we do take every day, in a hundred countries in every corner of every continent. There are dozens of countries that might be the target of foreign subversion. But clearly, we would rather live with such risks than attempt to occupy them. We take these risks because we cannot occupy the world and because we do not wish to become a garrison state; and also because we believe men and nations will not willingly choose to submit to other men from other lands.

I have described the action I believe our government should have taken in the winter of 1967, because there is much to be learned from the events of that time. Most of all, they teach us that for either side to put off negotiations, in the hope of military victory which will avoid the later need for compromise, is a tragic mistake. The passage of time will cause costs and casualties to mount on both sides, while hope of a negotiated settlement is postponed to an uncertain future. The actions I have outlined, the principles on which negotiations and a settlement must be based, I believe are still valid today. But

what is far less certain now is whether halting the bombing by itself will bring us to the negotiating table. Certainly a mere "pause" of a few days or even weeks is
highly unlikely to bring us to negotiations. In any case,
the winter of 1967 was a far better opportunity than is
apparent, just six months later, for negotiated settlement
of the war.

I continue to believe that the effort for negotiations,
including a halt in the bombing of North Vietnam,
should be made. If the passage of substantial time and
events proves that our adversaries do not sincerely seek
a negotiated solution, if discussions are used only as a
pretext to enlarge the conflict in the South, then we can
re-examine our entire military strategy in light of the
changing nature of the war. We should be generous in
our search for peace; but also mindful of the precedent
of Panmunjom. We must also realize, however, that the
success or failure of any effort for negotiations will depend, more than ever, on our attitude and over-all position at the time—both our public position, and that
which we put forward in secret messages and conversations.

Further we must realize that the hope of negotiations
depends also on the position of our adversaries, Another
year of combat and mounting destruction has almost
certainly further hardened opinion in North Vietnam,
much as in the United States it has led to successful calls
for greater military action. When the bombing was begun, the initial limitation on targets such as North Vietnamese industry, or the port of Haiphong and the city of
Hanoi, were justified on the sound basis that to destroy
too much would detract from our bargaining power:
Without "hostages" in the form of a threat of greater
damage in future, there would be little incentive for
the North Vietnamese to come to terms. Now almost
every target worth a bomb or a rocket has been struck.
None can say whether an offer not to bomb what remains
will be regarded by the North as worthwhile. Much of
the population of Hanoi and Haiphong has already been
evacuated.

Moreover, there are signs that our adversaries feel the
war in the South is going favorably to their cause. They

are receiving increased aid from the Soviet Union, in fact to such a degree that North Vietnam's resources are increasing rather than decreasing. Communist China, seemingly so paralyzed by internal chaos a year ago, has nevertheless maintained tens of thousands of support personnel in North Vietnam. There are strong indications that they have been joined by technicians and "volunteers" from other Communist nations; and U Thant tells us there will be more. Chinese airports are now being used for the North Vietnamese fighter planes, and North Koreans are flying them. Finally our adversaries may feel that an offer of negotiation, so close to our own elections, would be intended primarily for political effect in the United States—or that if the offer is serious, the terms will become more favorable as November 1968 gets closer. As I write, Soviet Foreign Minister Gromyko, in his opening address to the September 1967 United Nations General Assembly, seems to represent a new, unyielding Soviet posture; no longer promising negotiations in return for a bombing halt, but demanding full American withdrawal as the only way to peace, while pledging still more assistance to the North Vietnamese.*

We face an obdurate adversary, fired with hatred for the foreigner; backed, however reluctantly, by the great resources of the Soviet Union, with the masses of China looming behind. Our own vast resources, and even the great bravery of our soldiers, are able only to avert military defeat. Yet they do not preserve us as we were, for involvement and danger mount with every new day. Elsewhere the world goes on increasingly apart from us, and events of great moment pass us by. At home we are beset with dangers we hardly understand, as political leaders speak of our streets in a vocabulary learned from this faraway war.

* As witness to a further hardening of the Soviet position, Premier Kosygin stated in an interview published in Life in January, 1968, that "The U.S. wants to dictate its terms to Vietnam, but Vietnam is not a defeated country, and it will never be defeated. The U.S. cannot defeat Vietnam. And we, for our part, will do all we can so that the U.S. does not defeat Vietnam. American aggression will be met with growing rebuff. There are adequate forces in the world which will continue opposing American aggression."

But we are not trapped and hopeless. We are not paralyzed. We need not and cannot allow the decisions of others or the working of an inscrutable fate to pull us blindly ahead. Nothing in our position is more dangerous than the often-heard statement that the future is all in the hands of our adversaries. Such fatalism is the worst surrender of all.

The truth is that there is much we can do: not so much in four-point or five-point programs, but beginning with a change in attitude. We must recognize that the struggle in the South is just that—a struggle in the South. Such a reassessment would reach, at the outset, to the question of the Saigon government: ensuring its broadening to include now unrepresented elements of the South Vietnamese people, such as Buddhist organizations, labor unions, intellectuals, and civilian political leaders. With such an attitude, we would work to end harassment by the military and secret police, and restore the village and hamlet democracy that has been suppressed. This process would begin by ending the system of Saigon appointment of district and province chiefs which is central to the network of corruption and misgovernment in the countryside: ensuring that these officials are locally elected and responsible to the people, rather than to the senior military commander in the area.*

Recognition of the war's real character would also ensure attention to a *serious* program of social reform. I have outlined one possible program for land. Undoubtedly there are others, as well as programs to improve village life, cut down on corruption, ease the condition of millions of refugees, and make life in the cities more than a daily struggle against inflation and degradation. This is not just a matter of spending a few more billion dollars. It is primarily a matter of justice and decency within Vietnamese society.

It may be asked whether progress toward these objectives will not encounter strong resentment from the military and social ruling groups. Of course it will, as it

* Provision is made in the Constitution for a transition to elected district and province chiefs. The present government, however, has disregarded provisions of its own laws before. This statute must be enforced.

has in the past. But if these reforms are not initiated, there is neither prospect of success for our efforts, nor wisdom or purpose for our presence. The worst danger of making this our war is that our stake in it becomes greater than that of the Saigon government. When the regime refuses reforms, we are told that we cannot reduce our assistance because to do so would injure the war effort. But it is their war, and they must understand that refusing the necessary reforms will have direct and severe consequences. Continued support of a government that, after this long history and our patient effort, still refuses reform, is not pragmatic or tough-minded. It is ideological self-deception, and a surrender of American interests to a government that without our support would not survive a month. During the Diem period in 1961–63, we should have done far more than we did to move that government toward reform. Certainly from that experience, and the experience of the entire last decade, we should have learned our lesson.

Moreover, these reforms will be necessary whether or not negotiations take place. In fact, only real progress in the South, beginning at last to attract the support of the people—and not greater destruction in the North—offers a real prospect of convincing our adversaries that an early settlement is prudent. This would be especially true if all Vietnamese elements could be induced to participate in local elections; at present, of course, even "neutralists" are barred from such participation. Such social and political programs, if begun now and continued during negotiations, might well influence favorably the quality of any ultimate settlement.

Recognition of the character of the war would also affect our military effort, shifting its emphasis away from attacks on the North and combat by American forces, toward greater reliance on South Vietnamese action in the South. This means less concentration on American sweeps and search and destroy missions, and more on physical protection of the densely populated areas near the coast and the Mekong Delta. If sweeps are considered to have military value, let them be carried out by the South Vietnamese Army. Further, a greater burden of the military effort at the Demilitarized Zone should be assumed by the Vietnamese, with American Marines being gradually relieved. South Vietnam should have the total mobilization that they have so far refused to put into effect, and should begin to draft the tens of thousands of eligibles who up to the present time have been able to avoid service in the army. Thus we could serve our stated objectives, while conserving and protecting American lives, limiting further destruction of the South Vietnamese people by Americans, and assuring real security in the important areas of the country now under control. It is our cost, in money and lives, on which the enemy relies for his hope that we will grow tired. Lowering the war's cost to ourselves, while making clear our intention of remaining, is one sure way of convincing our adversaries that we can and will remain until a satisfactory resolution is assured. We should demonstrate clearly that this is a South Vietnamese struggle: that we are there to help but not to take over the country or the war from them.

Finally, agony and interest, the limited nature of our goals and the formidable consequences of rising war, combine to compel us to seek whatever new initiatives can resolve this conflict—honorably, justly, consistent with our aims, and in peace. Our adversaries, perhaps, will prove unreasoning and obstinate; and peace cannot come without them. Moreover, negotiations in and of themselves are not the answer but only the means to an answer. Failure to understand what we wish to accomplish, what is negotiable and what is not, can lead to a damaging and dangerous termination of any discussions that might ensue from an end of the bombing. But we cannot allow ourselves to be swayed by anxiety or anger, by false fears of humiliation or false hopes of victory. We seek, calmly and with confidence, what will advance our own interests, the peace and security of the world, and the benefit of South Vietnam. Above all we need the will for a peaceful settlement; and once we go to negotiations, we need the wisdom and persistence that will be required to find a satisfactory solution.

We owe no less to ourselves, to our people, and to those whose land we both protect and ravage. In that land, the stakes are very high: They are the home of the child in a jungle village, the hunger of a man driven from his farm, the life of a young American even now preparing for the day's battle. There is the national interest, and there is also human anguish. To protect the one and prevent the other, there is no effort too great for us to make.

The events of the last few weeks have demonstrated anew the truth of Lord Halifax's dictum that although hope "is very good company by the way . . . (it) is generally a wrong guide."

Our enemy, savagely striking at will across all of South Vietnam, has finally shattered the mask of official illusion with which we have concealed our true circumstances, even from ourselves. But a short time ago we were serene in our reports and predictions of progress. In April, our commanding general told us that "the South Vietnamese are fighting now better than ever before . . . their record in combat . . . reveals an exceptional performance." In August, another general told us that "the really big battles of the Vietnam war are over . . . the enemy has been so badly pummeled he'll never give us trouble again." In December, we were told that we were winning "battle after battle," that "the secure proportion of the population has grown from about 45 percent to 65 percent and in the contested areas the tide continues to run with us."

Those dreams are gone. The Vietcong will probably withdraw from the cities, as they were forced to withdraw from the American Embassy. Thousands of them will be dead. But they will, nevertheless, have demonstrated that no part or person of South Vietnam, is secure from their attacks: neither district capitals nor American bases, neither the peasant in his rice paddy nor the commanding general of our own great forces.

No one can predict the exact shape or outcome of the battles now in progress, in Saigon or at Khesahn. Let us pray that we will succeed at the lowest possible cost to our young men. But whatever their outcome, the events of the last two weeks have taught us something. For the sake of those young Americans who are fighting today, if for no other reason, the time has come to take a new look at the war in Vietnam; not by cursing the past but by using it to illuminate the future. And the first and necessary step is to face the facts. It is to seek out the austere and painful reality of Vietnam, freed from wishful thinking, false hopes and sentimental dreams. It is to rid ourselves of the "good company" of those illusions which have lured us into the deepening swamp of Vietnam. "If you would guide by the light of reason," said Holmes, "you must let your mind be bold." We will find no guide to the future in Vietnam unless we are bold enough to confront the grim anguish, the reality, of that battlefield which was once a nation called South Vietnam, stripped of deceptive illusions. It is time for the truth.

We must, first of all, rid ourselves of the illusion that the events of the past two weeks represent some sort of victory. That is not so.

It is said the Vietcong will not be able to hold the cities. This is probably true. But they have demonstrated despite all our reports of progress, of government strength and enemy weakness, that half a million American soldiers with 700,000 Vietnamese allies, with total command of the air, total command of the sea, backed by huge resources and the most modern weapons, are unable to secure even a single city from the attacks of an enemy whose total strength is about 250,000. It is as if James Madison were able to claim a great victory in 1812 because the British only burned Washington instead of annexing it to the British Empire.

We are told that the enemy suffered terrible losses; and there is no doubt he did. They cannot, however, be as devastating as the figures appear. The Secretary of Defense has told us that "during all of 1967 the Communists lost about 165,000 effectives," yet enemy main force strength "has been maintained at a relatively constant level of about 110,000–115,000 during the past year." Thus it would seem that no matter how many Vietcong and North Vietnamese we claim to kill, through some miraculous effort of will, enemy strength remains the same. Now our intelligence chief tells us that of 60,000 men thrown into the attacks on the cities, 20,000 have been killed. If only two men have been seriously wounded for everyone dead—a very conservative estimate—the entire enemy force has been put out of action. Who, then, is doing the fighting?

Again it is claimed that the Communists expected a

large-scale popular uprising which did not occur. How ironic it is that we should claim a victory because a people whom we have given sixteen thousand lives, billions of dollars and almost a decade to defend, did not rise in arms against us. More disillusioning and painful is the fact the population did not rise to defend its freedom against the Vietcong. Thousands of men and arms were infiltrated into populated urban areas over a period of days, if not of weeks. Yet few, if any, citizens rushed to inform their protectors of this massive infiltration. At best they simply shut their doors to concern, waiting for others to resolve the issue. Did we know the attack was coming? If so, why did we not strike first, and where were the forces needed for effective defense?

For years we have been told that the measure of our success and progress in Vietnam was increasing security and control for the population. Now we have seen that none of the population is secure and no area is under sure control. Four years ago when we only had about 30,000 troops in Vietnam, the Viet Cong were unable to amount the assaults on cities they have now conducted against our enormous forces. At one time a suggestion that we protect enclaves was derided. Now there are no protected enclaves.

This has not happened because our men are not brave or effective, because they are. It is because we have misconceived the nature of the war: it is because we have sought to resolve by military might a conflict whose issue depends upon the will and conviction of the South Vietnamese people. It is like sending a lion to halt an epidemic of jungle rot.

This misconception rests on a second illusion—the illusion that we can win a war which the South Vietnamese cannot win for themselves.

Two Presidents and countless officials have told us for seven years that although we can help the South Vietnamese, it is their war and they must win it; as Secretary of Defense McNamara told us last month, "We cannot provide the South Vietnamese with the will to survive as an independent nation . . . or with the ability and self-discipline a people must have to govern themselves. These qualities and attributes are essential contributions to the struggle only the South Vietnamese can supply." Yet this wise and certain counsel has gradually become an empty slogan, as mounting frustration has led us to transform the war into an American military effort.

The South Vietnamese Senate, with only one dissenting vote, refuses to draft 18 and 19 year old South Vietnamese, with a member of the Assembly asking "why should Vietnamese boys be sent to die for Americans." —While 19 year old American boys fight to maintain this Senate and Assembly in Saigon. Every detached observer has testified to the enormous corruption which pervades every level of South Vietnamese official life. Hundreds of millions of dollars are stolen by private individuals and government officials while the American people are being asked to pay higher taxes to finance our assistance effort. Despite continual promises the Saigon regime refuses to act against corruption. Late last year, after all our pressure for reform, two high army officers were finally dismissed for "criminal" corruption. Last month, these same two officers were given new and powerful commands. In the meantime, incorruptible officers resign out of frustration and defeat.

Perhaps, we could live with corruption and inefficiency by themselves. However the consequence is not simply the loss of money or of popular confidence; it is the loss of American lives. For government corruption is the source of the enemy's strength. It is, more than anything else, the reason why the greatest power on earth cannot defeat a tiny and primitive foe.

You cannot expect people to risk their lives and endure hardship unless they have a stake in their own society. They must have a clear sense of identification with their own government, a belief they are participating in a cause worth fighting for. Political and economic reform are not simply idealistic slogans or noble goals to be postponed until the fighting is over. They are the principal weapons of battle. People will not fight to line the pockets of generals or swell the bank accounts of the wealthy. They are far more likely to close their eyes and shut their doors in the face of their government—even as they did last week.

More than any election, more than any proud boasts, that single fact reveals the truth. We have an ally in name only. We support a government without supporters. Without the efforts of American arms that government would not last a day.

The third illusion is that the unswerving pursuit of military victory, whatever its cost, is in the interest of either ourselves or the people of Vietnam. For the people of Vietnam, the last three years have meant little but horror. Their tiny land has been devastated by a weight of bombs and shells greater than Nazi Germany knew in the Second World War. We have dropped twelve tons of bombs for every square mile in North and South Vietnam. Whole provinces have been substantially destroyed. More than two million South Vietnamese are now homeless refugees. Imagine the impact in our own country if an equivalent number—over 25 million Americans—were wandering homeless or interned in refugee camps, and millions more refugees were being created as New York and Chicago, Washington and Boston, were being destroyed by a war raging in their streets. Whatever the outcome of these battles, it is the people we seek to defend who are the greatest losers.

Nor does it serve the interests of America to fight this war as if moral standards could be subordinated to immediate necessities. Last week, a Vietcong suspect was turned over to the Chief of the Vietnamese Security Services, who executed him on the spot—a flat violation of the Geneva Convention on the Rules of War. Of course, the enemy is brutal and cruel, and has done the same thing many times. But we are not fighting the Communists in order to become more like them—we fight to preserve our differences. Moreover, such actions—like the widespread use of artillery and air power in the centers of cities—may hurt us far more in the long run than it helps today. The photograph of the execution was on front pages all around the world—leading our best and oldest friends to ask, more in sorrow than in anger, what has happened to America?

The fourth illusion is that the American national interest is identical with—or should be subordinated to—the selfish interest of an incompetent military regime.

We are told, of course, that the battle for South Vietnam is in reality a struggle for 250 million Asians—the beginning of a Great Society for all of Asia. But this is pretension. We can and should offer reasonable assistance to Asia; but we cannot build a Great Society there if we cannot build one in our own country. We cannot speak extravagantly of a struggle for 250 million Asians, when a struggle for 15 million in one Asian country so strains our forces, that another Asian country, a fourth-rate power which we have already once defeated in battle, dares to seize an American ship and hold and humiliate her crew.

And we are told that the war in Vietnam will settle the future course of Asia. But that is a prayerful wish based on unsound hope, meant only to justify the enormous sacrifices we have already made. The truth is that Communism triumphed in China twenty years ago, and was extended to Tibet. It lost in Malaya and the Philippines, met disaster in Indonesia, and was fought to a standstill in Korea. It has struggled against governments in Burma for twenty years without success, and it may struggle in Thailand for many more. The outcome in each country depends and will depend on the intrinsic strength of the government, the particular circumstances of the country, and the particular character of the insurgent movement. The truth is that the war in Vietnam does not promise the end of all threats to Asia and ultimately to the United States; rather, if we proceed on our present course, it promises only years and decades of further draining conflict on the mainland of Asia—conflict which, as our finest military leaders have always warned, could lead us only to national tragedy.

There is an American interest in South Vietnam. We have an interest in maintaining the strength of our commitments—and surely we have demonstrated that. With all the lives and resources we have poured into Vietnam, is there anyone to argue that a government with any support from its people, with any competence to rule, with any determination to defend itself, would not long ago have been victorious over any insurgent movement, however assisted from outside its borders?

And we have another, more immediate interest: to

protect the lives of our gallant young men, and to conserve American resources. But we do not have an interest in the survival of a privileged class, growing ever more wealthy from the corruption of war, which after all our sacrifices on their behalf, can ask why Vietnamese boys should die for Americans.

The fifth illusion is that this war can be settled in our own way and in our own time on our own terms. Such a settlement is the privilege of the triumphant; of those who crush their enemies in battle or wear away their will to fight.

We have not done this, nor is there any prospect we will achieve such a victory.

For twenty years, first the French and then the United States, have been predicting victory in Vietnam. In 1961 and in 1962, as well as 1966 and 1967, we have been told that "the tide is turning"; "there is 'light at the end of the tunnel' ", "we can soon bring home the troops—victory is near—, the enemy is tiring." Once, in 1962, I participated in such predictions myself. But for twenty years we have been wrong. The history of conflict among nations does not record another such lengthy and consistent chronicle of error. It is time to discard so proven a fallacy and face the reality that a military victory is not in sight, and that it probably will never come.

Unable to defeat our enemy or break his will—at least without a huge, long, and ever more costly effort—we must actively seek a peaceful settlement. We can no longer harden our terms everywhere Hanoi indicates it may be prepared to negotiate; and we must be willing to foresee a settlement which will give the Vietcong a chance to participate in the political life of the country. Not because we want them to, but because that is the only way in which this struggle can be settled. No one knows if negotiations will bring a peaceful settlement, but we do know there will be no peaceful settlement without negotiations. Nor can we have these negotiations just on our own terms. We may have to make concessions and take risks, and surely we will have to negotiate directly with the NLF as well as Hanoi. Surely it is only another illusion that still denies this basic necessity. What we must not do is confuse the prestige staked on a particular policy with the interest of the United States; nor should we be unwilling to take risks for peace when we are willing to risk so many lives in war.

A year ago, when our adversary offered negotiations if only we would halt the bombing of the North, we replied with a demand for his virtual surrender. Officials at the highest level of our government felt that we were on the edge of a military victory and negotiations, except on our terms, were not necessary. Now, a year too late, we have set fewer conditions for a bombing halt, conditions which clearly would have been more acceptable then. And the intervening year, for all its terrible costs, the deaths of thousands of Americans and South Vietnamese, has not improved our position in the least. When the chance for negotiations comes again, let us not postpone for another year the recognition of what is really possible and necessary to a peaceful settlement.

These are some of the illusions which must be discarded if the events of last week are to prove not simply a tragedy, but a lesson: a lesson which carries with it some basic truths.

First, that a total military victory is not within sight or around the corner; that, in fact, it is probably beyond our grasp; and that the effort to win such a victory will only result in the further slaughter of thousands of innocent and helpless people—a slaughter which will forever rest on our national conscience.

Second, that the pursuit of such a victory is not necessary to our national interest and is even damaging that interest.

Third, that the progress we have claimed toward increasing our control over the country and the security of the population is largely illusory.

Fourth, that the central battle in this war cannot be measured by body counts or bomb damage, but by the extent to which the people of South Vietnam act on a sense of common purpose and hope with those that govern them.

Fifth, that the current regime in Saigon is unwilling or incapable of being an effective ally in the war against the Communists.

Sixth, that a political compromise is not just the best

path to peace, but the only path, and we must show as much willingness to risk some of our prestige for peace as to risk the lives of young men in war.

Seventh, that the escalation policy in Vietnam, far from strengthening and consolidating international resistance to aggression, is injuring our country through the world, reducing the faith of other peoples in our wisdom and purpose and weakening the world's resolve to stand together for freedom and peace.

Eighth, that the best way to save our most precious stake in Vietnam—the lives of our soldiers—is to stop the enlargement of the war, and that the best way to end casualties is to end the war.

Ninth, that our nation must be told the truth, about this war, in all its terrible reality, both because it is right—and because only in this way can any administration rally the public confidence and unity for the shadowed days which lie ahead.

No war has ever demanded more bravery from our people and our government—not just bravery under fire or the bravery to make sacrifices—but the bravery to discard the comfort of illusion—to do away with false hopes and alluring promises. Reality is grim and painful. But it is only a remote echo of the anguish toward which a policy founded on illusion is surely taking us. This is a great nation and a strong people. Any who seek to comfort rather than speak plainly, reassure rather than instruct, promise satisfaction rather than reveal frustration —they deny that greatness and drain that strength. For today as it was in the beginning, it is the truth that makes us free.

Postscript

IF YOU FLY IN a plane over Europe, toward Africa or Asia, in a few hours you will cross over oceans and countries that have been a crucible of human history. In minutes you will trace the migration of men over thousands of years; seconds, the briefest glimpse, and you will pass battlefields on which millions of men once struggled and died. You will see no national boundaries, no vast gulfs or high walls dividing people from people; only nature and the works of man—homes and factories and farms—everywhere reflecting man's common effort to enrich his life. Everywhere new technology and communications bring men and nations closer together, the concerns of one more and more becoming the concerns of all. And our new closeness is stripping away the false masks, the illusion of difference that is at the root of injustice and hate and war. Only earthbound man still clings to the dark and poisoning superstition that his world is bounded by the nearest hill, his universe ended at river shore, his common humanity enclosed in the tight circle of those who share his town and views and the color of his skin.

Each nation has different obstacles and different goals, shaped by the vagaries of history and experience. Yet as I talk to young people around the world I am impressed not by the diversity but by the closeness of their goals, their desires and concerns and hope for the future. There is discrimination in New York, apartheid in South Africa, and serfdom in the mountains of Peru. People starve in the streets of India; intellectuals go to jail in Russia; thousands are slaughtered in Indonesia; wealth is lavished on armaments everywhere. These are differing evils, but they are the common works of man. They reflect the imperfection of human justice, the inadequacy of human compassion, the defectiveness of our sensibility toward the sufferings of our fellows; they mark the limit of our ability to use knowledge for the well-being of others. And therefore, they call upon common qualities of conscience and of indignation, a shared determination to wipe away the unnecessary sufferings of our fellow human beings at home and around the world.

Our answer is the world's hope; it is to rely on youth—not a time of life but a state of mind, a temper of the will, a quality of the imagination, a predominance of courage over timidity, of the appetite for adventure over the love of ease. The cruelties and obstacles of this swiftly changing planet will not yield to obsolete dogmas and outworn slogans. It cannot be moved by those who cling to a present that is already dying, who prefer the illusion of security to the excitement and danger that come with even the most peaceful progress. It is a revolutionary world we live in; and this generation, at home and around the world, has had thrust upon it a greater burden of responsibility than any generation that has ever lived.

"There is," said an Italian philosopher, "nothing more difficult to take in hand, more perilous to conduct, or more uncertain in its success than to take the lead in the introduction of a new order of things." Yet this is the measure of the task of this generation, and the road is strewn with many dangers.

First is the danger of futility, the belief that there is nothing one man or one woman can do against the enormous array of the world's ills—against misery and ignorance, injustice and violence. Yet many of the world's great movements, of thought and action, have flowed from the work of a single man. A young monk began the Protestant Reformation, a young general extended an empire from Macedonia to the borders of the earth, and a young woman reclaimed the territory of France. It was a young Italian explorer who discovered the New World, and the thirty-two-year-old Thomas Jefferson who proclaimed that all men are created equal. "Give me a place to stand," said Archimedes, "and I will move the world."

These men moved the world, and so can we all. Few will have the greatness to bend history itself, but each of us can work to change a small portion of events, and in the total of all those acts will be written the history of this generation. Thousands of Peace Corps volunteers are making a difference in isolated villages and city slums in dozens of countries. Thousands of unknown men and women in Europe resisted the occupation of the Nazis and many died, but all added to the ultimate strength and freedom of their countries. It is from numberless diverse acts of courage and belief that human history is shaped. Each time a man stands up for an ideal, or acts to improve the lot of others, or strikes out against injustice, he sends forth a tiny ripple of hope, and crossing each other from a million different centers of energy and daring, those ripples build a current that can sweep down the mightiest walls of oppression and resistance.

"If Athens shall appear great to you," said Pericles, "consider then that her glories were purchased by valiant men, and by men who learned their duty." That is the source of all greatness in all societies, and it is the key to progress in our time.

The second danger is that of expediency, of those who say that hopes and beliefs must bend before immediate necessities. Of course, if we would act effectively we must deal with the world as it is. We must get things done. But if there was one thing President Kennedy stood for that touched the most profound feelings of people across the world, it was the belief that idealism, high aspirations, and deep convictions are not incompatible with the most practical and efficient of programs—that there is no basic inconsist-

ency between ideals and realistic possibilities, no separation between the deepest desires of heart and mind
and the rational application of human effort to human
problems. It is not realistic or hardheaded to solve
problems and take action unguided by ultimate moral
aims and values. It is thoughtless folly. For it ignores
the realities of human faith and passion and belief,
forces ultimately more powerful than all the calcula-
tions of economists or generals. Of course, to adhere to
standards, to idealism, to vision in the face of immediate dangers, takes great courage and self-confidence.
But we also know that only those who dare to fail
greatly can ever achieve greatly.

It is this new idealism that is also, I believe, the
common heritage of a generation that has learned that
while efficiency can lead to the camps of Auschwitz or
the streets of Budapest, only the ideals of humanity
and love can climb the hill to the Acropolis.

A third danger is timidity. Few men are willing to
brave the disapproval of their fellows, the censure of
their colleagues, the wrath of their society. Moral courage is a rarer commodity than bravery in battle or
great intelligence. Yet it is the one essential, vital quality for those who seek to change a world that yields
most painfully to change. Aristotle tells us that "at the
Olympic games it is not the finest and the strongest
men who are crowned, but they who enter the lists. . . .
So too in the life of the honorable and the good it is
they who act rightly who win the prize." I believe that
in this generation those with the courage to enter the
moral conflict will find themselves with companions in
every corner of the world.

For the fortunate among us, the fourth danger is
comfort, the temptation to follow the easy and familiar paths of personal ambition and financial success so
grandly spread before those who enjoy the privilege of
education. But that is not the road history has marked
out for us. There is a Chinese curse that says, "May he
live in interesting times." Like it or not, we live in interesting times. They are times of danger and uncertainty, but they are also more open to the creative energy of men than any other time in history. And all of

us will ultimately be judged, and as the years pass we will surely judge ourselves, on the effort we have contributed to building a new world society and the extent to which our ideals and goals have shaped that effort.

Our future may lie beyond our vision, but it is not completely beyond our control. It is the shaping impulse of America that neither fate nor nature nor the irresistible tides of history, but the work of our own hands, matched to reason and principle, that will determine destiny. There is pride in that, even arrogance, but there is also experience and truth. In any event, it is the only way we can live.